CANNIBALIZING
THE COLONY

Purdue Studies in Romance Literatures

Editorial Board

Patricia Hart, Series Editor
Paul B. Dixon
Benjamin Lawton

Floyd Merrell
Marcia Stephenson
Allen G. Wood

Howard Mancing, Consulting Editor
Susan Y. Clawson, Production Editor

Associate Editors

French
Jeanette Beer
Paul Benhamou
Willard Bohn
Gerard J. Brault
Mary Ann Caws
Glyn P. Norton
Allan H. Pasco
Gerald Prince
Roseann Runte
Ursula Tidd

Italian
Fiora A. Bassanese
Peter Carravetta
Franco Masciandaro
Anthony Julian Tamburri

Luso-Brazilian
Fred M. Clark
Marta Peixoto
Ricardo da Silveira Lobo Sternberg

Spanish and Spanish American
Maryellen Bieder
Catherine Connor
Ivy A. Corfis
Frederick A. de Armas
Edward Friedman
Charles Ganelin
David T. Gies
Roberto González Echevarría
David K. Herzberger
Emily Hicks
Djelal Kadir
Amy Kaminsky
Lucille Kerr
Howard Mancing
Alberto Moreiras
Randolph D. Pope
Francisco Ruiz Ramón
Elżbieta Skłodowska
Mario Valdés
Howard Young

PSRL volume 45

CANNIBALIZING THE COLONY

Cinematic Adaptations

of Colonial Literature

in Mexico and Brazil

Richard A. Gordon

Purdue University Press
West Lafayette, Indiana

Copyright ©2009 by Purdue University. All rights reserved.

♾ The paper used in this book meets the minimum requirements of American National Standard for Information Sciences—Permanence of Paper for Printed Library Materials, ANSI Z39.48-1992.

Printed in the United States of America
Design by Anita Noble

Library of Congress Cataloging-in-Publication Data

Gordon, Richard A. (Richard Allen), 1969–
 Cannibalizing the colony : cinematic adaptations of colonial literature in Mexico and Brazil / Richard A. Gordon.
   p. cm. — (Purdue studies in Romance literatures ; v. 45)
 Includes bibliographical references and index.
 ISBN 978-1-55753-519-1 (alk. paper)
  1. Historical films—Mexico—History and criticism. 2. Historical films—Brazil—History and criticism. 3. Mexican fiction—Film and video adaptations. 4. Brazilian fiction—Film and video adaptations. I. Title. II. Series.
   PN1995.9.H5G65 2008
   791.43'6587202—dc22
                                                   2008043436

To Pili

Contents

ix **Acknowledgments**

1 **Introduction**

19 **Chapter One**
Re-creating Caminha: The Earnest Adaptation of Brazil's Letter of Discovery in *Descobrimento do Brazil* (1937)

47 **Chapter Two**
Exoticizing the Nation in *Cabeza de Vaca* (1991) and *Como era gostoso o meu francês* (1971)

79 **Chapter Three**
Reimagining Guadalupe in *Nuevo mundo* (1976) and *La otra conquista* (1998)

109 **Chapter Four**
Sor Juana Inés de la Cruz and the Retooling of a National Icon in *Ave María* (1999)

141 **Chapter Five**
Inverted Captivities and Imagined Adaptations in *Brava Gente Brasileira* (2000) and *Caramuru: A Invenção do Brasil* (2001)

177 **Epilogue**
The Unwieldy Dynamics of Anthropophagous Adaptations

181 **Appendix**
English Translations

197 **Notes**

235 **Works Cited**

253 **Index**

Acknowledgments

This book owes its existence to the help of many, many people. Those listed below are the ones I have been able to recall. The shortcomings that remain, in spite of their generous aid are, of course, mine alone.

This project's first life, as a dissertation, benefited immensely from the support, first and foremost, of Stephanie Merrim, who directed the project, and of Chris Conway and Luiz Valente, who provided careful readings and insightful suggestions. My gratitude, for various motives, goes out to the following friends, mentors, and family: Ana María Fagundo, Roberto Hozven, Wadda Ríos Font, Antonio Carreño, Geoffrey Ribbans, Beth Bauer, Marie Roderick, Julissa Bautista, Sandra Hombreiro, Angel Otero, Lucía Tono, Robert Moser, Dan Bautista, Amy Sellin, Domingo Ledezma, Anna Turner, Leigh Mercer, Goretti Ramírez, Michele Gardner, Yarí Pérez Marín, Jerelyn Johnson, José Santos, Patricia Hildebrand, Dick Gordon, Bill Black, Caryn Gordon, Susan Charette, Christine Charette, Lindsey Gordon, Lainey Gordon, Victoria Condon, and Mary and Dean Hildebrand.

I've incurred many debts during the transition from dissertation to book, as well. I thank the following people for their invaluable input and assistance: Robert Stam, Ana López, Kimberle López, Stephanie Dennison, Darlene Sadlier, Joanne Hershfield, Anne Marie Stock, Randal Johnson, Leila Lehnan, Cristina González, Tom O'Brien, Marcus Vinícius de Freitas, Hélder Garmes, Beth Newman, Bruce Levy, Luis Maldonado, Robert Howell, Nicolle Jordan, Elizabeth Russ, Rasma Lazda, Doug Lightfoot, Marguerite Itamar Harrison, Patrícia Sobral, Thomas Skidmore, Mark Lokensgaard, Vivaldo Santos, Kittiya Lee, the anonymous readers of the manuscript, and the many participants in various Spring Break Think Tanks over the years. It has been a pleasure completing this book at The Ohio State University. In particular, I thank the office staff—Susan Farquhar, Melinda Robinson, Tammy Jones, and Judy Manley—for their frequent support; the chair of the department, Fernando Unzueta, and Associate Deans Debra Moddelmog and Sebastian Knowles, for fostering an ideal atmosphere for research and teaching; and the following colleagues for

Acknowledgments

reflections on my work: Ignacio Corona, Pedro Pereira, Abril Trigo, Laura Podalsky, Maureen Ahern, Rebecca Haidt, Ileana Rodríguez, Frederick Aldama, and Jonathan Burgoyne. I would like to thank, for so many reasons, my dear friend Lúcia Costigan, the best colleague anyone could ask for. I could not have written this book without the constant friendship and collaboration, from graduate school until today, of two people in particular: Bill Worden and Lisa Voigt.

I would like to acknowledge the financial support in the form of grants from Brown University, Southern Methodist University, and The Ohio State University (College of Humanities).

I am grateful to the editors of *MLN* and *Torre de Papel* for permission to reprint parts of this work that have appeared previously in print. An early version of Chapter 1 appeared as "Recreating Caminha: The Earnest Adaptation of Brazil's Letter of Discovery in Humberto Mauro's *Descobrimento do Brasil* (1937)," *MLN* 120.2 (Mar. 2005): 408–36. © 2005 The Johns Hopkins University Press. A very early version of part of Chapter 2 appeared as "Exoticism and National Identity in *Cabeza de Vaca* and *Como era gostoso o meu francês*," *Torre de Papel* 10.1 (Spring 2000): 77–119.

I am grateful to the Centro Técnico Audiovisual in Rio de Janeiro, for permission to publish images of the *Descobrimento do Brasil* posters; the staffs at the Cinemateca do MAM, the Cineteca Nacional, FUNARTE, the Filmoteca de la UNAM, and IMCINE, for their assistance with the research for this project; and my editors, Patricia Hart and Susan Clawson, at Purdue Studies in Romance Literatures, for their crucial advice and patience.

Finally, and most importantly, I thank my companion, Pilar Chamorro, for her love and the countless ways that she has helped.

Introduction

The 1992 and 2000 quincentenaries of the arrival of the Spanish and the Portuguese in America prompted an explosion of rewritings and cinematic renditions of texts and figures from colonial Latin America. However, such critical and aesthetic negotiations with the colonial past are not simply a recent phenomenon in Latin America.[1] They are an enduring concern. *Cannibalizing the Colony* analyzes a crucial way that Latin American historical films, since the beginning of sound cinema, have grappled with the legacy of colonialism. Mexico and Brazil are the Latin American nations that have produced the greatest number by far of what I call "colonial" films, and are thus the focus of this study.[2] In these countries and elsewhere in Latin America cinematic engagements of colonial literature exemplify a shared, perennial interest in conversing with the colonial past in order to evaluate national identity. Mexican and Brazilian filmmakers in particular have transformed colonial narratives of European and indigenous contact into commentaries on national identity. This book focuses on the dynamics of cinematic adaptation and examines the processes through which filmmakers "devour" and "digest" artifacts from the colonial period in order to incorporate them into present-day understandings of these nations.

Cannibalizing the Colony considers diverse motivations for these filmic dialogues with the past, and places particular emphasis on the conceptions of identity that each filmmaker attempts to promote and the adaptational and cinematic strategies that he or she uses to construct a particular vision of the past and understanding of the present. Additionally, it examines how the directors attempt to control the way that spectators understand the complex and contentious roots of identity in Mexico and Brazil, especially in terms of the importance of indigenous populations and their relationship to Iberian colonizers. The different kinds of persuasive rhetoric employed—the ways that directors ensure the effectiveness of their message and entice viewers into sharing the stance on identity that they have fashioned—constitute one of the primary concerns of this book.

Despite drastically different contexts of production and ideological perspectives, the colonial films that I study all demonstrate an analogous approach to renovating their source text. These films neither revere the colonial source, nor invite the adapted text to speak for itself. Instead, they take tight control of their intertext and transform it into a calculated commentary on the nation. I call this process of domination "anthropophagous adaptation." The concept of cannibalism well captures the domineering role that colonial films tend to establish with their source texts and the governed fusion that results from the relationship. I derive my understanding of anthropophagous adaptation from Oswald de Andrade's 1928 "Manifesto antropófago," and the enduring theory of cultural cannibalism that it helped to spark in Brazil.[3] The strategies that Andrade proposes and enacts enable him to take control of the tricky but inevitable dynamic of transformation that results from intercultural contact across time or space.[4] The "Manifesto antropófago" ("Cannibal Manifesto")[5] prefigures (or inspires) the films not only in terms of strategy or form, but also with regard to content: much of Andrade's preoccupation and much of the fodder for his commentary is the colonial past.

Andrade taps into the symbolic appeal of the ritual cannibalism of the Brazilian Tupinambá, which holds that if the captured and assimilated enemy is consumed, his valor is absorbed. He declares that all of Brazil is (or should consider itself) indigenous. From that assumed subject position he adopts an aggressive stance toward colonial rule, some of its key figures and institutions, and their lasting legacy. However, the metaphor of anthropophagy allows Andrade to postulate not only destruction, but also absorption of certain valuable (i.e., nutritious) aspects of what is consumed.[6]

Andrade creatively navigates, with regard to the past and the present, the power dynamics of center and periphery, in intellectual, political, and artistic spheres. The films coincide largely with him in that they take an aggressive stance vis-à-vis products of colonial Latin America: texts or figures arising in colonial Latin America whose impact continues to be felt. The "enemy" that these Latin American historical films dominate, consume, digest, and absorb could be seen as the legacy of the colonialism that is embodied in written texts from the past. The films essentially do what Oswald de Andrade does and promotes: they consume, digest, and absorb remnants of colonialism. They take in the colonial sources and their centuries-long cadre of associations, discard or expel much, and digest the rest.

The political implications of these cannibalistic cinematic adaptations are diverse. Not all of the films are fighting against the perceived perennial oppression of colonialism. Some of them display a sort of nationalistic pride in the colonial period, while others treat the history of colonialism uncritically or ludically. The colonial films that I study here strive to determine the outcome of the necessary and continual convergence of past and present.[7] Of course, all of them hope to effect the maximum social impact through their interventions on identity. According to the postulates of anthropophagy, the strength of the cannibal increases on par with the strength of the enemy. In other words, the most influential transformations promise to be the ones that take as their object especially ingrained, pervasive, and nefarious symbolic remnants of colonialism. In this sense, many of the films can be seen as postcolonial acts of resistance which recognize that attempts to re-evaluate and comprehend (in both senses of the word) a postcolonial present perhaps necessarily involve a return to the colony. The colonial past—steeped in oppression, violence, and intercultural contact—is always present and influential; the films decide to take hold of this transhistorical intermingling. The concept of anthropophagy aptly evokes the rhetorical design of the films. They cannibalize the colony, apprehending and absorbing the insidious and potentially unwieldy symbolic aftermath of colonialism. Ironically, they implement dominating strategies as a means of denouncing a dominant and oppressive social phenomenon, which makes for fruitful complexities in the films' effects. Such strategies, for instance, can become tangled in their own rhetoric, and thus can undermine the effectiveness of the filmmakers' objectives.

Introduction

* * *

Existing trends in scholarship about Latin American film do not typically designate colonial cinema as a discrete category.[8] Those that do, by historians and specialists in cinema, tend to take a different approach from the one that I pursue. This is not, I would like to underscore, a comprehensive history of Latin American films about the colonial period.[9] Nor is it an attempt to evaluate the historical veracity of the films, their use in history classes, or the viability of Latin American colonial cinema as a form of historical discourse, which are among the most common goals of work done by historians on Latin American historical cinema.[10] Instead, *Cannibalizing the Colony* takes a cultural studies approach to colonial films. The book carries out a critical analysis of strategies of adaptation and interventions in identity. I study the dynamic at play, in several emblematic instances, between the colonial text and the film, and between the film and the society that produced it, in order to offer a clearer picture of the strategies that directors use effectively to devour the colonial texts and ensure their complete digestion. Such an approach to colonial films, I contend, helps to uncover the ways in which identity is negotiated in Latin America.[11]

Latin American filmmakers have looked to the colonial period throughout the twentieth century and into the twenty-first. My point is illustrated by scores of films from the silent period through the 1980s, as well as recent films that transcend the stimulus of quincentenaries, such as *La otra conquista* (*The Other Conquest*; Mexico, 1998, dir. Carrasco), *Cautiverio feliz* ([*Happy Captivity*]; Chile, 1998, dir. Sánchez), *Ave María* ([*Hail Mary*]; Mexico, 1999, dir. Rossoff), and *El bien esquivo* (*The Elusive Good* AKA *The Good Bastard*; Peru, 2001, dir. Tomayo San Román), *Roble de olor* (*Scent of Oak*; Cuba, 2002, dir. López), and *Eréndira ikikunari* ([*Eréndira, the Indomitable*]; Mexico, 2006, dir. Mora Catlett) in Spanish America; and in Brazil *Desmundo* (2003, dir. Fresnot), *Aleijadinho: Paixão, Glória e Suplício* (*Aleijadinho: Passion, Glory and Torment;* 2003, dir. Santos Pereira), *Gregório de Mattos* (2003, dir. Carolina), *Diário de um novo mundo* ([*Diary of a New World*]; 2005, dir. Nascimento), and *Cafundó* ([*Middle of Nowhere*]; 2005, dir. Betti and Bueno).[12] In all cases, the contextual catalysts for the production of Latin American films treating the colonial period have been distinct;[13] yet filmmakers have coincided in regarding the era as a particularly apt setting to reflect on identity and culture in the present. If Latin American historical films generally signal a desire for self-examination, I contend that colonial films, in particular, reveal an uncanny hunger to reach into the past to rethink the present. The principal films that *Cannibalizing the Colony* studies—*Descobrimento do Brasil* (*The Discovery of Brazil*; Brazil, 1937, dir. Mauro), *Cabeza de Vaca* (Mexico, 1991, dir. Echevarría), *Como era gostoso o meu francês* (*How Tasty Was My Little Frenchman*; Brazil, 1971, dir. Santos), *Nuevo mundo* (*New World*; Mexico, 1976, dir. Retes), *La otra conquista, Ave María, Brava Gente Brasileira* (*Brave New Land*; Brazil, 2000, dir. Murat), and *Caramuru: A Invenção do Brasil* ([*Caramuru: The Invention of Brazil*]; Brazil, TV 2000/Theaters 2001/DVD 2002, dir. Arraes)—epitomize this craving.

Latin American cinema has always exhibited interest in the connection between history and identity. In the 1930s and 1940s, for example, governments in both Mexico and Brazil capitalized on the currency of historical films. Recognizing the ideological sway of cinema and seeking to bolster their own visions of national identity, both governments encouraged historical films through tax breaks and direct financial backing. Under the Lázaro Cárdenas and Manuel Ávila Camacho administrations in Mexico (1934–46), as well as that of Getúlio Vargas in Brazil (1930–45, and again 1951–54), the State intervened extensively in the film industry with the explicit aim of utilizing cinema as a means to unify the nation (Johnson, *The Film Industry* 11, 51; Nájera-Ramírez 7). Colonial films such as *La monja alférez* (*The Lieutenant Nun*; Mexico, 1944, dir. Gómez Muriel) and *Descobrimento do Brasil* reflect governmental involvement in film during this period.[14]

Treatments of history in Latin American film took on a distinctly revisionist tone beginning in the 1950s. Inspired by Italian Neo-Realism, a socially critical cinematic movement, the founding directors of New Latin American Cinema and Brazil's *Cinema Novo* (including Nelson Pereira dos Santos, one of the directors whose work I study here) consistently confronted notions of national identity through their films, and often based such examinations on historical themes (Chanan 740–41; Pick

10–11). In the 1970s and 1980s, it was common for directors of New Latin American Cinema and *Cinema Novo* to carry out their commentaries on present-day politics and conceptions of identity through the revision of history (Stam and Xavier 309; Chanan 741). Brazilian filmmaker Glauber Rocha, for example, supported the validity and importance of revisionist approaches to history, arguing for the central role of the director in re-evaluating history (Chanan 742). Examples from this era of films set in the colonial period abound, and include *Pindorama* (Brazil, 1970, dir. Jabor), *Como era gostoso o meu francês*, *El jardín de tía Isabel* ([*The Garden of Aunt Isabel*]; Mexico, 1971, dir. Cazals), *El santo oficio* (*The Holy Office*; Mexico, 1974, dir. Ripstein), and *La última cena* (*The Last Supper*; Cuba, 1976, dir. Gutiérrez Alea), among many others.

Latin American directors' use of the past in order to comment on present-day identity and politics at times met with official resistance. Reminiscent of the interest of the Mexican and Brazilian governments with historical cinema in the 1930s and 1940s, the military dictatorship in power in Brazil in the early 1970s wanted to tap the usefulness of such films, and therefore conditionally backed their production. The government allowed certain historically removed re-creations or adaptations, even tolerating a degree of social critique (Stam and Xavier 309).[15] Consider the case of Brazilian director Nelson Pereira dos Santos, who successfully negotiated official cinematic policies in the early 1970s. Pereira dos Santos's film, *Como era gostoso o meu francês*, made during an especially repressive moment of the military dictatorship,[16] capitalized on the government's efforts to sponsor historical films.[17] By exploiting the government's recognition of the value of historical films, Pereira dos Santos and other *Cinema Novo* directors were able to instrumentalize the past as a means to interrogate national identity and politics, while circumventing extensive intervention through their oblique commentaries ("Nelson Pereira dos Santos" 134).

In conjunction with history, a concern about race has played a prominent role in Latin American cinematic treatments of identity.[18] In fact, among the very first historical films made in Mexico and Brazil are several that examine the indigenous population in the colonial period. A few examples from the silent period are *Cuauhtémoc* (Mexico, 1918, dir. de la Bandera), *Tiempos Mayas* ([*Mayan Times*]; Mexico, 1914, dir. Martínez de Arredondo), *O Guarani* (*The Guarani;* Brazil, 1912, dir. Benedetti), *O Guarani* (Brazil, 1916, dir. Capellaro), and *Iracema* (*Iracema*; Brazil, 1919, dir. Capellaro), none of which has been extensively studied.[19] The general lack of criticism on early Mexican and Brazilian films that thematize indigenous populations is partly explained by the dearth of extant silent films, a result of devastating fires at film archives in both nations. Still, as I will explain further on, even available films about the indigenous populations of Mexico and Brazil during their colonial periods have yet to receive adequate attention. *Cannibalizing the Colony*'s focus on such films aims to fill this critical gap.

Besides the thread of indigenous/European contact during the colonial period, Latin American colonial films coalesce along a number of other thematic lines. A few of the recurring topics are: indigenous and African resistance and rebellion;[20] indigenous and European captivities and captivations;[21] Creole struggles for independence;[22] the many Brazilian adaptations of José de Alencar's romantic novels, *Iracema* and *O Guarani*; the Catholic Church;[23] and women in colonial Iberoamerica.[24] Conspicuously absent are clusters of films treating the arrival of Europeans to the New World. Although Brazil produced *Descobrimento do Brasil* about Cabral's 1500 voyage to the New World, and Mexico demonstrated sporadic interest in the figure of Columbus (e.g., *Cristóbal Colón;* 1943), interest in the "discovery" of America has originated overwhelmingly in Europe and the United States.[25] Latin American directors have understandably avoided underscoring the conquest and conquistadors. They choose instead to revisit and highlight themes that embody a resistance to colonialism or an anticipation of a postcolonial era or ideology, topics that lend themselves to holding up the colonial period as a mirror for self-examination and as an allegorical lamp to illuminate present-day oppression analogous to that caused by colonialism. Films have tended to focus on the indigenous population and other subaltern or marginalized groups, and on strategies of resistance and struggles for independence or freedom. Such approaches to the past illustrate Latin American historical cinema's inclination to produce films that take a critical look at the issues of history and identity, rather than the escapist costume dramas, or the action-charged allegorical endorsements of official US policy or dominant ideologies so common to the Hollywood tradition.[26]

The films that I analyze here exemplify the topical tendency in Latin American film embodied by the thematic groupings above: each deals with emblematic figures or moments in the histories of Mexico and Brazil that lend themselves to interrogating colonialism and its aftermath. In that regard, *Cannibalizing the Colony* can be seen as a representative examination of Latin American colonial cinema, or even, in certain ways, of Latin American historical cinema in general. I would argue that the anthropophagous dynamic between the directors and their colonial sources exists in much of the historical cinema emerging from Brazil, Spanish America, and the Caribbean. Even films that call attention to their adaptational tactics and reveal the devices of their own cinematic historiography—and by extension historiography in general—capture and consume their source text, break it down and absorb it into an existing body.[27] The converse of the cinematic anthropophagy that I study herein would be films that realize a more egalitarian conversation with their historical source by taking steps to leave their resurrections open to multiple readings, or ones that promote a critical view of historiography, the study of which merits further research.[28]

Without exception, the directors I study choose sources ripe for resurrection, foundational and contentious texts and contexts: a letter of discovery, captivity narratives, the tale of a female figure already central to Mexican identity, and a story of indigenous rebellion. Through their varied contact with these iconic aspects of the colonial past—fertile patches of the historical landscape—the directors have enriched naturally suitable sites in order to revise the intricate ways that Mexico and Brazil are imagined. My goal is to uncover the nature of that reflection and to examine the methods of such retrospective journeys to the colonial period. A preliminary foray into *Cabeza de Vaca* and *Como era gostoso o meu francês* will bring into clearer relief the evocative dynamic at play in all of the films under consideration here.

Introduction

Directors Nicolás Echevarría and Nelson Pereira dos Santos, in their respective films, re-examine sixteenth-century narratives of captivity by dealing with elements central to conceptions of Mexico and Brazil: the indigenous population and the early interaction of European and American peoples. The directors' choice to adapt captivity narratives would appear to grow out of a concern with indigenous themes. Echevarría declares his passion, both in documentary and fiction film, with "los indios" ("the Indians") ("La conquista" 11). In an interview with Julianne Burton, Pereira dos Santos comments on the same theme in Brazil: "[I]t is clearer than ever that the indigenous tribes are an integral part of our history" ("Nelson Pereira dos Santos" 139). The collision of cultures portrayed by *Cabeza de Vaca* and *Como era gostoso* and the peculiar circumstances under which the European and Amerindian characters interact in the films urge contemplation of Latin America's colonial legacy. Cabeza de Vaca undergoes a profound and complex process of transculturation. His story inspires at least a partial shift in modern conceptions of identity in Latin America by centering the indigenous characters. The protagonist of *Como era gostoso*, Jean—a revision primarily of the sixteenth-century German explorer and writer Hans Staden—similarly experiences a cultural transformation while captive, and thus possesses an equivalent symbolic value. Echevarría and Pereira dos Santos resuscitate moments in which the colonizer and the colonized intersect in an inverted power dynamic, which in itself suggests a re-evaluation of the relative weight of indigenous and European elements with regard to national identity. Besides specifically lending the directors the opportunity to comment on indigenous populations in the past and, by inevitable extension, the present, the transculturation that Álvar Núñez and Hans Staden experience while held captive helps to erode Eurocentric notions of national identity in Latin America. These stories of early European explorers represent not so much conquest but encounter, interaction, and assimilation out of, rather than into the European cultural context: an appropriate setting for questioning the legacy of the "conquest."[29] Both Echevarría and Pereira dos Santos choose a fruitful context for their critique: tales that by their very nature help the directors to

Introduction

dispute entrenched visions of national identity, which relegated indigenous peoples to a subordinate position. By foregrounding the experience of European captivity, in which the traditionally marginalized indigenous captors are in a position of power, the directors privilege an indigenous perspective, and thus seek partially to displace Europeans from the center of concepts of identity.

I have given this brief example here because the captivity tales and their cinematic exploitation are paradigmatic of the dynamic at work in all of the films examined in the ensuing pages. Each of them amplifies the symbolic potential of the texts and figures that they choose to revive. The texts with which the filmmakers enter into dialogue already enjoy a symbolic cachet, having proven themselves significant to both the past and the present of the nations. The directors draw on what amounts to the mythic status of the stories that the colonial texts tell, and exploit the inherited malleability of existing cultural icons in the process of reconceiving the nations' cultural heritage, of making the past relevant for the present, and of shaping their own, new national icons.

I have sought to broaden the relevance of my reading of Mexican and Brazilian cinema's ubiquitous anthropophagous relationship with the colony by selecting films that represent a variety of both cinematic strategies and circumstances within which they were produced. Through these case studies, *Cannibalizing the Colony* clarifies how directors from these and other Latin American countries have attempted to retool the colonial past. Yet I also seek to demonstrate more generally the often underappreciated and untapped potential for studies comparing Brazil and Spanish America. In 2000, the *Journal of Latin American Cultural Studies* published—under the title "Do the Americas Have a Common History?"—a discussion that took place in 1941 between Roger Caillois, Pedro Henríquez Ureña, and Germán Arciniegas. Henríquez Ureña maintains that Brazil, "whose language hardly differs from Spanish [...] keeps itself apart from Spanish-speaking America [...] [I]n many respects Brazil remains unknown to Spanish America. Nevertheless, Brazil's similarities to the rest of Latin America—that is to say Spanish-speaking America—are great" (361–62). I would suggest that the separation to which Henríquez Ureña refers does not stem only from Brazil, and that we should be mindful of the facile propensity to level the rich linguistic, historical, and cultural distinctiveness of Brazil and the varied nations that make up Spanish America. Nevertheless, the Dominican intellectual underscores a real and lamentable mutual ignorance that historically has cauterized the borders that isolate the former Spanish and Portuguese colonies from one another. At a moment shortly after the release of Humberto Mauro's *Descobrimento do Brasil*, Henríquez Ureña insists that despite the many obvious differences that distinguish Latin American nations, a number of social and political parallels do exist and are worthy of study.

Around the same time that the cited discussion took place, plans were forming within the government of the United States to use cinema to promote a broader understanding of the connections among all of the nations of the Americas with a special and specific emphasis on Mexico and Brazil. In conjunction with US wartime support of the Mexican cinema industry,[30] Nelson D. Rockefeller's Office of the Coordinator for Inter-American Affairs arranged for Walt Disney to tour Latin America, a trip that sparked the production of *Saludos Amigos* (*Hello Friends*; 1943) and *The Three Caballeros* (1945) (Mora 73).[31] Although *The Three Caballeros*, which features Donald Duck and a Brazilian and a Mexican friend—José Carioca and Panchito—indulges in cultural stereotyping, it nonetheless attempts to paint a favorable picture of the two nations, and tries to avoid conflating the two cultures, as Hollywood has sometimes done. The Disney film also makes use of Brazilian Portuguese and Mexican Spanish, which manages to contribute to the story line and, at the same time, not frustrate, for lack of comprehension, either Donald or what we might presume to be the monolingual viewer from the United States.[32]

Henríquez Ureña's critique sadly still strikes a chord more than sixty years later, and such concerns continue to be voiced.[33] There persists a kind of myopia that often and unfortunately fortifies the separation of Spanish America and Brazil while also obscuring clear and compelling comparative possibilities, as Henríquez Ureña aptly observed in 1941. Yet there is currently a growing academic inclination to carry out comparisons of Brazilian and Spanish-American culture. *Cannibalizing the Colony* seeks to contribute to this international academic endeavor to promote comparative Latin American scholarship,

Introduction

specifically by highlighting one aspect of the cultural and intellectual connections between Mexico and Brazil. Notwithstanding the potential value of comparing Brazilian cinema to that of other Spanish American film-producing nations, there are strong motives for privileging Mexico in a comparative Luso-Hispanic study of Latin American colonial cinema. First, along with Cuba and Argentina, Mexico and Brazil are historically the most important film-producing countries in Latin America, and the Mexican and Brazilian cinema industries have at times found themselves intertwined. Mexican cinema, for example, for decades exerted influence over the rest of Latin America, including Brazil.[34] Also, despite their many historical, cultural, and political differences, the similarities between the two nations are compelling. Mexico and Brazil are two of the largest, most populous nations of Latin America, and they, like other Latin American nations, coincide in their longstanding tradition of concern over the definition of their identity, a subject intimately connected to their indigenous populations and to cultural hybridity. Even today, both nations continue to struggle with questions of assimilation as well as cultural and political independence of indigenous groups. The films studied in *Cannibalizing the Colony* are key symbolic sites of that continuing struggle. Most important, however, is the proliferation in these two nations of colonial films.

Although other Latin American nations have shown sporadic, and at times intense, cinematic interest in the colonial period, Mexican and Brazilian directors have consistently and frequently recognized the contemporary significance of their colonized past. In fact, the vast majority of Latin American films set in the colony were made in these two nations.[35] *Cannibalizing the Colony* explores the intrigue with the colonial period shared by directors from Mexico and Brazil, and examines the similarities and differences manifest in both the strategies that the filmmakers employ in their reactivation of the colony and the ideological implications of the films.

* * *

In Chapter 1, "Re-creating Caminha: The Earnest Adaptation of Brazil's Letter of Discovery in *Descobrimento do Brasil* (1937)," I query Humberto Mauro's adaptation of Pêro Vaz de

Introduction

Caminha's letter describing Pedro Álvares Cabral's arrival in Brazil. Mauro's film invokes an iconic moment in the history of Brazil: it is explicitly based on the 1500 "Carta" ("Letter") of the scribe Caminha, a founding text of Luso-Brazilian literature that depicts the initial encounter between the indigenous population of Brazil and the Portuguese. In this chapter, I evaluate how the director mines Caminha's narrative and inscribes his version of the tale onto his own historical context. Additionally, I look at the means by which Mauro strives to guarantee the success of his message—how he writes the rules for the game of persuasion and manipulation that he enacts. Finally, I address some of the motives and contextual factors that led to Mauro's calculated re-creation of Caminha, a re-creation collusive not only with Getúlio Vargas's government, but also with the Portuguese colonial presence in Brazil.

The second chapter, "Exoticizing the Nation in *Cabeza de Vaca* (1991) and *Como era gostoso o meu francês* (1971)," examines how a Brazilian and a Mexican director coincide in aggressively entering the polemical realm of exoticism as an adaptational and ideological strategy. The two films revisit sixteenth-century narratives of captivity, reproducing the rough story line of the sources, but stylizing them through the lens of the exotic. Nelson Pereira dos Santos's *Como era gostoso* transforms Hans Staden's sixteenth-century *Warhaftige Historia [...]* (*The True History and Description of a Country Populated by a Wild, Naked and Savage Man-munching People Situated in the New World, America*; 1557), while Nicolás Echevarría's *Cabeza de Vaca* finds inspiration in Álvar Núñez Cabeza de Vaca's well-known *Naufragios* (*Castaways: The Narrative of Álvar Núñez Cabeza de Vaca*; 1542 and 1555). The filmmakers draw on the colonial stories in order to model empowered, if doomed, indigenous resistance to colonizers. Their retellings resonate for a Brazilian present asphyxiated by dictatorship and a Mexican present resolved to transcend merely nominal pride in an indigenous heritage. I evaluate the ways in which both Pereira dos Santos and Echevarría use the tool of exoticizing— which I understand to mean a distancing that results from the hyperbolization of difference, regardless of agent or intentionality—as a cinematic strategy that enables them to morph the colonial texts into vehicles for their commentary. Much of my analysis focuses on the implications of how the directors make

Introduction

use of this device. I also consider such extratextual issues as Hollywood representational practices and the role of the government in how and why the films were made.

Chapter 3, "Reimagining Guadalupe in *Nuevo mundo* (1976) and *La otra conquista* (1998)," looks at two attempts to come to terms with one celebrated vision of the roots of mestizo identity in Mexico. Gabriel Retes's *Nuevo mundo* and Salvador Carrasco's *La otra conquista* offer stories that reconceive how a perennially powerful national icon, the Virgin of Guadalupe, may have entered the Mexican imaginary. In this chapter I study the nature of these adaptations, which domineeringly dialogue with both the Baroque text that helped to propagate the story of Guadalupe's apparition to Juan Diego in 1531 as well as the *Nican mopohua*, and also with the ubiquitous momentum of their legacy. To differing degrees both films indict European colonization on religious and ideological grounds. I consider how the films cinematically appropriate images of the Virgin in order to realize their critique of the colonial and modern origins of persistent and problematic aspects of politics and identity.

Chapter 4, "Sor Juana Inés de la Cruz and the Retooling of a National Icon in *Ave María* (1999)," analyzes Eduardo Rossoff's first feature film, which was released on the eve of a political changing-of-the-guard in Mexico. Rossoff, like the directors who revive Guadalupe, revisits an influential Mexican icon. In a free-form engagement of seventeenth-century sources, *Ave María* disrupts conceptions of Mexican identity by translating the historically *criolla* Sor Juana Inés de la Cruz into the *mestiza* María Inez. In this chapter, I explore the process and connotations of Sor Juana's transformation into an idealized representative of Mexican identity and probe the relevance of such a film for Mexico at the turn of the millennium.

Chapter 5, "Inverted Captivities and Imagined Adaptations in *Brava Gente Brasileira* (2000) and *Caramuru: A Invenção do Brasil* (2001)," examines two Brazilian films produced in a moment of reflection on the quincentenary of the Portuguese encounter with Brazil. Both of the films engage Brazilian conceptions of cultural mixture through liberal interactions with colonial history and literature. The films re-evaluate iconic moments, the eroticized birth of a happy, racially and culturally mixed nation, and the historically suppressed reality of a violent

Introduction

and problematic clash of cultures. Like several of the films studied in other chapters (e.g., *Como era gostoso, Nuevo mundo, La otra conquista*), these two films exploit the long-established and efficacious tendency to allegorize the nation through foundational couples, which Doris Sommer has studied in relation to nineteenth-century novels that embody "national projects [...] coupled with productive heterosexual desire" (2). Some of the films conjure this resonant tradition of allegorical romances in order to effectively debunk it. Others evoke it so as to bolster their own, similar national allegory.

Brava Gente, directed by Lúcia Murat, analyzes a case of indigenous captivity and revolt against Portuguese colonizers that is loosely based on a historical event. *Brava Gente* indicates that it adapts an eighteenth-century Portuguese account—which the film invents—*Viagem Filosófica à Capitania do Mato Grosso (Philosophical Expedition to the Captaincy of Mato Grosso)*, by Diogo de Castro e Albuquerque. The best-known source for the story conveyed by Guel Arraes's *Caramuru*, in turn, is an eighteenth-century retelling of a sixteenth-century tale of Portuguese and indigenous contact, José de Santa Rita Durão's 1781 *Caramuru: Poema Épico do Descobrimento da Bahia* [*Caramuru: Epic Poem of the Discovery of Bahia*]. However, this film, like *Brava Gente*, invents a primary intertext, one that *Caramuru* suggests was written by the sixteenth-century protagonists of the film. Similar to *Ave María*, this film, initially conceived and made as a TV miniseries to commemorate the quincentenary, establishes a rather abstract but nonetheless governing relationship with colonial sources, dealing with the tradition and myth surrounding a figure more than the historical figure himself. This chapter evaluates how Murat and Arraes cinematically corral history and legend in their drastically distinct but intersecting treatments of captivity, transculturation, and the notion of an imaginary adaptation.

The chapters of the book, in addition to moving chronologically with respect to the dates of the films and the texts on which they were based, treat colonial texts that generally, though not always, progress from collusive (e.g., a letter of discovery) to dissentient writings (e.g., the proto-feminism of Sor Juana) with regard to European colonial rule and the ideology dominant at the time. In similar fashion, the films that I examine begin with

Introduction

ostensibly slavish adherence and fidelity to their intertext, and culminate in more slippery connections to colonial sources. Some of the adaptations, as we have seen, go so far as to invent their own intertext. Whereas *Descobrimento do Brasil* makes explicit reference to Vaz de Caminha's letter and gives the impression of being a strict adaptation, *Ave María*, *Caramuru*, and *Brava Gente Brasileira* authorize their adaptations from a different angle. They participate in more free-form dialogues with respect to the colonial period, interacting not so much with literature as with biography, legacy, legend, and myth—a context perhaps more capable of a complete and convincing transformation, since the intertexts that the directors engage are often intrinsically pliable. Mauro's film in particular hopes to give the impression that the conversation flows only in one direction; he feigns that he is merely a submissive listener to Caminha's voice of truth. The later films contrive a cooperative interlocutor: an invented voice from the colonial period that will say whatever the director wants it to say. I argue that all of the directors, as they strive to create their vision of the nation, attempt to control and convert their colonial intertexts. To continue the conversational metaphor, all of the directors would hope to assume the role of ventriloquist.

The comparatively open-ended interfaces that the more recent films establish with the colonial period, however, risk provoking the implosion of the directors' persuasive edifices. When the films fail to dominate their source fully, that text, not entirely consumed by the film, may assert its voice and challenge its partially digested version. Robert Stam's notion of "intertextual dialogism" may help us to understand the perils, and potential, of these sorts of conversations. Later films, such as *Caramuru*, hazard such egalitarian interactions with intertexts but nonetheless attempt to retain firm control over the interpretive paths that they leave open. Arraes's film freely and openly or, if I may offer a neologism, seam*fu*lly, interweaves past and present through obvious anachronisms, a strategy that on the one hand enhances the film's use of the colony to address postcolonial identity, but on the other hand potentially compromises the endurance of its cannibalization. *Caramuru*'s approach to adaptation, perhaps unwittingly, relinquishes some control over its colonial subject. For example, viewers of the

DVD are provided with the opportunity to interrupt the film with sections of a comedic historical documentary. This tactic may encourage an intertextual dialogue, and may enable varied reflections on history and identity. Arraes's film thus straddles the border between the univocal dynamic studied by this book and another, more open-ended paradigm.

The eight films that I study all participate in a special kind of dialogue with their distant literary sources. The following chapters underscore how these filmmakers take control of the exchange, how they appropriate and transform a colonial intertext—rather than an intertext rooted, for example, in the moment of independence—as a vital step in affirming, in a postcolonial context, concepts of identity reconciled with a colonized past. I see the conversations as directed dialogues that often contain their own urgent and also seductive guides to understanding. The act of adapting taps and translates the distant voice, reorchestrating it in the recording.

Thus, *Cannibalizing the Colony* seeks to amplify the resonance not only of the anthropophagous dialogue that each director maintains with colonial literature, but also of the quiet, digestive conversation between Mexico and Brazil that takes place through the films. In that spirit, this chapter's preliminary reflections on these processes might be appropriately considered a *sobremesa*, which means literally "over [the] table" in both Spanish and Portuguese; and it has come to signify "dessert" in Portuguese and "after dinner conversation" in some dialects of Spanish. Hence, *sobremesa* semantically embodies the interconnectedness of Latin American culture that these films exemplify, and, additionally, encompasses the dual metaphor—consumption and dialogue—that I have used to describe the adaptational dynamics at work in the films. I have in this way sought to summarize the aftermath of the feast. Each of the chapters that follow traces and probes some salient feature of the exchanges that are taking place in these films, some aspect of how Mexican and Brazilian filmmakers have attempted strategically to transform colonial literature.

Chapter One

Re-creating Caminha

The Earnest Adaptation of
Brazil's Letter of Discovery in
Descobrimento do Brasil (1937)

Coinciding with the quincentenary of the Portuguese arrival in America in 1500, three Brazilian directors bookended the turn of the millennium with reconsiderations of the nation's colonial past. Luiz Alberto Pereira's *Hans Staden* (1999), Lúcia Murat's *Brava Gente Brasileira* (2000), and Guel Arraes's *Caramuru: A Invenção do Brasil* (2001) return to a long-standing tendency among Brazilian filmmakers to re-evaluate national origins and present-day conceptions of identity by probing the symbolic potential of the colonial period.[1] Such retrospective efforts to spark examinations of Brazilianness were monumentally inaugurated in sound cinema in 1937 by one of the nation's most renowned directors, Humberto Mauro.[2] Mauro's film revives Pêro Vaz de Caminha's *Carta*, which in 1500 announced the arrival of the Portuguese to the land that would become Brazil. In this chapter, I examine the director's reading and "writing" strategies in order to evaluate how he mines Caminha's narrative and inscribes his inevitably different but strikingly collusive version of the tale onto his own context.[3] I additionally look at the means by which Mauro strives to guarantee the success of his message, how he writes the rules for the game of persuasion and manipulation that he enacts. Finally, I address some of the possible motives and contextual factors that led to Mauro's calculated re-creation of Caminha.

On the first of May, in the year 1500, Caminha signed the letter to the Portuguese monarch Dom Manuel announcing Pedro Álvares Cabral's "accidental" arrival at the land that would be christened Brazil. However, it is possible that the fleet did not happen upon the continent as a result of an unplanned, month-long diversion from its intended course around Africa, as Cabral's scribe Caminha claims (156–57). Some have alleged that the Portuguese intended the revised trajectory and acted in

Chapter One

response to a concern that the Spanish would claim the entire New World.[4] If this is the case, Caminha's *Carta*, the official voice of the "discovery," offers more than a merely innocent description of the voyage. Indeed, the scribe's writing reveals objectives beyond documenting the presumably unintentional nature of Cabral's voyage to the Americas. He describes a land that possesses in abundance good, if savage, people, and Caminha urges the king that Portugal, having discovered a population primed for conversion to Christianity, should return with missionary expeditions. Caminha's text assigns no other value to the newly discovered land, thus discouraging possible fortune seekers. Moreover, by attributing to the Portuguese strictly evangelical motives in the New World, Caminha not only legitimizes their continued presence in the Americas but also succeeds in presenting his people as altruistic and devout.

After scant lines relating the progress and arrival of the Portuguese, Caminha immerses his readers in detailed descriptions of the natives and their initial interaction with the Europeans. The writer's focus shifts in the second half of the letter to a passionate preoccupation with evangelism. He explains that the indigenous population is predisposed to Christianity and advocates their conversion:

> Parece-me gente de tal inocência que, se homem os entendesse e eles a nós, seriam logo cristãos, porque eles, segundo parece, não têm, nem entendem em nenhuma crença. [...] E pois Nosso Senhor, que lhes deu bons corpos e bons rostos, como a bons homens, por aqui nos touxe, creio que não foi sem causa. Portanto Vossa Alteza, que tanto deseja acrescentar a santa fé católica, deve cuidar da sua salvação. E prazerá a Deus que com pouco trabalho seja assim. (170–71)[5] [1]

Caminha contributes to the construction of the image of "noble savage" by describing the indigenous people as innocent, simple, and free of other beliefs. Moreover, he insists that by God's own hand the natives have been made beautiful and therefore good. Hence, Caminha leads readers to conclude that God carried the Portuguese, a people dedicated to the expansion of Christianity, to this "new" land in order to realize the religious potential that He instilled in the natives.

Whether or not the Portuguese intended their westward journey and enlisted Caminha's written complicity, Dom Manuel of

Portugal did exploit the scribe's letter as propaganda directed at Spain and the rest of Europe in an attempt to legitimize and perpetuate the Portuguese claim to the lands. Upon receiving notification of Cabral's "discovery," Dom Manuel wasted no time in disseminating the news within and beyond the Iberian Peninsula through letters (Pereira 13). On August 28, 1501, in a missive to his uncle and aunt, King Ferdinand and Queen Isabel of Spain, the king declares that Cabral "chegou a uma terra que novamente descobriu," and there found "gentes nuas como na primeira inocência, mansas e pacíficas"; he goes on to write that it appears that God miraculously wanted them to find that land "porque é mui conveniente e necessária à navegação da Índia" (qtd. in Pereira 14–15) [2]. The quoted excerpts demonstrate how the Portuguese king parallels Caminha's argument in several respects. He insists to the Catholic Monarchs that Cabral encountered previously unclaimed land, but assigns it no worth beyond the innocence of the people, and continues his justification for the Portuguese presence in the New World by advancing a providential explanation for the turn of events. However, the king's reasoning differs from that proffered by the scribe: curiously, the Portuguese monarch suggests that God conjured for Cabral a colossal, but "convenient" and "necessary" detour: the Creator led the fleet all the way to the Western Hemisphere so that they might repair their ships and navigate to India by way of Africa. Dom Manuel paraphrases Caminha's letter with the aim of determining how others would conceptualize the newly claimed lands. In so doing, the king's writing anticipates the significance that others would assign to Caminha's foundational missive.[6] The symbolic terrain of the letter, first tested by Portugal's monarch, has proven to be fertile in subsequent commentaries on national identity in Brazil.

In 1937 Brazilian director Mauro follows the rhetorical path cleared by Dom Manuel, tapping the potential of Caminha's letter in his film *Descobrimento do Brasil*. As part of his strategic commentary on Brazilian identity, Mauro consistently, strictly, and even reverently seems to emulate the sixteenth-century text. The filmmaker takes great pains, both within his film and in promoting it, to convince the viewer that he indulges in no deviation from Caminha's *Carta*. Additionally, Mauro presents the letter as a privileged and correct depiction of the first moments of the Portuguese presence in the New World, and would have viewers

Chapter One

accept his film as a flawless cinematic transcription of a "true" text. *Descobrimento do Brasil* so gives the impression of faithfulness to its source that Hernani Heffner of the Cinemateca of the Museu de Arte Moderna in Rio de Janeiro writes that Mauro "logrou seu intento de adaptar com fidelidade e minúcia a carta" ["achieved his intention to adapt the letter with fidelity and in detail"] (19). However, I contend that the director transcends mere adherence to the minutiae of the letter in order to resuscitate, and even exaggerate, certain aspects of the text's ideology.[7] Mauro echoes but also shapes Caminha's perspective by exalting colonialism, Catholicism, the Portuguese and their justification for evangelizing the Amerindians, whom the film portrays as children in need of European tutelage.[8]

Some contemporaries of Mauro vehemently critiqued his adaptation of the *Carta*. Lourival Fontes, director of the Departamento Nacional de Propaganda ([National Department of Propaganda] D.N.P, later absorbed by the Departamento de Imprensa e Propaganda [Department of Printing and Propaganda]) of the Ministry of Justice, in a 1937 personal note to the director, lauded the film's "fidelidad historica e [a] sua orientação técnica" ["historical fidelity and technical capacity"] (qtd. in Schvarzman, *Humberto Mauro* 149). In the same year, Brazilian writer Graciliano Ramos condemned its perspective on the encounter, lamenting that the film presents to spectators "retratos desfigurados dos exploradores que aqui vieram escravizar e assassinar o indígena" ["disfigured portraits of the explorers who came here to enslave and murder the indigenous people"] (67), though he did coincide with Fontes in praising the film's quality. Ramos's anti-colonial stance was shared by others, including modernist writer Oswald de Andrade, whose 1928 "Manifesto antropófago" sought to expose the lingering effects of colonialism and evangelism in what would be Brazil (*A Utopia Antropofágica* [*Anthropophagous Utopia*] 47–52).[9] The surprising ideological disparity between Mauro and some of his contemporaries compels us to consider the circumstances that gave rise to an apparent apology for colonialism in an era of such consciously critical postcolonial voices.[10] What is more, *Descobrimento do Brasil*'s recent restoration and distribution in 1997—on the occasion of what would be the director's one-hundredth birthday and in anticipation of Brazil's own "quinto centenário" ["quincentenary"]—insert the film into a revised cinematic and cultural context and compound the need to re-evaluate Mauro's revival of the *Carta*.[11] In the ensuing pages I will explore how and why Mauro, well into the twentieth century, reproduces a sixteenth-century European explorer's narrative of discovery and attempts to authorize both the narrative and his reading of it.

* * *

The thrust of *Descobrimento do Brasil*'s portrayal of history and of the peoples that would constitute the modern nation is apparent: Mauro presents to the viewer indigenous peoples enthusiastic about a cultural and religious salvation generously extended by pious Portuguese. However, the ease with which we can trace the broad lines of Mauro's treatment of the *Carta* may distract the viewer from appreciating the rich and problematic complexity of the director's project. Mauro consistently combines his version of the *Carta* with techniques that seek to sanction his adaptation. For example, the action that Mauro presents on the screen often faithfully follows the letter, if you will, of Caminha's letter, in an attempt to inspire the viewers' trust in the veracity of the film's interpretation of the encounter. At the same time, through the frequent display in intertitles of Caminha's declarations and their subsequent representation, the film simultaneously posits the *Carta* as a true depiction of historical events and veils the director's own modifications. Consider as an initial illustration the cinematic representation of a central event rendered by Caminha: the moment of encounter between Cabral and the Amerindians. The sequence takes place shortly after the armada arrives at the coast, and Portuguese sailors have brought two native men aboard the ship. In his portrayal of the pair, Mauro looks constantly to Caminha, following even the smallest details of his lengthy description of them (158–60). The duration of the sequence, 10 minutes of a 60-minute film, indicates its importance within *Descobrimento do Brasil*'s argument. The end of Cabral's interview with the two men—a section of the sequence that lasts just under a minute—corresponds with the following quotation from Caminha's letter:

> Então estiram-se de costas na alcatifa, a dormir, sem buscarem maneira de encobrir suas vergonhas, as quais não eram fanadas; e as cabeleiras delas estavam bem rapadas e feitas. O Capitão lhes mandou pôr baixo das cabeças seus coxins; e o da cabeleira esforçava-se por a não quebrar.

Chapter One

> E lançaram-lhes um manto por cima; e eles consentiram, quedaram-se e dormiram. (160) [3]

The film reproduces many particularities of the action and mise-en-scène described by the text, such as how the Portuguese provided pillows and blankets for their guests. In so doing, Mauro labors to persuade Caminha's diligent reader of the care that the director has given to accuracy.

The director himself has said that in making *Descobrimento do Brasil*, "tentei contar o fato como se fosse um repórter filmando dentro do barco de Cabral" ("O Mundo" 206) [4]. Mauro even writes the Tupi dialogue for the film himself (Merten n. pag.); much later, he was also consulted by Nelson Pereira dos Santos and Paulo César Saraceni regarding Tupi dialogues for *Como era gostoso o meu francês* (1971) and *Anchieta, José do Brasil* (1976–77), respectively (Miranda 365). As part of his dedication to detail, Mauro also takes steps to portray accurately the dress and other aspects of native Brazilian culture,[12] markers to which some critics have referred when judging the historical film's fidelity (e.g., Merten n. pag.; Pina n. pag.; and Aquino n. pag.).[13] However, the film's air of accuracy surpasses a desire to produce a faithful historical re-creation. Rather, Mauro's evident quest for credibility hopes to lure the viewer into his representation of Caminha's text, and consequently into the ideology that the director embraces.

Although Mauro would have spectators believe that he transfers with disinterest the raw material of Caminha's letter onto celluloid, the director modifies the account such that the film not only emulates, but also reshapes the scribe's colonialist ideology. Mauro often stylizes Caminha's representation of the natives and of the events surrounding the so-called discovery of Brazil. Even where the director clearly follows the text, he often hyperbolizes Caminha's portrayal of the natives: Mauro draws on Caminha's touching, if sparse, description of the pillows and the blankets being used to "tuck in" the visitors on the boat, but the director adds his own flourish with several conjured details. Specifically, the actor who plays Cabral placing the pillows himself under the heads of the two men augments the text's positive representation of the Portuguese. Furthermore, a white-bearded priest pulls the covers up even more, and Cabral puts his finger to his lips to keep the soldiers from disturbing the adorable, prostrated pair. Heitor Villa-Lobos's score collaborates in Mauro's stylization of Caminha's text. When the two indigenous men meet Cabral aboard the ship, for example, the score first contributes a sense of distance and jocular exoticism with the orchestration and rhythms of a new musical theme at the beginning of the sequence that, apparently, are intended to sound native. As the two men drift peacefully off to sleep, the score shifts to a sentimental, European-style lullaby motif that confirms and reinforces the film's patronizing tone. In spite of the composer's and filmmaker's effort, *Descobrimento do Brasil*, as we have seen, did not always successfully draw viewers into its imaginary world and indoctrinate them. Instead of perceiving an idyllic and spiritually inspiring encounter of cultures—the end to which the film palpably tweaks the letter— novelist Graciliano Ramos interprets the aforementioned scene in 1937 critically. He condemns how Cabral covers the natives with the "delicadeza de mãe carinhosa" (67), and criticizes the "sorriso de condescendência babosa" of the Portuguese (67).[14] And in a comment replete with irony, Ramos also insists that the film portrays the Portuguese as saints and observes that they have "uma expressão de beatitude que destoa das façanhas que andaram praticando em Terras da África e da Ásia e por fim neste hemisfério" (67) [5].

By means of distinct *modi operandi*, Caminha and Mauro similarly strive to demonstrate a felicitous encounter as well as the necessity of the Portuguese colonial and evangelical project. An intertitle that does not derive from Caminha's letter states, "Os descobridores rasgam a matta virgem, a procura do lenho para a Cruz" [6], and initiates a thirteen-minute sequence that chronicles Mauro's version of the events leading up to and including the first mass held with the natives, a scene inspired by both Caminha and the 1861 painting *The First Mass*, by Victor Meirelles (Stam, *Tropical Multiculturalism* 8), which in turn derived from Horace Vernet's *Première Messe en Kabilie* (Stam, "Cabral and the Indians" 212).[15] Mauro's designation of the forest as "virgin" in the intertitle intensifies his continuing portrayal of the indigenous peoples, not to mention their land, as a *tabula rasa*, destined to receive and in need of the technological and religious influence of Portugal, a portrayal that the director carries to inflated conclusion during the Mass. Mauro not only links native to nature in his celebration of the Portuguese

Chapter One

possession and manipulation of the territory's raw materials, but also puts on display the awe-struck participation of the natives in the colonial enterprise.[16] In the film, as in the letter (168), the Portuguese construct a monumental cross, and although Caminha briefly mentions that some of the natives helped the Portuguese men to carry the cross (171), Mauro compounds the image of spontaneous collective servility by shooting only the Amerindians lugging the cross to its new site. Just as the camera cuts, in a shot/reverse shot from a slow tilt showing the legs then torsos of many indigenous men carrying something as-yet unseen, to a low-angle image of the men walking away from the camera, now clearly carrying a large cross, Villa-Lobos's score shifts from a light but intensifying instrumental theme to exuberant but sacred-sounding choral music. With an inspired and exultant thematic shift, the composer encourages the raising of the cross, a crucial scene in the film and one that Caminha only touches on in the letter (172).

In the sequence that follows the encounter scene on the ship, Cabral goes ashore with the two indigenous men who had slept on board. In both the film and the letter, the two men are clad in "sua camisa nova, sua carapuça vermelha e um rosário de contas brancas de osso" (160) [7]. The Portuguese ask them to signal to the two hundred naked men[17] on the beach to put down their weapons (160), a request with which the men on the beach comply. Caminha soon announces the quick departure of the two indigenous men ("Dali se partiram os outros dois mancebos, que os não vimos mais" [161]) [also in 7], but not before they shed the trappings of Portuguese "civilization."[18] In the film, however, the two men never leave. Mauro incorporates them into his sign system, and utilizes them up until the end. Their continued presence indicates the director's insistence on indigenous collusion with the conquest and religious conversion. The final moments of the film confirm once again this tactic, as one of the indigenous men from the ship scene is depicted kissing a crucifix. Toward the end of the mass, the film converges visually on the young man's gesture of reverence. Following a medium long shot that frames several standing priests to the right and a line of Brazilians to the left waiting to kneel before the clergy, the director cuts to a medium close-up of the priest offering a small cross to the genuflecting man, and then to a high-angle close-up of the indigenous man's face, hand, and the cross, as if seen from the point of view of a standing Portuguese onlooker.

The landing party's arrival ashore precedes a series of events with no textual foundation. After a ceremonial exchange of headgear and weapons, there is a high-angle close-up of Cabral's hand deliberately shaping an indigenous hand into a European handshake. Mauro fabricates here, albeit in general agreement with Caminha, an emblem of an allegedly peaceful and egalitarian union of two cultures. In service of his apology for the conquest, the director suggests that the Portuguese bring an offer of partnership and cooperation. And Cabral seals the agreement on European terms, with a European gesture. The act of teaching the indigenous man how to greet in a European fashion reinforces the teacher/student, parent/child, wise/ignorant dichotomies that pervade the film.

Even as Cabral and the Brazilian are shaking hands, the viewer notices shadows traversing the screen of many men carrying barrels. One of the film's many intertitles soon recalls the textual inspiration for the apparently spontaneous and cooperative behavior "… e então se começaram de chegar muitos; e … tomaram barris e encheram-nos" (160) [8]. However, Mauro sidesteps the explanation that follows in the text: The indigenous men carried the barrels with the hope of receiving some reward or to initiate trade.[19] In the film, a succession of several and varied shots are interwoven to document a seemingly endless, altruistic procession of barrel-carrying Brazilians as they make their way to a ship: an eye-level long shot of the line of men with barrels traversing the screen from left to right; a low-angle extreme long shot of the same men silhouetted winding their way from left to right toward the camera and then beginning to pass close in front of the camera; a low-angle, deep-focus shot that shows members of the procession from far to close as they snake their way across the screen toward the camera; a brief variation on the previous shots; and finally, an extreme long shot of the burdened men walking away from the camera along the beach toward a Portuguese ship visible in the distance. The enthusiasm of the indigenous men confirms *Descobrimento do Brasil*'s insistence on the positive native reaction to the Portuguese presence, and suggests the origins of an equal, predestined, smooth, and cooperative spirit. Mauro's reading of Caminha leads to another related and inevitable

Chapter One

interpretation, that the passive indigenous population accepts as natural a relationship based on servility.

Generally, *Descobrimento do Brasil* manifests its vision of the origins of the Brazilian nation by displaying favorable indigenous reactions to the Portuguese and portraying a nascent peaceful, but paternal, relationship. The romanticized dynamic that Mauro reproduces, following Caminha, implicitly elevates the Portuguese and debases the Brazilians. Although the *Carta* tends to (problematically) praise certain qualities of the indigenous people that the expedition encounters, it occasionally also offers an explicitly negative description, as in the case of predictably referring to the Brazilians' barbarism (161).[20] In reference to the prompt disappearance of the familiar pair of Brazilians, the scribe makes this comment:

> Os outros dois, que o Capitão teve nas naus, a que deu o que já disse, nunca mais aqui apareceram—do que tiro ser gente bestial, de pouco saber e por isso tão esquiva. Porém e com tudo isto andam muito bem curados e muito limpos. E naquilo me parece ainda mais que são como aves ou alimárias monteses, às quais faz o ar melhor pena e melhor cabelo que às mansas, porque os corpos seus são tão limpos, tão gordos e formosos, que não pode mais ser. (166) [9]

Here, Caminha conflates praise and denigration in an exoticizing association of the native Brazilians with birds and wild animals. By means of an addition to the narrative, Mauro reads with the grain of the letter's intent. The following three intertitles, which appear in close succession, and the corresponding images in the film, illustrate the director's technique:

> ... e ... andavam muitos dêles, dançando e folgando. (165)
>
> Mestre João encontra, com seu astrolábio, 17 gráus austraes de latitude.... Diogo Diaz ... meteu-se a dançar com êles ... dando salto real. (165–66)[21] [10]

Mauro took the first and third intertitle from the same paragraph in Caminha's text, and invented the second intertitle. The paragraph from which Mauro quotes reads:

> Além do rio, *andavam muitos deles dançando e folgando*, uns diante dos outros, sem se tomarem pelas mãos. E faziam-no bem. Passou-se então além do rio *Diogo Dias*, almoxarife

> que foi de Cacavém, que é homem gracioso de prazer; e levou consigo um gaiteiro nosso com sua gaita. E *meteu-se com eles a dançar*, tomando-os pelas mãos; e eles folgavam e riam, e andavam com ele muito bem ao som da gaita. Depois de dançarem, fez-lhes ali, andando no chão, muitas voltas ligeiras e *salto real*, de que eles se espantavam e riam e folgavam muito. E conquanto com aquilo muito os segurou e afagou, tomavam logo uma esquiveza como de *animais monteses*, e foram-se para cima. (165–66; my emphasis) [11]

The director chose not to include the end of Caminha's description, where he refers to the natives as "animais monteses." However, the added intertitle and the accompanying, contrived cut to Mestre João and his *astrolábio* help the film nonetheless to contrast analogously "civilization" and "barbarism." First the film presents presumably "barbaric" dancing, then a "civilized" concern about science, and finally a child-like, unconcerned play. Whereas Caminha equated barbarism with animals, Mauro saw fit to activate another opposition, science vs. native dancing, in order to achieve a similar goal within his own context.

Throughout the film, Mauro presents viewers with natives who are inexplicably stricken with Christian devotion.[22] In one of the rare glimpses of a female in *Descobrimento do Brasil*, the director extracts—but also partially covers up, as it were—another moment from Caminha (173) and indulges in a symbolic veiling of nudity with a shining white cloth, a lesson in Christian modesty. However, where Mauro articulates acts of devotion, Caminha admits mere mimicry or ambivalence. According to the *Carta*, despite kissing the crucifix some of the natives simply departed in the middle of the service because it was too hot (172). Caminha's narrative also admits that the naked woman responds to the priest's morally edifying efforts with indifference, making no attempt to keep the lesson in modesty from slipping to the ground: "não fazia grande memória de o estender bem, para se cobrir" (173) [12]. The film, in contrast, in a medium long shot of Mauro's miraculously proselytized female character backed by companions, shows her reaching out longingly for the resplendent fabric while she securely clutches the sheet that now thoroughly envelops her.

Mauro's avoidance of the natives' nudity aligns his adaptation with the first printed version of the letter, for these same

Chapter One

passages were excised from Father Manuel Ayres de Casal's 1817 edition. The topic of nudity in general illustrates how Caminha and Mauro reach analogous destinations by way of diverging paths. Caminha waxes repeatedly, often with tongue in cheek, about the Brazilians' beautiful, well-formed bodies, and even indulges in double-entendres about the women's vaginas, e.g., "suas vergonhas [eram] tão altas, tão cerradinhas e tão limpas das cabeleiras que de as muito bem olharmos, não tínhamos nenhuma vergonha" (161); and with respect to one of the women, he declares that "sua vergonha (que ela não tinha) era tão graciosa, que a muitas mulheres da nossa terra, vendo-lhe tais feições, fizera vergonha, por não terem a sua como ela" (161) [13]. Caminha's playfully euphemistic, if sexualizing and exoticizing, descriptions disappear in Mauro's version, which rarely even presents the viewer with a Brazilian woman. In order successfully to celebrate Catholicism, the director chose not to take the same representational path as the sixteenth-century scribe. For Caminha, a rapt and repeated fascination with the genitalia of the Brazilians did not conflict with his plea for the conversion of the natives. Mauro, on the other hand, felt compelled to "cover up" completely this very prevalent, rather prurient aspect of the scribe's text.

Only by means of plotting differently the elements that he lifts from the letter can the filmmaker convey a message that runs roughly parallel to Caminha's. Mauro, for example, does not communicate the core of his argument for evangelization by means of the same details that Caminha selects in order to achieve his similar goal. The scribe supports his plea with the assertion that God's will brought the Portuguese to Brazil. In contrast, Mauro augments the textual description of the scene around the cross in order to animate the image of a peaceful and Christian birth for Brazil.

During the encounter scene aboard the ship, Mauro's two indigenous men likewise demonstrate a spontaneous fascination with the rosary held by one of the priests, a symbolically suggestive aspect of the film for which the director finds inspiration in the text (159). By means of the portrayal of the pair's interest in the rosary, Mauro once again associates the Portuguese with a charitable and innately embraced evangelical project. The director chips away at the letter's characteristic ambiguity and focuses the viewer's interpretation; Mauro never lets slip an opportunity to execute and authorize his message, even if it means communicating a more colonialist message than did Caminha himself. The narrative passage that treats the rosary does draw attention to the indigenous men's interest in it, but Caminha attributes the pair's apparent intrigue not to a religious epiphany as the film implies, but to a desire to initiate trade. Moreover, Caminha calls attention to the inherent ambiguity of the actions of the native men, and recognizes that the Portuguese understood only what they wanted to understand ("Isto tomávamos nós assim por assim o desejarmos" [159]) [14]. Where Caminha admits that he may be wrong, Mauro confidently presents his telling of the events as infallible. The director's modifications to the letter in these scenes unambiguously celebrate a native population predisposed to Catholic devotion and European guidance.

Descobrimento do Brasil follows and focuses on the *Carta* as well by tightly weaving religion with the State and by presenting Portuguese colonization as positive and predestined, a stance embodied even in the film's distribution. Figures 1 and 2, promotional posters for *Descobrimento do Brasil*, illustrate how essential the culminating, evangelical sequence of Mauro's film was to the manner in which the producers of the film wished to market the project. Both of the stylistically distinct posters foreground a priest and a tall cross. Figure 2 links Church and State in its depiction of massive Portuguese ships that loom over a scene in which the priest, backed by soldiers, blesses a genuflecting indigenous man, while a group of natives appear to await, with downcast eyes, their chance to kneel before the European colonizers. Figure 1 reflects Mauro's reading of Caminha with a stylization of a similar scene. The poster features cartoon-like silhouettes of a priest, the cross, and a group of indigenous people. Dotted lines emanating from the crucifix suggest divine illumination. The priest, as if already (inevitably) present on land, opens his arms toward the Portuguese fleet in a gesture that welcomes the Europeans to the New World.[23]

We have already seen some key elements of the game of persuasion that Mauro plays. His dedication to details, for example, helps to lend his views a veneer of objectivity. Within this context of credibility the director then develops the ideological content of the film, which, as we have seen, consists generally of a positive view of the Portuguese, a paternalistic

Chapter One

Fig. 1. Poster for Humberto Mauro's *Descobrimento do Brasil*. Courtesy of the Centro Técnico Audiovisual, Ministério da Cultura, Rio de Janeiro, Brazil. Rpt. by permission.

Fig. 2. Poster for Humberto Mauro's *Descobrimento do Brasil*. Courtesy of the Centro Técnico Audiovisual, Ministério da Cultura, Rio de Janeiro, Brazil. Rpt. by permission.

view of the Brazilians, and the celebration of a glorious and welcome introduction of Catholicism into the newly discovered land. Mauro attempts to ensure the success of his presentation of Brazilian history and identity in a number of ways. The first frames of the film try to prime the viewer's reading of *Descobrimento do Brasil* by invoking with an opening credit the names of several intellectuals (who are also cited on one of the posters), which assures spectators that Mauro's adaptation adheres to rigorous academic standards. Both the poster and the opening credit read: "Collaboração intellectual e verificação histórica" [15], and display the names of three well-known scholars: Edgard Roquette-Pinto, Affonso de E. Taunay, and Bernardino José de Souza.[24] Before the film commences, then, would-be expert witnesses testify to the validity of the director's views on Brazil.[25] The poster and the credits work in extratextual conjunction with—indeed as a guarantee for—Mauro's vast persuasive apparatus within the film.

The lack of dialogue in *Descobrimento do Brasil*'s initial scenes works in concert with Mauro's authorization of the film's version of history. The director exploits silence by assigning unusual communicative responsibility to exaggerated facial expressions, a technique that, like the intertitles, recalls the silent film era.[26] For example, moments after a member of the crew declares that he has spotted land, the camera lingers in a medium shot on the scribe/witness Caminha, as he contemplates, in an awe-struck pose, an image of the cross, to which the film then cuts in an eyeline match. The way that the filmmaker shapes his actors' faces, as in this scene, leaves no room for misinterpretation. The cast never fails to hammer home the director's points with their mutely effusive reactions. In a shot of Portuguese children and their dog on board Cabral's ship, as well, the camera lingers for several seconds, thereby lending the image a photographic stillness that insists on the shining countenance of the virtuous, yet apocryphal, children. Through their expression Mauro deploys the pair as stand-ins for the kind Portuguese.

Also within the opening sequences of the film, Mauro infuses light with persuasive, ideological value. During the film's nocturnal prelude, the camera studies the steps of a crewmember who ushers away darkness by methodically lighting a torch and then a lantern, and then slowly circulating through the ship, as a muted and stately section of the score accompanies his passage. The director treats the procession of light as an introduction to the fleet's journey, which links the Portuguese, and in particular their endeavor, to the notion of illumination or enlightenment, in the cultural, intellectual, and religious sense. Immediately following the announcement that land has been sighted, the film solidifies the suggested symbolic associations of light. The director surrounds Caminha, in the shot referenced earlier, with a luminous halo as the scribe absorbs the portentous news of the arrival in the New World. The timing of the illumination implies the complicity of some supernatural force in the Portuguese colonization of the land. The film reinforces the implication with an image that comes shortly after Caminha's apparent epiphany. After cutting to the image of the cross that Caminha contemplates, the following shot broadens the viewer's perspective, framing the scribe from behind in a medium shot before panning to the left to expose a kneeling priest. The director now displays from behind Caminha praying with the wizened priest, and spotlights on the wall before and between the pair both a cross and a weapon, signaling the connection between Church and State.

The halo around Caminha's head in the land-sighting scene anticipates the final moments of the later encounter scene on the ship. As Cabral puts the two indigenous men to bed, the director illuminates the men, which stresses that the initial military and political Portuguese contact with natives has culminated in their Christianization. The image that Mauro composes, similar to the promotional poster mentioned earlier, solders evangelism and conquest and assists in the film's apology for colonialism: *Descobrimento do Brasil* not only celebrates Christianity but also the Portuguese presence in the New World.

As I have already suggested, Mauro's use of intertitles seeks to authorize the film's message by reinforcing the impression of accuracy and objectivity. Every three minutes or so a quotation from Caminha's letter (or occasionally another descriptive text) materializes on the screen, and the subsequent images purport to re-create what the writer describes. Mauro's choice of utilitarian quotations that leave little room for interpretation (e.g., "houvemos vista das ilhas"; "seguimos nosso caminho"

Chapter One

[16]) implies a solid textual basis for the film and helps to persuade the viewer of the trustworthiness of the adaptation. Similar to other tactics that we have seen, Mauro would appear to be declaring through such intertitles that he adapts Caminha transparently, and that he has lent the viewer the means by which to judge the film's portrayal of the distant events. The director validates his view of the past by taking the position that subjectivity does not plague his retelling of history. Take the intertitle that reads "[...] ... 21 de Abril, topamos alguns sinais de terra" [17] and its subsequent representation in a simple close-up of the surface of the water strewn with twigs and other debris. Such verifiable correspondence encourages the viewer to infer that the film is objective. In the closing shots of the film, the director again explicitly connects the text to its adaptation. Several interior medium long shots that show Caminha reading the letter aloud to Cabral and several others are intercut with medium close-ups displaying his listeners' reactions and with close-ups of the letter itself that concretize the association of the film with the letter. *Descobrimento do Brasil* additionally insists on the veracity of Caminha's (and by extension the film's) account by exposing to the viewer the unequivocal assent of the writer's companions: as Caminha reads his account, his listeners thoughtfully and frequently nod their approval of the scribe's interpretation of the events.

Nevertheless, Mauro's attempt to claim adaptational innocence through the use of intertitles dissolves upon closer examination. One notices, for instance, that the first half of the film contains intertitles corresponding only to the initial paragraphs of Caminha's letter. In fact, the first eleven of twenty-two intertitles are a virtually seamless quotation from the straightforward beginning of the narrative. The last eleven intertitles follow a different pattern: the director selects them from among the many remaining, richly descriptive pages of the letter. Mauro quotes extensively at first in order to infuse his film with authority and to give the impression that he always and only follows Caminha precisely. Yet the vast and hidden textual gaps between the quotations in the second half of the film reveal that Caminha says much that Mauro does not communicate. The spaces that Mauro creates leave ample room for him to shape people and events, a freedom that the director exercises under the rubric of exactitude.

Mauro intersperses quotations from Caminha's letter with several intertitles of his own composition, which subtly contribute to the director's casting of the letter. The filmmaker surrounds his additions with the same air of detached accuracy that the intertitles from Caminha's text enjoy. The director does demarcate the created intertitles with a different, but notably archaic, font: a Gothic script reminiscent of early printed documents. Perhaps the choice of font attempts to compensate for sacrificing the implication of historical authenticity that the intertitles taken directly from Caminha's letter lend the film. Some of the invented intertitles include: "Monte Pascoal" ["Mount Easter"], "O degredado Affonso Ribeiro" ["The Convict Affonso Ribeiro"], and "19 de Abril de 1500 Domingo de Páscoa" ["April 19, 1500, Easter Sunday"]. The factual tone of this last intertitle, which appears early in the film, associates it with the descriptive intertitles taken from Caminha's text and therefore attempts to lend credence to the loaded scene that follows. Immediately after the intertitle disappears, the viewer witnesses a rare moment of speech in the film: one of the (many) priests on the voyage is giving a pre-arrival sermon, about which Caminha's letter mentions no details. The sermon culminates in a cry about the "glória da Igreja e de Portugal!" to which one of the men responds, "Viva Portugal!" [18]. The rapt and frenzied crew rewards that exclamation with a crescendo of cheers. The invented intertitle and subsequent spurious scene advance but also augment the pro-Portuguese and pro-Catholic perspective of Caminha's letter.

Another invented intertitle announces the previously mentioned smiling children, the "Filhos de Ayres Correia" ["Sons of Ayres Correia"], whom Mauro captures, in a portrait-like medium shot, in the act of lovingly caressing their dog. Caminha does mention Correia (159), but his children play no part in the letter, nor do any of Mauro's other embellishments regarding the mundane details of life on board the ship during Cabral's westward journey. The director furthers the illusion of adaptational precision by implying that he has diligently scoured the text for its arcane yet revelatory facets.[27] And at the same time, the shot of Correia's children gives the Portuguese a face of benevolence and beatific innocence. Mauro buttresses through cross cutting the implication of a textual source for the charged shot in question. The sequence begins with a close-up of

Caminha's notebook, and then of Caminha himself, serious and engaged in writing. Mauro then cuts to an image of the children, returns to Caminha, and finally rests on the Portuguese youth with their faithful (but cinematically invented) dog. The shots of Caminha and his text inextricably anchor Mauro's cinematic adaptation in yet another way to its ostensibly exclusive textual basis. The scenes that represent the text of invented intertitles establish an important precedent: the director links intertitles—already clearly connected to quotations from Caminha—with a departure from the letter, thus broadening his license to shape the story of Brazil's birth, while perpetuating the impression of accuracy that Mauro has established through the film's touted ties to the letter. As a result of his use of intertitles and other cinematic techniques Mauro attempts to narrow the avenues of interpretation left open to the viewer.

The opening scenes of the film, which reflect the roles that the director assigns to the intertitles, are a case in point. Whereas Caminha gives only schematic information about the voyage before the fleet's arrival to Brazil, Mauro engages in an extensive cinematic prelude. As with the fabricated intertitles, the director's creative protraction of the events—which tends to expose his agenda—is punctuated by suggestions of historical or adaptational exactitude. Throughout the representation of Cabral's westward journey, for example, Mauro presents to the viewer frequent close-ups of scientific instruments and navigational notation. The film's references to navigation, which are entirely absent from Caminha's text,[28] collaborate with the air of attention to detail that the director creates. Mauro's exhibition of science also quickly associates the Portuguese with the superior technology of European civilization, a move that comes to fruition later in the film when the director juxtaposes a Portuguese man using an astrolabe with Brazilians engaged in carefree celebration.

By means of the system that I have been examining, the filmmaker presents his viewers with an apparently infallible version of the dawn of modern Brazilian history. Upon *Descobrimento do Brasil*'s release in 1937, the success of Mauro's efforts to persuade becomes clear. The press praised the film's historical fidelity (Heffner 19), a compliment that Luís de Pina echoed years later, in 1989. Pina additionally described the first part of the film as a "descrição quase documental da aventura" (n. pag.) [19], which parallels Mauro's own declaration, quoted above, that he attempted to film as if he were a reporter on board Cabral's ship. And in 1997 reviewers of the restored version of the film surprisingly labeled *Descobrimento do Brasil* a "documentary," which may indicate that Mauro's attempt to present his vision of Brazil as true and unbiased has once again found purchase (Aquino n. pag.; Merten n. pag.).

Through his adaptation of Caminha's *Carta*, Mauro gives life to the scribe's vision of the encounter, modifies it, and authorizes his own stylization of the letter. We have seen that Mauro, even more than Caminha, exalts the Portuguese, condescends to the natives, and implies not only that the natives desire both religious and technological aid from the Portuguese, but also that they eagerly accept a subordinate role in a nascent European-dominated society. We have also witnessed how the director reinforces Caminha's insistence that God intended for the Portuguese to colonize the territory. As author Graciliano Ramos writes in his 1937 review of the film, "a intenção dos criadores da melhor película brasileira não foi denegrir o invasor: foi melhorá-lo, emprestar-lhe qualidades que ele não tinha" (67) [20]. Moreover, the director takes care to present his interpretation as unassailable by means of a convoluted but smoothly executed persuasive apparatus. What motivated such a skewed foundational portrait in an era also populated by voices critical of colonialism, like those of Ramos and Oswald de Andrade? And why does Mauro take such care in convincing us of the validity of his reading of Caminha?

We have already glimpsed a few of Mauro's apparent motives for the way that he adapted the *Carta*. His knowledge of the Tupi language and his lauded attention to ethnographic details suggest a genuine interest in indigenous culture. Mauro also seems to indicate an enthusiasm for documentary-like filmmaking apart from what I have termed his quest for credibility. However, the filmmaker's interest in documentaries—which he directed for many years after 1937 while working for the government-run Instituto Nacional de Cinema Educativo (INCE [National Institute of Educational Cinema])—stemmed from his desire to educate the masses.[29] Mauro explicitly insisted on the educational value of cinema, in particular feature-length films, and argued that "'[e]ducar é fazer com que o cidadão adquira hábitos que tenham significação na sociedade em que ele vive. [...] [O] sujeito não pode se educar sozinho. O sujeito pode se instruir sozinho, mas se educar sozinho é impossível'" (Mauro, qtd. in Souza 90) [21]. So, in what way did he want to educate the masses? The preceding examination has shown that Mauro charged what is for some his documentary-like reproduction of Caminha with a calculated message and persuasively mobilized that message in order to instill in his viewers a particular outlook on the encounter of Portuguese and Amerindians, one that perpetuates the myth of a modern Brazil born of a peaceful union of peoples. The film also obviously desires to promote Catholicism and champion the Church's historical attempt to convert indigenous peoples, which may be due in part to Mauro's own religious leanings.[30] What we know of the director's personal motives partially accounts for the film's ideology, but it fails to explain adequately what appears to be a crafted piece of propaganda that advances a problematic portrayal of the Portuguese and the Amerindians.

Certain aspects of the socio-political context in which Mauro produced *Descobrimento do Brasil* help to illuminate the director's depiction of Brazilian identity. Mauro in 1937, like King Manuel in 1500, manipulates Caminha's letter in accordance with the goals of the government: the director's motives dovetail nicely with those of the Brazilian State.[31] Through his film Mauro participated in composing and propagating a myth of Brazilian national origins consistent with several aspects of the vision and policies of Getúlio Vargas, who was in power from 1930 to 1945 and again from 1951 to 1954 (the dictatorial Estado Novo ran from 1937 to 1945). The markers of government involvement contained in the opening credits of *Descobrimento do Brasil* provide a starting point for situating the film within its political and ideological context. The credits explicitly point to a direct connection with the government of Vargas: the film received funding from the Ministério da Educação [Ministry of Education] and the Instituto Nacional de Cinema Educativo. What is more, one of the scholarly authorities cited in the credits and in the distributional poster, anthropologist Roquette-Pinto, had profound ties to the State. When the time came to organize the INCE, Vargas's Minister of Education and Public Health, Gustavo Capanema, chose *Descobrimento do Brasil*'s own Roquette-Pinto to head the fledgling institute.[32] Upon assuming control of the INCE, Roquette-Pinto wasted no time in enlisting Mauro to run the technical side of the organization (Autran 471).[33] Even before joining the INCE, Roquette-Pinto had a hand in censorship: he headed the Comissão Federal de Censura [Federal Cenorship Commission], formed in 1932 by governmental Decree 21.240 (Gatti and Simões 115), which sought in part to promote a unified sense of patriotism.[34]

Descobrimento do Brasil's insistence on a peaceful and united national foundation clearly coincides with the government's own project to persuade the public. Partly by way of propaganda pamphlets, the state attempted to instill in Brazil's youth pride in a unified nation. One text, produced by the Departamento Nacional de Propaganda and titled *O Brasil é Bom* [*Brazil Is Good*], tells its young readers that Brazil is one large family. It additionally insists on the equality of all (productive) Brazilians, no matter what their race may be: "O Brasil é bom porque não faz distinções de raças. Porque não tem preconceitos de côr, nem de religião" (n. pag.)[35] [22]. The unifying catechism culminates in the following exclamation: "Hoje, só ha um Brasil, só ha uma bandeira, só ha um Chefe! Eis porque o Brasil de hoje é diferente do Brasil de ontem. Eis porque já podemos afirmar, com júbilo e entusiasmo patriótico, que o BRASIL É BOM" (n. pag.) [23].

Vargas sought to "educate" the population in part by way of Brazil's history. In a 1940 pamphlet produced by the Departamento de Imprensa e Propaganda, *Brasil dos Nossos dias* [*The Brazil of Our Time*], the voice of the government refers to a decree that sought "a proteção ao patrimônio histórico e artístico nacional," which "sobressai pela sua especial significação" (13)[36] [24]. Another slightly later pamphlet (from circa 1940),[37] produced by the D.I.P., *Quem foi que disse? Quem foi que fez?* [*Who Said It? Who Did It?*], appears to be describing the project of Mauro's *Descobrimento do Brasil* when it insists on the value of revisiting historical moments in an entertaining way, and on the capacity of such retellings to promote patriotism and a "civic spirit" among the masses:[38]

Chapter One

> Recordar os grandes feitos da história, de maneira amena, pitoresca, ou mesmo anedótica, constitue, sem dúvida, um serviço útil prestado à cultura popular e ao aprimoramento do espírito cívico das massas. [...] [P]rocuramos, aqui, veicular ensinamentos de caráter patriótico, de sentido construtivo, noções e ensinamentos que se podem fixar, sem esfôrço, na memória de tôda gente, de moços e de velhos. (5) [25]

In the opening chapter of the pamphlet, Vargas's government explicitly invokes Caminha, referring to him as "prophetic" and using him, for his recognition of the abundant natural resources to be found in Brazil, as a means to encourage a sense of economic unity among Brazilians: "A carta de Pero Vaz Caminha, o primeiro documento escrito sôbre a terra brasileira, é um hino à beleza da natureza selvagem e à exuberância do Brasil primitivo. Não tiveram os brasileiros, por muitos e dilatados anos, visão tão aguda quanto a do profético escrivão de Cabral" (7)[39] [26].

It was by means of intervening in the cinema industry and in cultural production at large that the government hoped to influence the population's perception of the nation and its history (Fausto 376).[40] *Brasil dos Nossos dias* writes that with respect to culture "pode dizer-se que nenhum govêrno tivera ainda a compreensão das nossas necessidades, nem sentira a importância dêsse problema, como o fez o Presidente Getulio Vargas" (Departamento de Imprensa e Propaganda, *Brasil* 13) [27]. Vargas designated the cinema as one of the primary vehicles with which to "educate" the people of Brazil, which coincides with Mauro's outlook on the educational value of feature-length films. In order more fully to exploit cinema's propagandistic potential, and to communicate more efficiently "a proper image of the country," on January 13, 1937, Vargas established the INCE, which recommended clear, unambiguous, logical, dynamic, and interesting films (Johnson, *The Film Industry* 55). The qualities that the INCE sought in Brazilian cinema and the aims of Decree 21.240 would appear to coincide in an appeal for cinematic propaganda, an appeal to which *Descobrimento do Brasil* responded, especially through its thorough avoidance of ambiguity.

Descobrimento do Brasil combines the recognition of the lessons to be taught by history and the acknowledgment of the educational potential of cinema as a conduit for those lessons.

As the primary forces behind the INCE, both Roquette-Pinto and Mauro collaborated professionally to construct an official version of Brazilian history and identity, which evidently began with their work on *Descobrimento do Brasil*. Mauro hoped cinematically to craft for Brazil a glorious birth, one characterized by the willing (and divinely inspired) union of two peoples, an origin myth of which the nation could presumably be proud. The government's insistence on the importance of pride among Brazilians in a unified nation may help us to understand Mauro's characterization of the encounter. However, even in the scenes that most heavy-handedly attempt to represent equality, the privileging of the Portuguese prevails, as in the scene in which Cabral, recently on shore, shapes an indigenous hand into a European handshake. The evident desire to praise the Portuguese—combined as it is with a paternalistic view of the natives—seems to derail the film's attempt to celebrate the sort of egalitarian union of cultures that Vargas was urging his people to embrace.

Vargas's views on the Catholic Church, an organization that shared a symbiotic relationship with the government (Fausto 333; Miceli 51, 163), may shed some light on the film's characterization of the Portuguese, who were, of course, the messengers of Christianity in what would become Brazil.[41] Nevertheless, the hyperbolic exaltation of the Portuguese remains seemingly incongruous, given the long-standing tension between Brazil and Portugal and the deep-rooted inclination among many Brazilians to deny the Iberian branch of their heritage in the name of their own cultural independence. However, at the time that the film was made, the traditional rejection of the Portuguese was diminishing, within both intellectual circles and the government. The positive portrayal of what the film presents as the initiation of a cultural partnership encourages all racial constituencies of the nation—including the once reviled Portuguese—proudly to unite, and follows ideas being advanced at the time by intellectuals such as Roquette-Pinto himself and the sociologist Gilberto Freyre. Roquette-Pinto argued, for example, against the idea that miscegenation—to which the film only alludes through the harmonious "marriage," as it were, of Europeans and Amerindians—led to degeneracy (Skidmore, *Black into White* 187). Freyre is similarly known for his favorable evaluation of Brazil's cultural miscegenation.

Chapter One

His 1933 volume *Casa Grande e Senzala* argues that Brazil's harmonious hybridity grew from "um ambiente de quase reciprocidade cultural que resultou no máximo de aproveitamento dos valores e experiências dos povos atrasados pelo adiantado" (91) [28]. By way of his ideal of harmony within an ideology of cultural superiority/inferiority, Freyre, like INCE's Roquette-Pinto, would appear to inspire the film's romanticized vision of a nascent hybrid Brazil.

However, assuming that Mauro attempts to do justice to Roquette-Pinto's and Freyre's arguments, how do we reconcile the film's efforts to present a conjugal coexistence of two cultures with what amounts to a beatification of the Portuguese and the infantilization of the indigenous peoples? After all, in many ways Roquette-Pinto and Freyre exemplified the fight against racism in Brazil and, as we have seen, Mauro himself shows some sympathy for the indigenous point of view.[42] We can begin to resolve the apparent conflict by considering some of the premises of Freyre's argument. The writer lauds his nation's hybridity and harmony, but places the constituent parts of Brazil's unique cultural combination within a hierarchy: a presumably advanced people (the Portuguese), in terms of religion and culture, form the trunk of a tree that history has grafted with relatively more backward, though not entirely unappreciated, indigenous and African elements. Thomas Skidmore points out that Freyre's commentary on identity did not "promote [...] racial egalitarianism. Rather, it served to reinforce the whitening ideal" ("Racial Ideas" 22).[43] Freyre's centering of the European contribution to Brazilian society intersects with other contemporary reflections on the history and composition of the nation, such as that which the historian Sérgio Buarque de Holanda offers in *Raízes do Brasil* (1936). Holanda places the Portuguese at the core of Brazilian identity: "Nem o contato e a mistura com raças indígenas ou adventícias fizeram-nos tão diferentes dos nossos avós de além-mar como às vezes gostaríamos de sê-lo [...] Podemos dizer que de lá nos veio a forma atual de nossa cultura; o resto foi matéria que se sujeitou mal ou bem a essa forma" (11) [29]. In the end, despite Roquette-Pinto's belief in the beauty of Brazilian racial hybridity, what seemed most strongly to influence Mauro's adaptation of Caminha's narrative was a renewed pride in the Portuguese—and by extension, Catholic—contingent of Brazilian identity.

In 1937, Freyre was sent by Vargas's government to Portugal to research materials relating to the discovery of Brazil. In one of the speeches that he wrote to be delivered during his voyage, Freyre emphasizes the proud unity of the Lusophone world (*Conferencias* 5), and attributes it to the influence of the cordial Portuguese, "o mais cristão dos colonizadores modernos nas suas relações com as gentes consideradas inferiores" (*Conferencias* 7)[44] [30]. Freyre's apology for the Portuguese colonization of Brazil underscores their exceedingly Christian nature and praises them for what amounts to a paternalistic benevolence toward people considered inferior. Though religion draws the Portuguese-speaking world together, indigenous Brazil remains happily in a subordinate position; former Portuguese colonies share a diverse culture, but one that Freyre enthusiastically describes as "sob o predomínio de Portugal e do cristianismo" ["dominated by Portugal and Christianity"] (*Conferencias* 33).

Freyre also recognizes that what he calls "nacionalistas lusófobos do Brasil" ["Lusophobe Brazilian nationalists"] still exist, but are "reduzidíssimos" ["very reduced"] (*Conferencias* 17). He signals a desire for cooperation between the two nations that is so strong that any mutual antagonism that still exists will not prevail (*Conferencias* 76). Freyre's sentiments reflect an on-going effort in the 1930s between Portugal and Brazil to improve relations. During Portugal's celebration in 1940 of the formation of the country in 1140 and their independence from Spain in 1640 after 60 years of political control that began in 1580, the Portuguese dictator Antônio Salazar declared that they could not do without Brazil's participation (Rego 58). He insisted that the South American nation is owed "reverência especial" ["special reverence"] and characterized Portugal's attitude toward Brazil in terms of "terna e carinhosa solidaridade" ["tender and affectionate solidarity"] (Rego 58), a comment that tellingly recalls Graciliano Ramos's critique of *Descobrimento do Brasil*'s maternal Cabral. During the 1930s and 1940s Brazil reciprocated with similar goodwill, signing in 1933 an economic accord and in 1941 the Acordo Cultural Luso-Brasileiro [Luso-Brazilian Cultural Accord], which the director of Brazil's Departamento de Imprensa e Propaganda signed. Indeed, Brazilian efforts to strengthen ties with Portugal intensified during the Vargas regime (Cervo and Magalhães

271–72). The whitening tendency among Brazilian intellectuals in the 1930s and the close ties between Brazil and Portugal at the time that Mauro made *Descobrimento do Brasil* help to explain the film's ideology. For Mauro, patriotism and the praise of the Portuguese were not mutually exclusive.

Mauro and Roquette-Pinto began to work at the heart of the institution that controlled educational cinema in Brazil before the release of *Descobrimento do Brasil*. Hence, the brand of history offered by our director and his happy gathering of intellectuals not surprisingly coincides with the State's idea of the past and the myth that they wished to construct about Brazilian identity, as well as with the government's suggested means to communicate such an ideal. Following others, Mauro injects the *Carta* with foundational significance and attempts to present peaceful unity and the triumphant birth of a nation proudly based on miscegenation. However, by means of his purportedly faithful transposition of Caminha's letter, the director ultimately also perpetuates the historical oppression of the indigenous population of Brazil and suppression of their culture. Mauro's unswerving and uncritical adoption of the overall ideology of Caminha's portrayal of the conquest exalts colonialism, albeit among the powerful postcolonial protests of writers like Ramos and Andrade. The context of Brazil in the 1930s under Getúlio Vargas was ripe for the reappearance of Caminha's letter, as well as certain aspects of its ideology. Mauro's stylized re-creation of Caminha's letter contributed to Vargas's goals. However, *Descobrimento do Brasil*'s propagandistic lack of ambiguity ironically tips the comparatively balanced representational scale proposed by the *Carta*. The complex and sometimes playful and open-ended *Carta* invites and awaits—in this current era of intense cinematic interest in Brazil's past—another re-creation.

Chapter Two

Exoticizing the Nation in *Cabeza de Vaca* (1991) and *Como era gostoso o meu francês* (1971)

In one of the final scenes of *Cabeza de Vaca* (1991), Nicolás Echevarría's liberally conceived cinematic adaptation of Álvar Núñez Cabeza de Vaca's sixteenth-century *Naufragios* (1542 and 1555),[1] the four protagonists of the film—Cabeza de Vaca, Castillo, Dorantes, and his African slave Estevanico—have just arrived at an outpost on the Western coast of New Spain after eight years of migration and captivity, and gather around a campfire with a band of raucous Spanish soldiers who solicit tales of the travelers' adventures.[2] The film had begun with the group's arrival earlier that day and continues with a flashback occupying the remainder of the film that starts with their shipwreck, in 1527, off the coast of Florida. The castaways, on the beach and dressed in rags, are attacked by indigenous people, who subsequently sell the survivors into slavery. Eventually, Cabeza de Vaca is released from captivity and wanders west until he finds his three friends, who are being held captive within what is portrayed to be a nefarious cannibalistic tribe. Shortly afterwards, another native group rescues the four men. The protagonists eventually find signs of Spaniards, and the flashback converges with the initial scene, in 1535, at the Spanish encampment.

Close to the campfire that night, in a scene with no relation to *Naufragios*, Castillo and Dorantes are clothed and contentedly reassimilated, while Cabeza de Vaca and Estevanico, still in indigenous attire, sit skeptically on the outskirts of the circle. After relating to the soldiers the typical stories of secret riches, Castillo and Dorantes weave myths that take on a distinctly sexual and abnormalizing tone. One of them speaks of a potion, for example, that gives one "la fuerza jodedora de veinte asnos" ["the fucking power of twenty donkeys"] and claims that he was "obligado a parearme con mujeres de tres tetas" ["forced to mate with three-titted women"]. Playing on the currency of the exotic, here embodied by the depiction of a strange and shocking yet alluring other, Castillo and Dorantes succeed in sparking the interest of their captivated audience. Cabeza de Vaca and Estevanico view the hyperbolic performance with disdain, and the protagonist proposes to his companion that they tell what happened. Thus, in order to critique an exoticizing discourse, the film shows the protagonist condemning two characters who systematically marginalize indigenous women through denigrating sexualization and deformation. Although exoticizing is by no means an immutable universal, my use of the term here has in mind a hyperbolization of difference, regardless of agent or intentionality, that leads to distancing. Generally, in this chapter, it refers to Eurocentric representational practices with regard to indigenous people.

The buildup in the film to this condemnatory moment is complex and potentially unwieldy. The perspective and gaze of the protagonist have been the factors responsible for framing and producing the film's visual orientation and ideology, which is manifest in *Cabeza de Vaca*'s characterization of indigenous characters. And up to this point, the camera, following Cabeza de Vaca's lead, has tended to alienate the natives encountered, generally showing them to be bizarre, fragmented, and depraved beings. In this sense, the campfire scene serves as a metafictional microcosm of the film's own process of representation. The film itself, in a sustained departure from the source text—which, as I will argue below, exoticizes less than one might expect for a sixteenth-century account by a European in the Americas—has othered the indigenous characters as a means of displaying what Cabeza de Vaca will denounce at the end of the film.

From his detached, marginal position at the edge of the campfire, a wiser Cabeza de Vaca incredulously hears an inflated re-enactment of the film's visual construction of indigenous characters. The abnormalizing and distancing of the indigenous characters is spoken here, not shown, bringing it to the surface for the hero of the film and, one would hope, for the spectator. The protagonist's perspective still guides the film, but it now seems to suggest that the viewer take a step back and look at the film's portrayal of indigenous people from the outside, as Cabeza de Vaca demonstrates. The doubt cast by his reformed

Exoticizing the Nation

gaze on the re-enactment of what has been at least superficially the film's own paradigm of portrayal tries to enact a belated destabilization and interrogation of that same paradigm.

Some twenty years earlier, and working within quite distinct cinematic, historical, and political genealogies, Brazilian filmmaker Nelson Pereira dos Santos bases his *Como era gostoso o meu francês* (1971) on another sixteenth-century narrative of captivity, Hans Staden's *Warhaftige Historia [...]* (1557; trans. as *Viagem ao Brasil*).[3] The film begins as Jean, the protagonist, is condemned by the French and pushed off a cliff, a fall that he manages to survive. A tribe of cannibals called the Tupinambá captures him and, after nine months during which he becomes integrated into the community, largely through his intimate relationship with a woman from the tribe, the community eventually eats him. Like Echevarría, Pereira dos Santos interacts extensively with conceptions of the exotic in his representation of the Tupinambá. *Como era gostoso* clearly sensationalizes the cultural difference implicit in cannibalism, for example, but the director's strategy differs from the one described above. Rather than condemning a Eurocentric point of view, as Echevarría appears to do, Pereira dos Santos embraces what for the spectators would likely be the shocking, alien connotations of cannibalism.

A sequence near the end of the film, which I will discuss in detail later, suggests one of *Como era gostoso*'s manipulations of the associations of cannibalism. The day before his execution, Pereira dos Santos displays Jean—after querying his female companion Seboipep, about how the process will be of killing and eating him—sensuously frolicking with her as she explains the tradition. The film confounds spectator expectations by drastically resignifying a cinematic love scene. It depicts the Tupinambá's anthropophagy by way of this startling irony. At the same time, however, the film generally portrays the Tupinambá as a cultural benchmark, presenting their cultural practices as contextually justified,[4] thereby urging the viewer to identify with the tribe.[5] In other words, *Como era gostoso* treats cannibalism as exotic while simultaneously encouraging spectators to accept the Tupinambá as their representative. In so doing, the film inscribes itself within a long-standing strategy in Latin America of self-exoticizing, which appropriates an alienating tag and proudly recasts it.[6] *Como era gostoso* thus echoes not only the Indianist celebration of indigenous culture carried out by the Brazilian Romantics, but also, of course, the *modernista* embrace of indigenous Brazilian anthropophagy. However, I am reading the film's use of cannibalism not necessarily as a proposal to assume anthropophagy as a cultural strategy;[7] in my reading, the film does that itself with regard to its adaptation, but does not necessarily urge spectators to do the same. Rather, I am looking at cannibalism in Pereira dos Santos's film as the vehicle of a self-othering strategy, a particular approach to reconfiguring Brazilian identity through the transformation of a colonial text.

Como era gostoso and *Cabeza de Vaca* coincide in essaying a critique of colonialism that depends, as in other films about the colonial period (or "colonial" films, as I call them), on dominating the source texts; in these cases, however, the tamed intertext is refocused through the lens of the exotic. Though the outlines of the plots remain intact, the filmmakers unsparingly reconfigure the content of these evocative tales of European captivity. The scenes that I have briefly outlined illustrate two fundamental approaches to representing identity by capitalizing on and manipulating ways in which indigenous peoples have been portrayed in an exotic light generally, but not necessarily in the intertexts on which the films are based. *Cabeza de Vaca*'s display and subsequent critique of exoticizing and *Como era gostoso*'s self-exoticizing are central to Echevarría's and Pereira dos Santos's films. However, both films show signs of both strategies. The directors interact with what has been deemed shocking or bizarre in varied and complex ways. One of the subtleties that has started to emerge in the scenes that I have discussed so far involves the object treated: people in *Cabeza de Vaca*, and a cultural practice in *Como era gostoso*. Moreover, both approaches depend simultaneously on distancing or othering indigenous characters even while encouraging identification with them. For example, while Pereira dos Santos plays on the shock of cannibalism, he also insists on presenting the Tupinambá tribal practices as a cultural norm in order to stimulate sympathy toward them. In the case of *Cabeza de Vaca*, Echevarría anticipates his final critique of a denigrating European perspective with some images late in the film of indigenous people whom the camera does not other. Although the complexities of the directors' strategies contribute to the aesthetic and ideological richness of the films, the same complexities also potentially become problematic or contradictory. This chapter asks to what extent Echevarría and Pereira dos Santos carry out effective confrontations with traditional, oppressive representations. In other words, I ask if the films manage to accomplish the goal outlined by Edward Said: "Perhaps the most important task of all would be to undertake studies in contemporary alternatives to Orientalism, to ask how one can study other cultures and peoples from a libertarian, or a nonrepressive and nonmanipulative, perspective" (24). I also address whether or not the films run the risk of perpetuating negative stereotypes by maneuvering through the possible minefield of exoticizing. In sum, the ensuing pages evaluate to what degree the films' arguments are ultimately consistent or contradictory.

A continuation of my discussion of Echevarría's film will introduce some of the issues that arise from both *Cabeza de Vaca*'s and *Como era gostoso*'s multivalent approaches to revisiting history in order to revise present-day notions of identity. Although *Cabeza de Vaca*'s attitude toward indigenous people changes as the film progresses, the camera, in my analysis, responds sluggishly, painting a relatively uniform picture until late in the film, when *Cabeza de Vaca* indirectly attempts to erase the exotic rubric.[8] The final images of natives abandon the film's marginalizing aesthetic. Assuming that the film intends and achieves a final reversal of this perspective, such a strategy appears ineffective, as criticism of *Cabeza de Vaca* persistently infuses the entire film and the director with general, ethnographic, and anthropological authority.[9] Any of the thesis-driven adaptations of colonial literature studied in this book—such as Humberto Mauro's celebration of the Portuguese arrival in Brazil, in his *Descobrimento do Brasil*—which I call "anthropophagous adaptations," for the way they dominate and digest their sources, typically strive for such a qualification. Yet one can only suppose that Echevarría would hope that spectators recognize the difference between the portrayal of the indigenous people during most of the film and the culminating reversal of that policy.

According to Kevin Thomas, for example, the audience is "transported to another world" where the film "[brings] to life [...] the rich and varied details of the costumes, crafts and customs of the native people" (17). Similarly, "Strat" states that Echevarría has "convincingly re-created the world of the long-gone Indian tribes of Florida and Louisiana" (54). Elsewhere, a critic points to "well-researched scenes of Native American life" (Fernández 72). Another review, having in mind the 1992 movies on Columbus, is entitled, "Finally, an *Honest* Portrayal

Chapter Two

of the New World" (Carr 32; emphasis in original). And in one interview with Echevarría, a question begins with the statement: "Hay muchas secuencias que parecen filmadas por un documentalista de 1530" (Interview 11) [31], which recalls Mauro's declared attempt in his 1937 *Descobrimento do Brasil,* to film as if he were a reporter on Cabral's ship ("O Mundo" 206). Notwithstanding rigorous research, abundant faithful ethnographic details, and some changes in how the film depicts indigenous people toward the end, we must read the anthropological authority heaped on Echevarría in the context of his admission that he is inventing peoples and that his interest lies in mysticism, rather than ethnography (Echevarría, Interview 11). Many critics have been apparently blind to the film's consistent and exaggerated objectifying of women that precedes (and perhaps overwhelms) its critique in the campfire scene, as those quoted above problematically apply the label of "anthropological" to the film as a whole.

However abrupt and tardy *Cabeza de Vaca*'s final shift in its perspective toward the depiction of indigenous characters and culture, and despite the resulting questionable interpretations of the film, the campfire scene does imply that the film attempts to confront the colonial and ongoing tendency to view indigenous peoples as strange others. Indeed, both of the films at hand do clearly intend to advance anti-imperialist, pro-indigenous ideologies, or at least ones that encourage broad social symbolic identification with indigenous groups from the past.[10] Echevarría's film has certainly been received in such a way. Jay Carr calls *Cabeza de Vaca* "one of the great anti-imperialist movie epics" (32), and Joanne Hershfield maintains that the film "attempt[s] to respond to T. Minh-Ha's injunction to 'recreate without recirculating domination'" ("Assimilation" 9).[11] Such readings of Echevarría's film find compelling support in one of *Cabeza de Vaca*'s final and most powerful images, where a crane extreme long shot shows dozens of indigenous slaves bearing the burden of a mammoth cross. The camera follows them as they march to a snare drum from the left to the right of the screen and away, toward a dark, looming storm. The scene may represent an intertextual reference to the remarkably similar scene from *Descobrimento do Brasil* that I discussed in Chapter 1. In Mauro's film, however, the burden seemed happily assumed by a miraculously indoctrinated indigenous population. Given *Cabeza de Vaca*'s critical reception, it appears that Echevarría realizes, through the protagonist's attitude in the campfire scene, a successful reversal of the film's previous visual exploitation of indigenous women, and a consequent debunking of the same practice. It remains to be seen if sparse minutes of skepticism can effectively undo the impression left by an hour and a half of sexualizing and marginalizing, controlled and condoned by the protagonist of the film, especially if spectators' perspectives become aligned with that of Cabeza de Vaca, and they feel sympathy for this character, a situation that I believe the film tries to create.

We should bear in mind that many viewers of *Cabeza de Vaca* may not have read the source text, and the stakes with regard to commenting on the past through the present would be similar for spectators viewing an entirely fictional story based in sixteenth-century New Spain—excepting, of course, the authorizing benefit of a "based-on-a-true-story" claim and the potential for quick audience engagement when the cinematic object is even a vaguely familiar historical figure. Still, we might consider that Álvar Núñez's sixteenth-century narrative is an odd site for the enactment of Echevarría's strategy; *Naufragios*, given its relative lack of detailed descriptions of women, is better suited to be a counter-example against which to measure instances of the exoticizing of women in other early colonial historiography. The entire negative representational paradigm apparently put into question in the campfire scene is invented by the filmmaker, having little, if any, precedent in *Naufragios*. Indeed, the sixteenth-century narrative, which paints a far less sensationalistic picture of the natives that the explorer encounters, more clearly encourages a re-examination of otherness than the film would appear to do. Sexualizing and marginalizing depictions of indigenous women certainly exist in the writings of other sixteenth-century historiographers, such as Columbus or Oviedo. One of Álvar Núñez's most scandalous descriptions of women is actually rather tame, reading simply: "Las mujeres cubren sus vergüenzas con yerba y paja" (126); Oviedo, in contrast, expresses, as do Castillo and Dorantes in the campfire scene, his fixation on the indigenous women's breasts: "[E]llas no quieren […] empreñarse, para que pariendo se les aflojen las

Chapter Two

tetas, de las cuales mucho se precian, *y las tienen muy buenas*" (79; my emphasis). Columbus provides a quintessential othering description of the native women, speaking of their "muy fermosos cuerpos y muy buenas caras, los cabellos gruesos cuasi como sedas de cola de cavallos e cortos" (110–11) [32]. Echevarría's counterintuitive revision of *Naufragios* may lead a viewer familiar with the sixteenth-century narrative to ask what the filmmaker's motive would be for transforming the text as it does, when other colonial narratives might have lent themselves much more fluidly to representing the typical othering gaze of the colonizer.

Also, we must ask if Echevarría's apparent desire to discredit exoticizing encompasses all forms and manifestations of it. If so, the strategy would seem to be in conflict with the film's portrayal of magic. For in addition to othering indigenous women, Echevarría surrounds with an air of strangeness the treatment of magic and mysticism, aspects of indigenous culture particularly fascinating to and respected by Echevarría (Echevarría, Interview 11). "Esa fue mi pasión: los indios," comments Echevarría, "[y] sobre todo, no la cuestión indígena a nivel etnográfico o folclórico, sino la mística y la técnica para lograr el éxtasis. Esa fue mi obsesión" (Interview 11) [33]. Instead of forming part of the depictions that the film presumably questions in the end, the treatment of magic in *Cabeza de Vaca* appears to participate in a strategy of self-alienation, similar to *Como era gostoso*'s portrayal of cannibalism. Echevarría exalts indigenous mysticism as a positive aspect of indigenous culture, which corresponds to the director's interest in mystical, psychedelic experiences. Can Echevarría's apparently contradictory tactics be reconciled when viewed in terms of the film's treatment of indigenous society as a whole?

The issues raised by the preceding discussion of Echevarría's film emblematize some of the complexities that inform my examination of how both *Cabeza de Vaca* and *Como era gostoso* selectively consider, interrogate, and appropriate the exotic. Thus far I have suggested that the directors' strategies manifest themselves in different contexts and in different ways and largely determine the nature of the films' portrayal of indigenous peoples. Echevarría and Pereira dos Santos alternately engage the exotic in relation to magic, women, and cannibalism. I have pointed out the two main strategies that the directors

Exoticizing the Nation

implement in conjunction with the preceding categories: they either appropriate and exalt elements of indigenous identity within a strategy of self-exoticizing or they display exoticizing in order to criticize it. The paths taken by the two directors both diverge and intersect. If only one strategy or message cannot consistently be identified in these films, perhaps the explanation lies in the directors' attempts to confound reductive perceptions of identity and reject the notion of a single source for it. Contradictions within the films may derive from the complexities of society and identity themselves. However, the possibility remains that in their complicated treatment of long-standing Eurocentric practices of representing other peoples, the directors of *Cabeza de Vaca* and *Como era gostoso* may advance conflicting premises that compromise their ideological stance, thereby nullifying the communicative potential of the films, and impeding their attempt to revise present-day conceptions of identity.

The following pages trace, examine, and compare how Echevarría and Pereira dos Santos revise sixteenth-century narratives of captivity. Parsing my study into the films' respective representations of cannibalism, magic, and women, I will focus on how *Cabeza de Vaca* and *Como era gostoso* attempt to transform conceptions of indigenous populations, and, in a broader sense, of national identity.

As I have already mentioned, Pereira dos Santos capitalizes on the image of cannibalism as an exotic cultural practice. He appropriates a conventional, externally applied, negative label and replays it hyperbolically as a positive aspect of indigenous and, by extension, of Brazilian identity as part of an overall strategy to critique colonialism and its contemporary corollaries by encouraging identification with archetypal victims of colonization. In my view, the director assumes, rearranges, and exalts a cultural practice that the film also, at times, depicts as disturbing and bizarre. In order for this self-othering to be effective in a revision of national identity, however, the group whose cultural practice the film dissociates must be a viable representative of the self, which, in relation to *Como era gostoso*, is Brazil. Hence, the success of this strategy hinges on the general treatment of the Tupinambá. The Brazilian audience must accept the indigenous characters as their symbolic surrogate and then embrace cannibalism as a proud aspect of how

Chapter Two

Brazil imagines itself. *Como era gostoso* therefore positions the Tupinambá as the core of a Brazilian self at the same time that it generally distances and discourages identification with the Europeans in the film. Nonetheless, as we will see, an otherwise clear distinction between Europeans and Tupinambá is blurred by the provocative figure of Jean and the implications of his complexity.

Como era gostoso favors the Tupinambá by exposing the duplicity and gratuitous cruelty of nearly all of the Europeans appearing or referred to in the film. For example, the director includes occasional intertextual intertitles displaying quotations by sixteenth-century Europeans. In possible intertextual dialogue with *Descobrimento do Brasil*,[12] Pereira dos Santos reconfigures the purpose of the intertitles implemented by the director who has been called the grandfather of *Cinema Novo,* Humberto Mauro, by juxtaposing exclamations about the savage barbarism of the natives with images of deceitful Europeans and reasonable Tupinambá, whose customs and their contextual justification Pereira dos Santos systematically displays for the audience.[13] Whereas Mauro finds authority in historiography, Pereira dos Santos reads European versions of historical events with a critical eye. By marginalizing the European contingent of Brazilian national identity, the film inevitably brings indigenous aspects of identity to the center.

Some critics have suggested that the tendency to question identification with Europeans extends to the film's protagonist, Jean.[14] Yet I argue that Jean acts not merely as a representative of the collective of Europeans, but also, and unquestionably, as an individual whose image and purpose in the film are consequently complex. He is an in-between character who is wronged and distanced by the French colonizers and partially assimilated into Tupinambá culture, for which he shows some respect. The presence of the French protagonist in fact broadens *Como era gostoso*'s treatment of Europeans, and complicates the dynamics of spectator identification, and the film's related proposals for how diverse Brazilian spectators might take cues from the film in terms of identity and politics. Of course Jean, unlike his relatively forthright captors, partakes in subterfuge and hardly embodies the archetypical hero. Yet his surprisingly open attitude toward cannibalism, which I will discuss in a moment, already enhances his role in the film's message. Indeed, partly by presenting Jean's ironic, partial acceptance of his captors' cultural practices, the director suggests a generous evaluation of Jean, and reinforces the film's favorable representation of the Tupinambá. Rather than eliminating any chance that the audience might identify with the Frenchman—a tactic that might hope to employ Jean as the primary vehicle with which to distance Europeans—*Como era gostoso* arguably laces Jean's character with suggestions of tragic irony, rooted in the difference between the way that Hans Staden's narrative and Pereira dos Santos's film present the confusion over their protagonists' nationality.

Because the tribe that captures both Staden and Jean, the Tupinambá, is an ally of the French and an enemy of the Portuguese, the fate of the captives hinges on how the Tupinambá interpret the foreigners' nationality. The fact that the tribe finds both the colonial text's and the film's protagonists working for the Portuguese as artillerymen complicates their plight. Let's consider how Staden and Jean become associated with the Portuguese, and the consequences of that association. Whereas Staden says that he asked the Portuguese for permission to stay and work for them in that capacity for two years (57),[15] Jean, after being expelled by his French compatriots, is captured by the Portuguese and forced to man the cannons in battle. In both instances, when the Tupinambá capture the men, their context suggests Portuguese nationality. At first Staden tries to explain that he is German and a friend of the French (72). He later claims that he really is French, that he has a brother who seeks his return (83), and that the Portuguese forced him to be an artilleryman (78), launching a convoluted series of lies that evolve during the narrative and result, in tandem with his supernatural influence, in his eventual release to his "French brothers" (118). Jean, on the other hand, who really is French, has two failed opportunities before the realization of his fate to prove that he is French and, as such, the ally of his captors. When the Tupinambá initially find him and order him to stand with some Portuguese soldiers, they insist that he speak in order to determine his identity. Jean utters some French words and repeats, pointing at himself, the word *maír*, the Tupi word for "French," but to no avail.[16] Later, an old Frenchman, negatively portrayed in the film, comes to visit the tribe and, despite Jean's justified attempt to have the man confirm his identity, the old man calls

Chapter Two

him Portuguese and the tribe sentences him to the assimilation process that will result in his consumption.

A series of coincidences trap Jean and determine his destiny. Since he is deemed to be from an enemy group, Tupinambá culture expects him to assimilate gradually and completely with the tribe (de Sousa 92). In a sense, however, the real assimilation takes place at the moment of his death, when the Portuguese identity with which his circumstances have stamped him converges with his reality. Tradition requires that Jean, before the chief of the Tupinambá will finish the ceremony, say that his Portuguese comrades will avenge his death. He is left with no alternative than to end his life playing the role of a Portuguese soldier. After initially refusing to carry out the last requirement of the ceremony, Jean blurts out the obligatory declaration of vengeance, adding his own ominous twist: that his comrades will avenge him to such a point that not one of them will be left. The director displays the realization of Jean's prophecy in the final shot of the film, of a beach, accompanied by an intertitle from 1557 by Governor Mem de Sã, stating that in a battle with the Tupiniquin he fought such that not one of them was left and their bodies were strewn along the beach.[17] Although circumstances thrust a Portuguese identity on him, Jean grabs control of that identity toward the end of the film by expanding the script given to him, and derives a degree of empowerment from the prophetic transformation that he enacts. Compared to Staden's story, Jean's does approximate tragedy. However, the ending of the film shifts a degree of Jean's tragic appeal to the Tupinambá, a group that merely realizes their cultural traditions, yet faces—as Jean's prophecy reminds us—a destiny of destruction. Hence, without completely eliminating sympathy for Jean and consequently questioning a reductive, solely indigenist view of identity, the film does favor the Tupinambá.

Pereira dos Santos solidifies his tendency to favor the Tupinambá in several other ways. In fictionalizing Staden, for example, the director removes emphasis from his point of view and transfers it to the Tupinambá, whose leader in the film is a concrete historical figure, Cunhambebe (Staden 76). In contrast to its presentation of the Tupinambá, the film presents the Portuguese as nameless, generally faceless enemies. Also, the audience hears very little Portuguese, despite *Como era gostoso* being a Brazilian film.[18] The implied linguistic norm for Brazil thus shifts from Portuguese to Tupi. In addition, Jean's partially positive attitude toward Tupinambá culture and his process of assimilation into it manages to normalize the tribe on the whole, encouraging identification with them.

Distinct from the film's representation of the Tupinambá, even from Jean's perspective, Staden's account of his captivity tends to portray the Tupinambá and in particular their anthropophagous practices in a negative light, and Staden writes of resisting assimilation at every turn. He consistently refers to his captors as "selvagens" ["savages"] and represents their cannibalism as barbaric. Moreover, throughout the narrative Staden shows God to sympathize with the Christians and denounce the savages, regardless of their tribe. God's influence, along with Staden's resulting righteous condemnation of cannibalism, comes gradually into play throughout his captivity.[19]

In *Como era gostoso*, however, Jean reacts in the opposite way, for the most part, to cannibalism and Tupinambá culture. Not only does he fail to demonstrate revulsion toward their anthropophagy but, even after becoming aware that he will be the object of the tribe's tradition, he actively seeks to understand his captors' culture rather than scoffing at or rejecting cannibalism outright. For example, early in the film, after the Frenchman refuses to confirm Jean's identity and save him, he asks Seboipep to explain about the Tupinambá worldview. And much later the ironic scene in which Jean and Seboipep frolic as she explains the details of Jean's fate begins with a subdued conversation about the ritual. Although a sense of self-preservation and the connected attempts to escape are clear motives for Jean, a close examination of the character's reactions to his circumstances exposes a respect for and desire to learn about Tupinambá customs. The degree to which the audience sympathizes with Jean determines the persuasive sway of his respect for the tribe.

Jean's perspective on his presence within the tribe and its cannibalistic practices emerges early in the film. Shortly after Jean is brought to the Tupinambá village, a woman named Seboipep is assigned to him to act as his "wife," an integral aspect of the tribe's custom of assimilating into their culture the prisoners whom they plan to eat (de Sousa 92). The next day, a visiting Frenchman explains to Jean that Seboipep will, in fact, act as his wife, but also will not hesitate to eat him at the appropriate time. The captive appears to take the tribe's anthropophagy in

Chapter Two

stride, accepting his role and actively pursuing his indoctrination and assimilation. Jean accepts the companionship of Seboipep not, at first, in a sexual sense, but as a vehicle to realize his apparently honest desire to learn about the history and customs of the Tupinambá. The scene in which he first solicits information about the tribe and encourages Seboipep to help him with one of the first steps of assimilation—the removal of all body hair—emblematically departs from Staden's account. At the beginning of his stay with the tribe, Staden relates, the women try to shave his beard and he steadfastly refuses them permission to do so, attempting to maintain the "mark of his difference" (Staden 70; de Sousa 93). Jean, on the other hand, while relaxing in the hammock with Seboipep, both of them romantically playful, asks her to speak of her people. After she has explained some of their customs, he happily submits to the removal of the hair on his body. The film shows Jean expressing a genuine, not feigned, interest in assimilation.

In general, the film avoids vilifying not only the Tupinambá but also Jean, thereby encouraging the audience to avoid a Manichean evaluation of Europeans and Amerindians. This leaves the possibility open of revising—rather than entirely rejecting—hybrid conceptions of identity. The fact that the film privileges the Tupinambá without completely demonizing the Europeans allows spectators to envision a plural and inclusive sense of Brazilianness centered—more than just nominally, as in traditional Indigenist views of Brazilian identity dating back famously to the Romantic period—on indigenous culture. Although there is no offspring from the union of Jean and Seboipep, the absorption through cannibalism of this somewhat positively portrayed character represents a degree of symbolic fusion of European and indigenous elements.

I have looked at some of the means by which *Como era gostoso* favorably portrays the Tupinambá—and even to a certain degree their cannibalism—in order to position them as acceptable representatives of the Brazilian self. I will now consider another other side of Pereira dos Santos's strategies of representation: how the director sensationalizes anthropophagy through shock, mystery, and sexualizing. In one of the last scenes in the film, for example, during the feast after Jean's execution, the director inserts a shot of Seboipep's face between shots of the chief exploding two cannons backward over his shoulders. We see her from the side placing meat into her mouth, and as she chews she turns to the camera, which zooms in with an extreme close-up of the top portion of her face. A still of this final image of the scene appears on the cover of a US version of the VHS (New Yorker Video), lending it the importance of representing how the film wishes to market itself abroad.[20] One review of *Como era gostoso* describes the shot: "a lovely woman looking directly into the camera as she eats—a shot that resembles an airline poster that would sell us a tropical vacation—is a further allurement" (Griffith 12). The references to a "tropical vacation" and "allurement" suggest that the film not only has successfully underscored the exotic, but has embellished it with sexual overtones, the importance of which I will discuss in detail later. There is mystery in this scene. The shots show no dismembered body parts. The camera only alludes to them. Pereira dos Santos consistently presents cannibalism as a contextually justified cultural process, but when it comes to the actual act, he exploits its shocking potential through the half-hidden suggestion of the final step: the audience only sees the eyes of the woman, Seboipep, as she feasts on her husband. Earlier in the film we find another example of the association of cannibalism with shock. During a ceremony in which Cunhambebe (Jean's captor and the chief of the tribe) declares the Frenchman's fate and doles out promises of body parts, the audience learns that the neck will go to Seboipep, an eventuality suggested in a previous scene: while Jean is sleeping, after his first day with the tribe, Seboipep, holding vigil by his hammock, creeps over and bites suggestively into Jean's neck, startling him from sleep. Again, the film reinforces the sensationalistic appeal of cannibalism by tying it to shock, mystery, and sex.

Como era gostoso again emphasizes these associations in the late beach scene mentioned earlier in which Jean learns what will become of his neck. Jean's ironic attitude of acceptance with regard to Tupinambá culture culminates here, and provides another example of exploiting the scandalous potential of cannibalism. I will now return to that scene and discuss it in somewhat more detail. After the ceremony in which the chief bequeaths Jean's meat and tells him that they will eat him the following day, Jean asks his wife to explain what they will expect him to do at the feast. Seboipep takes him to the beach and while Jean smiles and listens, she speaks of what will

61

happen before the ceremony's culinary finale. When she comes to the moment in which custom dictates that he be hit over the head and killed, he gets up and merrily mimics this aspect of the ritual with her. They fall to the ground, rolling around erotically in each other's arms and laughing while Seboipep exclaims, and Jean repeats: "Meu pescoço! Meu pescoço!" ["My neck! My neck!"] At this point in the film, Jean's validating acceptance of cannibalism and the director's desire to make it provocative converge in a moment bordering on grotesque, yet effective, absurdity. Jean's incongruous reaction to Seboipep's exclamation "Meu pescoço!" both perpetuates the film's positive perspective on Tupinambá culture consistently reinforced by the captive's willing assimilation into the tribe and enhances cannibalism's shock value within the film through the victim's light-hearted, playful reaction to the notion of his wife savoring his separated neck.

The success of *Como era gostoso*'s self-othering through cannibalism, we have seen, depends on two vital tactics. Pereira dos Santos echoes the historical European impressions of anthropophagy by lacing it with mystery, sexuality, and an underlying desire to shock. At the same time, the film's overall portrayal of the Tupinambá establishes them as a viable symbolic agent of Brazil. Hence, the director posits indigenous culture as a symbolic core of Brazilian national identity.

On the surface, the treatment of cannibalism in *Cabeza de Vaca* appears to self-exoticize as well. The film offers unquestionably strange, fragmented, and shocking cannibals. However, it becomes increasingly clear, during the cannibalism scene halfway through the film, that such a reading is untenable. Cabeza de Vaca, after being released from his initial captors and wandering west for quite some time, stumbles on an indigenous encampment in the desert where a tribe holds captive three of his companions and several members of another tribe that the film treats as friendly. As soon as he arrives, the cannibals tie the protagonist to a post like the other prisoners. Soon a ceremony begins: a large cauldron boils in the background while women painted blue emerge from tents and begin to dance around the captives, rubbing their naked bodies against the men and screaming tauntingly.[21] At one point, amid a flurry of cackling and confusion, a captive is untied, bashed over the head, and dragged toward the boiling water. In the nick of time, members of the friendly tribe arrive and liberate their fellow tribesmen as well as Cabeza de Vaca and his companions. As we see here, *Cabeza de Vaca* shrouds its cannibals in a strange and thoroughly nefarious light. Spectators cannot assume that the film seeks through cannibalism to other a self, as these demonic cannibals are unlikely representatives of the Mexican population. It is doubtful that spectators would identity with them.

Whereas the Tupinambá plausibly represent Brazil, the cannibals in *Cabeza de Vaca* lack the same value. Not only does the film leave the cannibals undeveloped as characters, but it portrays them as cruel, psychotic, and unjustified enemies of the hero of the film, and juxtaposes them with what Echevarría presents as a kind and reasonable tribe, one that rescues and befriends the Spaniards. As Pereira dos Santos does to a larger extent with the Tupinambá, the director of *Cabeza de Vaca* favorably portrays the friendly tribe, and develops its members as characters within the film. The friendly tribe, which later plays an important part in signaling the Spaniards' inhumane treatment of the local indigenous population, much more believably represents a postulated Mexican self. Nonetheless, as I will argue, this tribe still retains an exotic air until very late in the film.

Also, and importantly, the suggestion of cannibalism in *Cabeza de Vaca* is an add-on to the sixteenth-century *Naufragios*, perhaps used merely as a sensationalistic hook for the audience or as a way to introduce the friendly tribe and inspire sympathy for them. Álvar Núñez does mention cases of Spanish cannibalism in his narrative, as in the following statement: "[Y] los que morían, los otros los hacían tasajos; y el último que murió fue Sotomayor, y Esquivel lo hizo tasajos, y comiendo de él se mantuvo hasta 1 de marzo" (87) [34]. Yet he never makes reference to anthropophagy in any indigenous group with which he comes into contact,[22] despite his detailed descriptions of indigenous customs, and even the extremes of eating habits: "[Y] su hambre [es] tan grande, que comen arañas y huevos de hormigas, y gusanos y lagartijas y salamanquesas y culebras y víboras, que matan los hombres que muerden, y comen tierra y madera y todo lo que pueden haber, y estiércol de venados, y

Chapter Two

otras cosas que dejo de contar, y creo averiguadamente, que si en aquella tierra hubiese piedras las comerían" (89) [35].

Since *Cabeza de Vaca*'s depiction of its indigenous cannibals fails to inspire sympathy, they remain, as I have suggested, improbable representatives of the Mexican self, and cannot as a result contribute to a self-exoticizing strategy. Consequently, one may be tempted to see the film's portrayal of the cannibals in terms of the possible critique suggested by the campfire scene at the end of the film: to recall, *Cabeza de Vaca*, through the protagonist's late skepticism, appears to criticize the distancing Eurocentric practices that the film shows and employs. However, Cabeza de Vaca's attitude in the campfire scene cannot possibly undo the alienating, negative portrayal of the cannibalistic women. The hyperbolically exotic nature of these contrived characters exceeds the representation of a colonial Spaniard's visual perspective. Their presence in the film, therefore, derives from other concerns (i.e., a desire to provide a contrast for the other tribe, a desire to titillate). The consequences of their inclusion in the story remain to be considered.

The cannibals do still inevitably, albeit partially, embody the indigenous aspect of Mexican national identity. In one respect, their presence may emphasize the cultural diversity of the indigenous population of North America. However, I believe the way that the film portrays the cannibals may provoke a different effect. It manages to perpetuate the marginalization of the indigenous population. Echevarría's grip on representational alienation as a tool to treat identity begins to loosen, and the treatment of cannibalism scene is set free and turns against the argument of which it forms part. The result of the cannibalism scene, then, runs counter to any attempt to engage the exotic in a way that strengthens the indigenous image within Mexican national identity. Instead, it merely serves to perpetuate stereotypes. The film's sensationalistic hook ends up snaring itself, rather than its audience.

In its treatment of magic and mysticism, however, *Cabeza de Vaca* does coincide with *Como era gostoso*'s self-othering use of cannibalism. At the same time that *Cabeza de Vaca* makes magic seem strange, it also holds it in high regard, portraying it as a norm within its cultural context, and associating it with characters that the film treats kindly and with whom, for the most part, it encourages the audience to identify. Hence,

Cabeza de Vaca presents the characters associated with magic as plausible representatives of the nation, allowing the distancing sensationalization of magic to act as self-exoticizing. Generally, Echevarría displays magic as a positive aspect of indigenous and, by extension, national identity.

As with cannibalism in *Como era gostoso*, *Cabeza de Vaca* links its presentation of magic to the protagonist's process of assimilation. Toward the beginning of the film, Cabeza de Vaca is sold as a slave to a brooding but ultimately respectable and kind shaman, who does not appear in *Naufragios*. The shaman's assistant—also an addition to Álvar Núñez's narrative—is a more problematic figure whom I will discuss in greater detail later. After a miserable initial period and one desperate attempt at escape, the mood lightens and Cabeza de Vaca eventually becomes the shaman's apprentice, a change marked by the Spaniard uttering his first words in the language used by the shaman. At this point in the film, the protagonist begins to participate without resistance in indigenous culture, and undergoes a mystical indoctrination into the shaman's arts. Cabeza de Vaca's assimilation climaxes when, in a drug-induced mystical frenzy—part of what gives the film's treatment of magic an exotic feel—he manages to heal the eye of a man who was injured by a spell performed by the shaman himself. When Cabeza de Vaca wakes up the next morning, his master releases him from captivity and sends him on his way. The director establishes the role of magic in *Cabeza de Vaca*, then, through its association with a benevolent teacher and its acceptance by the hero of the film.

Throughout the remainder of the film, the protagonist and the film itself embrace magic and its basis in mysticism as normal. As in *Naufragios*, *Cabeza de Vaca*'s protagonist becomes a renowned healer, though the explanations suggested for his powers differ from those offered by the narrative. In both the narrative and the film, the protagonist passes through a process of initiation, and the healing that he performs is treated as real. Whereas in the film Cabeza de Vaca eventually participates willingly in the exploration of the healing arts, *Naufragios* understandably suggests that the explorer resists his shamanistic catechism. Álvar Núñez writes that "nos quisieron hacer físicos sin examinarnos ni pedirnos los títulos, porque ellos curan las enfermedades soplando al enfermo, y con aquel soplo y las manos echan de él la enfermedad" (78) [36]. He and his companions laugh at the proposition, and the tribe deprives them of food, he says, until they agree to participate. Along with the threat, Álvar Núñez writes that one of the indigenous men also attempts to persuade them with reason:

> Y viendo nuestra porfía, un indio me dijo a mí que yo no sabía lo que decía en decir que no aprovecharía nada aquello que él sabía, ca las piedras y otras cosas que se crían por los campos tienen virtud; y que él con una piedra caliente, trayéndola por el estómago, sanaba y quitaba el dolor, y que nosotros, que éramos hombres, cierto era que teníamos mayor virtud y poder. (78) [37]

In the end, Álvar Núñez and his friends submit to their transculturation and eventually all become healers: "venimos todos a ser médicos, aunque en atrevimiento y osar acometer cualquier cura era yo más señalado entre ellos" (99) [38]. Shortly after agreeing to be healers, Álvar Núñez explains that God's will produces their success: "Quiso Dios nuestro Señor y su misericordia que todos aquellos por quien suplicamos, luego que los santiguamos, decían a los otros que estaban sanos y buenos" (79) [39]. As Álvar Núñez's and his friends' fame for healing grows, *Naufragios* suggests that, even among the indigenous peoples, their power derives from God and not magic: "Luego el pueblo nos ofreció muchas tunas, porque ya ellos tenían noticia de nosotros y cómo curábamos, y de las maravillas que nuestro Señor con nosotros obraba" (94) [40]. While the narrative attributes the success of the acts performed by the protagonist of *Naufragios* to God, the film shows the power of Cabeza de Vaca's healing to come only from the magic taught to him by the shaman. Throughout *Cabeza de Vaca* the power of magic goes unquestioned, implying that supernatural acts form part of the film's reality.

Echevarría first presents the effectiveness of magic in a sequence perhaps in part based on the sixteenth-century narrative. In *Naufragios*, the writer says that he tries to escape from one of his captors three times, "y todos me anduvieron a buscar y poniendo diligencia para matarme" (92). The protagonist of the film also attempts to escape, but instead of pursuing him the shaman brings him back by a magic spell. Critics have rightly pointed out that the editing techniques implemented in the escape attempt sequence make the magic used seem real for the spectator. By means of intercutting between a lizard tied to a rope and the protagonist desperately running away, the director creates an analogy between the reptile and Cabeza de Vaca. When the shaman blows on the lizard, for example, the film cuts to Cabeza de Vaca being hit with a gust of wind, suggesting a causal relationship between the acts of the shaman and what the protagonist experiences. When the beast runs in progressively smaller circles around the stick to which the rope is connected, Cabeza de Vaca's movements mirror those of the lizard, bringing him back to the shaman. Echevarría does not depict magic from the outside as a belief or a possibility, but from within as a foundation for the perception of the world of the film as a whole—the quintessence of traditional "magical realism." He offers magic as a norm or a standard, albeit mystical and bizarre, lending it credence and respectability, which, again, recalls *Como era gostoso*'s presentation of cannibalism. The reception of the film as authoritative, ethnographic, and documentary-like, to which I referred in the opening section of the chapter, perhaps reflects the success of *Cabeza de Vaca*'s magical realist aesthetic. On the other hand, it may merely imply that the film is heir to a context of reception that sees realism in Latin America only when it is magical.

Echevarría treats magic as normal within its social context and portrays it positively by associating it with the kind shaman and showing the protagonist embrace the indigenous practice. Nevertheless, *Cabeza de Vaca* also ties magic to mystery, shock, and strangeness. The shaman's assistant, Mala Cosa, perhaps the prototypical other, is at the core of the alienation of the shamanistic arts in the film. This character has surely inspired some critics to call the film bizarre. He has been described as a "sidekick" with a "crazed sense of humor" (Thomas 17), a "screeching dwarf" (Denby 59), and "an armless dwarf who could have been imagined by Luis Buñuel" (Canby 12). The squat, round armlessness of Mala Cosa merely embellishes his disturbing strangeness, which the viewer perceives through his seemingly demented tormenting of Cabeza de Vaca. Although Mala Cosa undeniably serves a purpose in the film, enhancing the connection of magic in *Cabeza de Vaca* to a distancing difference, the director's construction of the character remains problematic.[23]

Chapter Two

Early in the film, one of the Spaniards, in disgust, gives the character the name "Mala Cosa" ["Bad Thing"], a name that points to an interesting reversal of a scene found in the original narrative. Late in Álvar Núñez's account, a native tells the protagonist and his companions of an evil, bearded man who lived beneath the earth and who used to come to their village and commit heinous acts of violence, terrorizing the people of that tribe (99–100). One of the notes in Roberto Ferrando's edition of *Naufragios* postulates that the text plays out a common myth: "el misterioso hombre blanco y barbudo llegado del Este" (100) [41]. Following Ferrando's reading, then, the name "Mala Cosa" in the book would refer to a terrorizing and murdering European man.[24] Echevarría offers the inverse of this interpretation of *Naufragios*, retaining the name and its negative connotations, but attributing them to a monster-like, sadistic, indigenous character who screams and laughs incessantly and spits food at Cabeza de Vaca. The addition to the film of a bizarre, cruel, grotesque, and fragmented character may aid in making magic seem alien, but the director's negative twisting of the Mala Cosa from *Naufragios* seems to collide head-on with any attempt to imagine indigenous peoples at the center of Mexican identity. Whereas the filmmaker encourages the audience to identify with the shaman, he demonizes Mala Cosa and deforms him into precisely the sort of negative representation apparently criticized by the protagonist (and the film) in the campfire scene. Echevarría's nefarious character complicates and perhaps nullifies the apparent self-exoticizing presentation of magic, spilling into a basically negative portrayal that, as in the case of the demonic cannibals, may be beyond redemption or reversal.

Stallybrass and White's discussion of the "grotesque body" sheds light on Echevarría's conflictual insertion of Mala Cosa. They identify an "inner complicity of disgust and desire which fuels its crises of value" (20). In the film, Mala Cosa's disgusting allure helps to alienate magic, but at the same time it also contributes to *Cabeza de Vaca*'s borderline dysfunctionality, if you will. On a different note, recalling Vincent Canby's suggestion that Mala Cosa could have been imagined by Buñuel, James Clifford provides the basis for another reading of this character, as a manifestation of surrealism, which he defines in the following way: "an aesthetic that values fragments, curious collections, unexpected juxtapositions—that works to provoke the manifestation of extraordinary realities drawn from the domains of the erotic, the exotic, and the unconscious" (118). Clifford continues: "To think of surrealism as ethnography is to question the central role of the creative 'artist,' the shaman-genius discovering deeper realities in the psychic realm of dreams, myths, hallucinations" (147). Given Echevarría's fascination with and the value he places on mysticism and shamanism, it is possible that his creation of the bizarre, fragmented character forms part of a "surrealist ethnographic" strategy to discover underlying truths, to indirectly ferret out and postulate aspects of indigenous identity, rather than merely defame the indigenous imagination through a diabolical character.

Later in the film, Mala Cosa's role shifts somewhat when the protagonist begins to look upon the armless dwarf with kinder eyes. However, the change takes place only after Cabeza de Vaca "nourishes" his captors with a show of "civilization." I refer to the episode in which the shaman retrieves Cabeza de Vaca from his escape attempt through magic. The protagonist drops weeping at the feet of his captors, who laugh at and ridicule the beaten man. In a response generally uncharacteristic of *Naufragios*, the protagonist cries out: "¡Porque soy más humano que vosotros!" [42]. And shortly afterwards, grasping for some symbol of his now distant world, Cabeza de Vaca recites a popular ballad. Only now does the laughter of his captors subside, their eyes welling up with tears. The film treats European culture here as a force capable, as it were, of soothing the savage beast.[25] Mala Cosa, while retaining his over-played alien sheen, sheds some of his cruel, monstrous, negative aspects. Cabeza de Vaca, and consequently the audience, sees his humanity, but only as a result of what the film treats as a powerful emblem of the protagonist's culture. The following scene shows Cabeza de Vaca completely assimilated into the shaman's culture and suddenly speaking his masters' language. Mala Cosa becomes more potentially representative of Mexican identity. Yet the manipulation of Mala Cosa remains riddled with questionable implications that may ultimately vitiate *Cabeza de Vaca*'s attempt to position indigenous culture, through a self-othering depiction of magic, as an exalted element of a Mexican hybrid national identity centered on indigenous culture.

In contrast, by downplaying indigenous magic, *Como era gostoso* contributes to its attempts to encourage identification

Chapter Two

with the Tupinambá, which works in tandem with its treatment of cannibalism. The director selectively exalts certain aspects of what is conventionally considered exotic in indigenous culture and de-emphasizes others. At the same time that the director hyperbolically marginalizes and lauds the real, cultural practice of cannibalism, he dismisses the supernatural and links it to simple trickery on the part of a European, reinforcing the positive presentation of the Tupinambá.

Jean claims magical powers in order to deceive and attempt escape. He invokes magic as a ploy, a fiction implemented to change the way that Cunhambebe perceives him. Staden, as well, makes pragmatic use of "magic," or rather, of the power to influence divine wrath and clemency. While it is true that *Naufragios* also attributes the protagonist's healing powers to God, as distinct from Álvar Núñez's account Hans Staden's "powers" are consistently associated with revenge and with the effort to manipulate his standing among the Tupinambá in order to achieve his release. Jean's use of "magic" is also tied to an escape attempt, and plays out in the following way. Cunhambebe, angered by an old French trader's refusal to supply him with gunpowder, directs his fury at Jean. In his desperation, the prisoner conceives of a plan, and promises to provide the chief with gunpowder, a plan that manages to delay his execution. Incidentally, the entire magic/gunpowder sequence, central in the film, is added to Staden's narrative, in which the chief already has gunpowder (63). Having seen a gold coin adorning the navel of his wife, Seboipep, Jean learns from her that there is a large stash of treasure near the village. He determines to retrieve the gold and trade it for gunpowder from the old Frenchman. Based on what Seboipep has taught him about Tupinambá culture and religion, he will claim that in secret union with one of their gods he conjures gunpowder from a thunderstorm. His plan works perfectly, but the chief remains unsatisfied and immediately demands more gunpowder. In a difficult situation, Jean complies and insists that he can create more gunpowder even without a thunderstorm. Later, having killed the old Frenchman and kept both the gold and the gunpowder, Jean tries to escape. In line with the opposite ways in which the two films deal with magic, while Cabeza de Vaca's flight is curtailed with a spell, Jean is more realistically shot in the leg by his wife and taken back to the village.

Jean's implementation of "magic" primarily serves to contribute to the film's overall suggestion of European duplicity vis-à-vis Tupinambá integrity, to a generally positive portrayal of the tribe that contributes to the effectiveness of *Como era gostoso*'s selective self-alienation. While Echevarría has at his disposal a context of reception in which the perceived cultural value of "magical realism" is well entrenched, the Brazilian context places less importance on indigenous magic than it does on cannibalism. Pereira dos Santos effectively uses the film to reposition the role traditionally played by magic and mysticism in conceptions of indigenous identity.

I now turn to *Como era gostoso*'s and *Cabeza de Vaca*'s varied interactions with the representation of indigenous women, and to how the directors' portrayal of women contributes to their overall commentary on national identity. To differing degrees and to disparate ends, both films confront the processes through which indigenous women have been objectified and marginalized. Where does the treatment of women fall in relation to the directors' two principal strategies seen so far—self-exoticizing and the display of exoticizing in order to criticize it? Does the representation of women in the films work in conjunction with the directors' attempts to re-examine and reposition the significance of indigenous populations in conceptions of national identity, or does it contradict or compromise the directors' strategies? An examination of how Echevarría and Pereira dos Santos exploit the male gaze will help to address the preceding questions.[26]

The representation of indigenous women in *Como era gostoso* has two primary roles. First, the film solidifies its attempt to inspire identification with the tribe by avoiding a representation that would cast the indigenous women as exotic others. Jean's non-objectifying gaze helps to achieve such a goal. Discussions of erotic or sexual aspects of the film stem primarily from an obsession, among reviewers, with the nudity of women in *Como era gostoso*. One review from *Village Voice* reads: "About three-dozen actors covered with reddish urucum juice run around starkers with three-dozen women outfitted in G-strings—not the relatively modest variety on strippers, but the type you find on guitars" (Allen 66). Of course, such a comment conceivably says more about the perspective of the reviewer—who fails to recognize the implications of Jean's neutral gaze—than that of the film itself.

However, it might be argued that by openly displaying the bodies of both men and women, Pereira dos Santos attempted to pique a depraved interest in *Como era gostoso* among more priggish international audiences. Indeed, a 1971 review points out that the film was "[p]resumably refused by Cannes for Indian nudity" (Rev. of *Como era gostoso o meu francês* 14 July 1971 n. pag.). Nonetheless, I would contend that while *Como era gostoso* may use cannibalism as a hook, the film treats nudity as contextually natural, as an aspect of Tupinambá culture so unremarkable as to almost pass without notice (except by the occasional reviewer).[27] As the same review that was just quoted writes, the film's display of nudity "is all ethnically sound and never exploited" (n. pag.). The film does not fall into the trap of representing women in such a way that would perpetuate the Hollywood proclivity for sexualizing and objectifying the female body.

At the same time, however, Pereira dos Santos also ties women to the film's treatment of cannibalism. In the character of Seboipep, *Como era gostoso* intermingles the normalizing treatment of nudity and the sensationalizing of anthropophagy. Throughout the film, Jean's companion Seboipep's lack of attire is in no way over-played. Nonetheless, in the beach scene, the shocking juxtaposition of eroticism with Seboipep's explanation to Jean of how he will be eaten the next day, and his subsequent agreeable participation in the execution ceremony, constitute a recruitment of the woman in order to contribute to the film's alienating treatment of cannibalism. The result is a profitable push-and-pull, a revolted identification with indigenous culture.

The second way in which Pereira dos Santos represents indigenous women converges with *Cabeza de Vaca*'s reversal strategy. As in Echevarría's campfire scene, the Brazilian film exoticizes through an objectifying male gaze and subsequently condemns such a practice. Jean, in preparation for his plan to trade gold for gunpowder, signals to the old Frenchman the gold coin in his wife's belly as proof of a nearby treasure. The camera moves in from a medium long shot of the three to a close-up of her torso as the old man polishes the coin in her navel. It is evident that the Frenchman expresses excited interest—in the woman at first, and then in the coin. In contrast, however, to *Cabeza de Vaca*, where the sexual alienation of women originates in the positively portrayed protagonist himself, the sexualizing, avaricious gaze in *Como era gostoso* stems from a character painted as secondary, negative, and foreign, from the perspective of both Jean and the Tupinambá. The old Frenchman's othering gaze serves merely to highlight Jean's and the film's non-objectifying treatment of women.

Whereas *Como era gostoso* sparingly uses the othering of women in its commentary on identity, *Cabeza de Vaca* inundates its representation of women with objectifying and abnormalizing, presumably in order to critique the same in the final campfire scene. From the first moments of the film, after Cabeza de Vaca's shipwreck off the coast of Florida, the camera follows, often with eyeline matches, the perspective and gaze of the protagonist, who is always portrayed favorably and with whom the viewer is consistently urged to empathize and identify. One critic points to the film's "búsqueda de hacer partícipe al espectador" (Aviña 12) [43], and the director achieves this participation in part by ensuring that the viewer see exactly what and how Cabeza de Vaca sees. The visual orientation of *Cabeza de Vaca* follows the protagonist's gaze, which tends to sexualize indigenous women, and is frequently a function of Cabeza de Vaca's shock. The first example of how the protagonist's perspective controls the presentation of the indigenous women in the film occurs immediately after Cabeza de Vaca has been sold into slavery. After a loud frantic shot that frames the caged Spaniards screaming to each other as Cabeza de Vaca is dragged from the tent, the film cuts to near silence and a glimpse of a long shot of a lone, naked indigenous woman, who is standing on a balcony of a hut poised above a river bridge and looking down. Cabeza de Vaca's masters, the shaman and Mala Cosa, are taking him downriver, and the image of the woman recedes through the top of the screen as the camera pivots down to rest on a close-up of Cabeza de Vaca's face. The spectator sees him at this point face-up in the boat as he stares with wide-eyed wonder at the woman before glancing at his captor standing in the bow, to whom the film obediently cuts, framing him in a medium shot. The sequence of the shots and the curiously exaggerated shock on Cabeza de Vaca's face, draw attention from the outset to the privileging of his alienating visual perspective with regard to women and establish the tone that will dominate almost the entire film.

The cannibalism scene in *Cabeza de Vaca* described earlier amplifies and suggestively problematizes the eroticizing and marginalizing portrayal of women in the film. Here the women, most of them covered entirely in blue paint, tease and torment the soon-to-be victims. The camera fragments and fetishizes the first woman to emerge from a tent, focusing only on her blue legs as she rises and walks slowly forward. The film cuts to a medium close-up of one of the bound indigenous men, whose eyeline suggests that he had been looking at the legs of the woman who rose from the tent. For a moment he diverts his gaze, and when he looks back the camera cuts to the legs of three women slowly walking in time to the beat of a drum. The ritualistic scene that follows is characterized by a sexualized violence. The women smile, seeming to indulge in their position of power, as they caress and rub their naked bodies against the bound men. The scene's erotic overtones and the importance of unsolicited domination in the ritual suggest a paradigm of female-to-male rape. Seen in this way, the sequence acts as a possible reversal of or resistance to the film's tendency to objectify women: the cannibals, presumably living within a matriarchy, may aggressively be appropriating and exploiting the male tendency to gaze upon them as sexual objects, much like Mala Cosa armors himself through shock and cruelty. Almost in defiance of *Cabeza de Vaca*'s treatment of them, the characters turn on the film through, if you will, their own metafictional instance of self-alienating, and rebel against the protagonist's and the film's treatment of indigenous women.

The scene culminates in a provocative way. As members of the friendly indigenous tribe arrive, attack, and begin the release of the captives, the leader of the cannibals, aware of her imminent defeat, makes one final and desperate attempt to bring to fruition their paradigm of representational resistance. Consistent with the suggestion of rape, the woman's last act is to shove an arrow into the chest of one of the young men. The young man survives, however, as does the male-oriented objectifying perspective of *Cabeza de Vaca*. Although the cannibalism scene apparently problematizes and renders heterogeneous the film's alienating representational practices, the contestatory potential of the defiance of the women disappears.

We must keep in mind that the film vilifies the cannibals. They are the enemy, as seen through the eyes of Cabeza de Vaca, the hero of the film. In effect, the cannibalism scene depicts indigenous women as merely bizarre, cruel, and sexually depraved others. Moreover, the director smoothes over the suggestiveness of this encounter with the subsequent image of a stereotypical, sexually submissive indigenous woman. After escaping from the cannibals, Cabeza de Vaca and his companions travel to the village of their newfound friends. Upon entering the village, one of the Spaniards is immediately given the gift of a female companion. The film cross cuts between Cabeza de Vaca conversing with several indigenous men and the demure and silent woman offering herself to the other Spaniard: she caresses the Spaniard and prostrates herself in willing and glossy-eyed submission. Although the protagonist's gaze here does not objectify, the film still indulges in the portrayal of the woman as a sexual object. It might be argued that the gift of a female companion is another instance of contact between *Como era gostoso* and *Cabeza de Vaca*. One review comments that Jean "gets along well, even beds down with a local widow" (Rev. of *Como era gostoso*), and de Sousa adds that, for Jean, "becoming Tupinambá is a seductive experience" (92). However, the film's treatment of Jean's relationship with Seboipep and its consummation is far more neutral than the reviews suggest. As opposed to *Cabeza de Vaca*'s concubine scene, neither the camera nor Jean's gaze distances or objectifies Seboipep.

Shortly after the concubine scene in *Cabeza de Vaca*, an apparently dead woman arrives in the village and Cabeza de Vaca manages to revive her. Here we have one of the few scenes with a direct link to *Naufragios*. However, in an ironic, yet emblematic reversal, the person healed in the book was a man.[28] The film transforms him into an adorned and naked woman, who draws both Cabeza de Vaca and, consequently, the camera, close in. Once again, the gaze orienting the visual perspective of the film in this scene is Cabeza de Vaca's, and its object an eroticized other.

Chapter Two

The campfire scene at the end of the film, in which Cabeza de Vaca seems to place in doubt the colonial (and Hollywood) representational tendencies with regard to indigenous women, attempts to act as a critique of the othering that the director presumably mirrors through his representation of women in the film. Yet *Cabeza de Vaca* infuses Álvar Núñez's narrative with women characterized by deformation, sexualization, and a general display of hyperbolized difference. It is only through the protagonist's implied skepticism in one of the final scenes that the film retrospectively cocks its cinematic eyebrow at itself.

Through its treatment of indigenous women, *Cabeza de Vaca* enacts a kind of colonizing aesthetic in which the film's sixteenth-century textual inspiration arguably never indulged. The film ultimately ends up tripping over conflicting premises. Whereas the portrayal of magic may represent an empowering instance of self-alienating, thereby positioning one aspect and vision of indigenous identity as a positive contribution to Mexican national identity, *Cabeza de Vaca* clearly contradicts itself through its representation of women, failing to achieve its attempted critique of Eurocentric representational practices. Consciously or subconsciously, Echevarría reproduces Hollywood's traditional objectification of women on the screen.

* * *

As I have pointed out at several junctures in my analysis, almost all instances in which the directors engage in exoticizing represent changes to the narratives on which they are based. Because much of the original narratives obviously had to be left out of the films, any addition to the stories is necessarily intentional, calculated, and indicative of the films' ideological perspectives. By way of these transformations, *Como era gostoso* and *Cabeza de Vaca* revisit and attempt to revise conceptions of national identity, capitalizing on the symbolically charged, destabilizing context of captivity narratives. The directors position the indigenous groups that appear in the films, and to a certain degree the Europeans being held captive, as representatives of their respective nations. The specific ways in which the films represent the indigenous characters expose the directors' commentary on national identity.

Separated by twenty years and considerable historical and cultural differences, both films confront a similar situation through similar means: they address the contribution of indigenous peoples to national identity by reintroducing captivity narratives into the popular imagination. Basing their commentary on elements of indigenous culture historically treated as exotic—cannibalism, mysticism, indigenous women—the directors alternately self-exoticize and critique exoticizing. Pereira dos Santos manages to change Staden's narrative effectively, using the exotic with positive precision in his commentary on Brazilian national identity. Echevarría, on the other hand, manipulates *Naufragios* unevenly. *Cabeza de Vaca*, though always complex, intriguing, provocative, and suggestive, generally creates a tangled and problematic ideological web, within which the director unwittingly falls victim to and reinforces the damaging yet pervasive appeal of Eurocentrism. This reading of *Cabeza de Vaca* underscores one of the pitfalls of the anthropophagous adaptations that Latin American colonial films tend to carry out. Precisely because the films attempt to craft a focused, unassailable message out of a complex and elusive colonial vestige, their persuasive devices may occasionally backfire. The one unwavering connection between *Como era gostoso o meu francês* and *Cabeza de Vaca* is the importance that Pereira dos Santos and Echevarría place on a continuing re-examination of their respective histories and a thoughtful consideration of the part played by indigenous groups in how Brazil and Mexico are imagined.

Chapter Three

Reimagining Guadalupe in *Nuevo mundo* (1976) and *La otra conquista* (1998)

> For Hidalgo and his ragtag army of Indians bent on revenge for centuries of oppression, as for Emiliano Zapata's *sureños* fighting for land and liberty, Guadalupe symbolized liberation and native rights. For others Guadalupe has had various meanings: indigenism, religious syncretism, respect for cultural autonomy, the struggle for human dignity, or, conversely, submission and subjugation, whether of Indians or women. Most frequently Guadalupe is associated with *mexicanidad*.
>
> Stafford Poole
> *Our Lady of Guadalupe*

Nicolás Echevarría's well-known *Cabeza de Vaca* is not alone among recent Mexican films in reformulating national identity through a return to the colonial period. Two other Mexican films that bracket the decade of the 1990s have carved out a corner of this cinematic zeitgeist. Juan Mora Catlett's *Retorno a Aztlán* (1990) and Salvador Carrasco's *La otra conquista* (1998) address the suppression of indigenous memory and recuperate pre-Columbian and early colonial indigenous history. If Echevarría's commentary capitalizes on "the other side of the conquest" in order to combat the residue of colonialism in Mexican society, *La otra conquista* confronts, consumes, and reconfigures a still-powerful icon of Mexican hybrid identity rooted in colonial culture, the Virgin of Guadalupe, who represents a symbolic fusion of the Virgin Mary with the Aztec goddess Tonantzin.[1] Like several other contemporary Mexican films that treat the colonial period, such as Eduardo Rossoff's *Ave María* (1999)—which enters into an intertextual conversation with seventeenth-century poet Sor Juana Inés de la Cruz—*La otra conquista* dialogues with literature written by people of European descent. In so doing, these films tackle and transform a part of the colonial period's discursive legacy in Latin America.

This chapter examines how *La otra conquista* and a much earlier film, Gabriel Retes's *Nuevo mundo* (1976)—which was released briefly in 1976 and then banned by the Mexican government until 1992[2]—transform the story of Guadalupe and intervene on deeply ingrained understandings of Mexicanness. When *Nuevo mundo* was re-released in 1992, one of the reviews was careful to point out that this film was not, like many, produced in conjunction with the *quintocentenario* (A.F.P. 3). The same can be said for *La otra conquista*, which arrived in theaters in 1998. As director Carrasco has said:

> Deseamos subrayar la actualidad de estos temas, la continuidad de los problemas abordados en la película, ya que el proceso de mestizaje y el sincretismo—y la violencia implícita en dichos procesos—no pertenecen sólo al pasado o a un momento ya superado de la historia de México. Espero que *La otra conquista* contribuya al diálogo sobre una realidad vigente de la que somos parte todos los mexicanos. ("Entrevista" n. pag.)[3] [44]

Such is the perennial preoccupation over Guadalupe, and what she represents in Mexican society.

By engaging Guadalupe the filmmakers are addressing one of the primary symbolic sources of mestizo identity not only in Mexico, but in many areas of Latin America.[4] Despite their disparate dates of release, these two films offer a particularly felicitous opportunity for comparison, and not merely because both films reconstruct Guadalupe. They also consciously reflect on the very process through which icons of identity are constructed. Through their versions of the story of the Virgin of Guadalupe, *Nuevo mundo* and *La otra conquista* envisage two distinct ways in which a figure may begin to reside in a nation's imaginary.

The literary intertext that I will take into consideration in my analysis of both of these films—one of the chief sources through which the tale of Guadalupe was promulgated—is the document known as the *Nican mopohua* [*Here Is Recounted*], a Nahuatl text most likely written in the mid-seventeenth century by the vicar of Guadalupe, Luis Laso de la Vega.[5] The text recounts the apparition of the Virgin to the indigenous man, Juan Diego, in 1531, on Tepeyac Hill (in present-day Mexico City), the place in which some scholars believe there was a temple dedicated to Tonantzin. The impact that this version of Juan Diego's story has had on conceptions of Guadalupe in Mexico is evident in the films' allusions to it. In fact, I would argue that any return to the emergence of the figure of Guadalupe in Mexican society necessarily engages this Baroque text and the mark that Guadalupe has left through it in collective memory. In order to articulate a fresh and powerful conception of Mexican identity within the symbolic territory occupied by the Virgin, her existing incarnation within the national imaginary must first be devoured. And that is what these films do from distinct angles and to different degrees: they revise long-held beliefs and replace them with others.

Nuevo mundo and *La otra conquista*'s attempts to reconfigure Guadalupe's syncretic and political character coincide strategically, at times, with the *Nican mopohua*'s own inscription of the figure on the Mexican imaginary. The title of the book of which the *Nican mopohua* forms a part is Luis Laso de la Vega's 1649 poetic account called *Huey tlamahuiçoltica* ["By a great miracle," or "Very miraculously"]. The description of the Virgin's appearance has been dubbed with that section's opening words, *Nican mopohua*. Stafford Poole argues that, despite being written in Nahuatl, "the story itself is European in form and substance. It follows closely the standard genre of miraculous appearances" (28). This rhetorical hybridity lays the foundation for the text's multi-pronged persuasive efforts to promote a Christian figure that it overlays with indigenous cultural markers. Broadly speaking, the text promotes identification with the protagonist, Juan Diego, telling the story of the apparition and his attempts to convince the Archbishop, Don Fray Juan de Zumárraga, of the truth of his account. The poem's omniscient narrator declares the truth of the apparition in the first lines of the text, and subsequently records the speech of Juan Diego as he, alone, encounters the Virgin on Tepeyac Hill. Yet the Archbishop is skeptical of the tale. Readers of the poem witness

Chapter Three

the construction of Juan Diego's case: his return, re-encounter, and retrieval of irrefutable proof that he has interacted with the Virgin Mary. The exigent Archbishop's acceptance of Diego's story provides a model of reception for the audience of the text. The Archbishop character has endorsed the syncretic figure that the text constructs. Like the *Nican mopohua*, the films remold Guadalupe's syncretic nature and likewise arm their texts with a persuasive apparatus to promote their vision.

According to Poole, Guadalupe was a crucial catalyst for "criollo self-esteem" (156) vis-à-vis Spain.[6] He writes that "[b]y the 1680s the news of the apparitions had reached Spain, where there was at least one effort to demean their importance and to appropriate them for Spain itself. Perhaps even at that early stage there was concern about the political potential of the Dark Virgin" (156). Though Guadalupe was not the only "dark" Virgin, Poole's comment does highlight how indigenous/European cultural fusion lent itself to strategies of resistance. We should, however, recall that the Creoles, who embrace what they see as a cultural, political, and perhaps even racial difference, will in fact be the white perpetuators of a system that will continue to resemble colonialism in its treatment of indigenous peoples. So, on the one hand, Guadalupe has in fact long been used to confront the colonizer, but on the other hand, she was appropriated by the colonizer's progeny. In this respect, we can see a political dimension to Guadalupe's syncretic nature: she combines colonialism with resistance to colonialism. *Nuevo mundo* and *La otra conquista* exploit her long-standing, yet compromised, or whitened, symbolic potential for resistance, and turn it against that aspect of her that may still act as a proxy for colonialism.

Both *La otra conquista* and *Nuevo mundo* illustrate a revisionist approach to colonial writing and identity that might be termed anti-adaptation. In contrast with Humberto Mauro's *Descobrimento do Brasil*, Echevarría's *Cabeza de Vaca*, or even Nelson Pereira dos Santos's *Como era gostoso o meu francês*, these films do not explicitly confront their colonial intertext. The fact that they choose not even to replay the well-known tale of Juan Diego that the *Nican mopohua* sings also underscores the malleable nature of national icons, their state of eternal flux, a dynamic that will be similarly germane in Rossoff's contemporaneous Mexican film *Ave María*, and in Brazilian filmmaker Guel Arraes's later *Caramuru: A Invenção do Brasil* (2001). Although I would not argue that these films represent the latest stage of a teleology within Latin American colonial cinema,[7] they do represent a significant cluster of films that manifest a rather free-form, but ultimately dominant engagement of well-known figures from the colonial period. Such films help to expose one general approach to cannibalizing the colony, one that involves skillful negotiation of both history and myth.

In different ways, *Nuevo mundo* and *La otra conquista* imply that their fictionalizations are grounded, at least partly, in history.[8] Such authorizing stratagems are not uncommon among makers of historical films that seek to persuade. Retes and Carrasco, in effect, recognize the fertile and fruitful interstices between history and myth.[9] They attempt to capture the confidence of viewers through, for example, allusions to verifiable events or figures. Subsequently, they exploit this acquired license once again to great effect in reshaping mythical or iconic figures. Such is the nature of their revision of Mexican history and identity. The films do redraft received renderings of history, yet neither of them pretends to offer a definitive version of events. Carrasco has said that one should approach the theme of the Conquest "de una manera absolutamente sincera y respetuosa, en el sentido de que esta película no pretende ser la versión definitiva o la 'nueva historia' de la post-conquista" ("Entrevista" n. pag.) [45]. These films would appear to suggest that more than one version of history is not only possible, but also valuable. Though the origins of identity markers such as the Virgin of Guadalupe are shrouded, their vague genesis does not make them less formidable. On the contrary, the uncertain emergence of icons, the impression of always having existed, imbues them with an unimpeachable air. If, on one side, an icon appears untouchable, its obscure outline also enables, and even facilitates its reimagining. Retes and Carrasco exercise this invitation to reinvent Guadalupe. In consuming her, they nourish their novel conceptions of Mexican identity and its relationship to the past.

These cinematic Guadalupes remain, as always, symbols of cultural fusion.[10] The filmmakers reshape her in order to inspire resistance or compromise. Broadly speaking, their reinventions

Chapter Three

of the story of Guadalupe differ in this way: *Nuevo mundo* seeks to expose the figure as a subjugating influence over indigenous people consciously devised by Spaniards, while *La otra conquista* underscores, through the invention of an entirely different story, the continuing value of a Guadalupe-like character as a conciliatory symbol of mestizo identity in Mexico.[11]

Nuevo mundo describes a cruel and corrupt Church in early sixteenth-century New Spain that manufactures the myth of the Virgin of Guadalupe. This film postulates that the story has no basis in reality: ecclesiastical officials in the film manufacture the apparition of a Virgin so that the Spanish might more easily subdue an indigenous population poised for insurrection. *Nuevo Mundo* shows a priest compel an indigenous painter, Manuel, who knows the story of the apparition to be false, to paint the image, using an indigenous model, and propagate the myth of the figure.[12] In the end, despite attempted rebellion by indigenous groups, the influential icon is shown to take root among the people, and the Church murders both the priest and the indigenous painter in order to guarantee the endurance of their deception.

Through various means, the first part of *Nuevo mundo* promotes spectator identification with an indigenous population faced with sadistic colonizers. For the purposes of this analysis, I make a distinction between sympathy—immediately solicited through the display of sadistic Spaniards—and identification. It is one thing to recognize the plight of an other; it is something entirely different for an audience to accept an individual or group as their symbolic proxy. *Nuevo mundo* plays with language and camera work to align gradually the spectator's point of view with that of the indigenous population with which they presumably sympathize.

Nuevo mundo makes palpable Spanish cruelty from the opening moments of the film. Concomitantly, the action inspires sympathy for the oppressed indigenous population of Mesoamerica. Yet the cinematic establishment of Mexico's symbolic representative and the way that the film proposes that the viewer adopt the indigenous population's point of view is more complex than the film's heavy-handedness would appear to indicate. The film achieves these goals through the disruption of spectator expectations. Through linguistic and visual shifts,

Nuevo mundo creates a tension that destabilizes, to a degree, established perspectives and ultimately encourages viewers to adopt as their own an indigenous perspective.

The first words spoken in the film are in Nahuatl, and the opening sequence records a confrontation between members of an indigenous village and a party of Spanish clergy, escorted by rifle-armed soldiers, which is just arriving in the region. The film starts with an extreme long shot, from the perspective of a native village, of a large party led by Spaniards arriving; a carriage and many on foot move toward the camera as it, slowly, also advances until the carriage nearly fills the screen. The film then cuts to a long shot within the village, and again the visual perspective is of one who might be watching the Europeans arrive. Despite this partial alignment with the point of view of the indigenous, the untranslated Nahuatl precludes spectators who do not understand that language from fully sharing their perspective. Nonetheless, the Spaniards' behavior would still provoke the pre-identification state of sympathy.

A deep-focus extreme long shot shows an old indigenous leader, armed with a bow, emerging from a building, center-left, while two Spanish soldiers are seen from the back, closer by, on either side of the screen. After a few moments, the old man talks to a Malinche-like figure who is translating for the Spaniards. Notably, the shot/reverse shot medium close-ups that document their short conversation, and put the spectator visually into each of their places, are the most intimate exposure to characters that the audience has yet seen, which reinforces the proposal, first implied through visual point of view of the opening shots, to identify with the indigenous figures. She translates into Spanish, in indirect discourse, the man's inquiry: "Que ¿por qué los van a juzgar? Que los dejen en paz ..." The priest responds: "¿Por qué están abandonando los pueblos?" [46] His preoccupation with indigenous flight recalls, and perhaps even winks at, the famous ending of Álvar Núñez Cabeza de Vaca's account of his captivity and long voyage through North America that culminated in his re-encounter with Spaniards led by Nuño de Guzmán, the cruel governor of the northern frontier province of New Spain, Nueva Galicia. Cabeza de Vaca tells of the governor's efforts to enlist him, because of his influential position among the indigenous people, to secure the return of

Chapter Three

the natives who have taken refuge in the hills. *Nuevo mundo* likewise shows a colonial power that has managed to scatter, through cruelty, their would-be work force. The indigenous man in the film responds by killing the Malinche figure, which sparks a short skirmish during which the old man is also killed. What initial identification the audience may have felt for these figures is quickly frustrated by their deaths.

The title sequence follows, and accompanies a series of shots that confirm the expectations that the opening scene proposes. Soldiers round up indigenous slaves and begin to torture them. The wickedness of the Spaniards is emphasized in a scene that epitomizes *Nuevo mundo*'s shocking implementation of graphic violence coupled with callousness. The titles close with a long take that displays, in an extreme long shot, Spaniards fording a river, and backs away as they come to shore, eventually exposing and centering on a small European house with a fenced area and surrounded by several horses and soldiers. Although this scene is similar to the movie's first shot in that it shows the arrival of Spaniards from afar, rather than from their point of view, this time the space from which we see is a European encampment. The perspective with which spectators are encouraged to identify remains ambivalent and varied. After the final title appears there is a fade out and fade in of the same view of the house. The camera, as if adopting the perspective of a curious onlooker—one would assume a Spanish onlooker, as the indigenous people in this place are prisoners—moves in closer to the house, ultimately framing a seated priest getting a haircut to the left. A soldier arrives from the right with two indigenous men in tow with blood stains tracing a line down their chins and covering their shirts. The soldier declares that they cut out their own tongues, and in this way manifests a damning collusion between soldiers and priests. The cruel behavior of the Spaniards is constantly reinforced during this first part of the film through vivid depiction of rape, and detailed portrayals of torture. Seen in this way, the film divorces modern Mexico from its Spanish side, and proposes exclusive identification with the indigenous population of Mesoamerica, though at this point still assuming, confirming, and yet challenging a European spectator perspective.

Shortly after the arrival of the ecclesiastical party at a Spanish village, one scene features a close-up traveling shot moving to the right across a line of indigenous people passing rocks from hand to hand. The shot then pans out to show dozens of natives occupied in this way, tracing a path up a hill in the distance that is topped with a cross. The coordinated labor of the indigenous people, here obviously forced, recalls a scene from Brazilian director Mauro's 1937 recounting of the Portuguese arrival in Brazil, in which an enthusiastic population helps to unload Pedro Álvares Cabral's ship, passing barrels from man to man. In Retes's film, the stones that the men pass along clearly indicate that they are building a church, the location and emblem of the spiritual indoctrination of indigenous Americans. Once again, a compelling intertext is found in Mauro's film, which depicts the first mass held in Brazil in 1500, which itself revisits the mise-en-scène of Victor Meirelles's 1861 romantic rendering of the scene in his painting *The First Mass*. In *Descobrimento do Brasil*, the filmmaker's goals are accomplished by postulating an indigenous people who happily haul a massive wooden cross to the top of the hill. Rather than following the implications of Mauro's film, *Nuevo mundo* anticipates Echevarría's 1991 *Cabeza de Vaca*. Retes overlays indigenous participation in the construction of a church with an exposé of their state of slavery exposing once again in this way the collusion of Church and State.[13]

The construction sequence in *Nuevo mundo* culminates inside the building that safeguards not only the apparatus of religious indoctrination, but also that of ruthless subjugation. The mise-en-scène of the interior of the church correlates with the torture taking place within and starkly contrasts with the brightly lit exterior. The camera frames shadowy space, dimly lit by several torches placed around the perimeter of the small room. Clergy are clustered around a table and at the several torture stations packing the room where men and women are being interrogated with the help of an interpreter. Several priests and others are occupied with torturing indigenous men and women in order to discover how many indigenous people are part of the insurrection. One of the priests tells another that the natives that they are torturing die before they are able to reveal how many rebels there are. When they splay a naked woman on a two-meter-tall wooden wheel and begin to stretch her to death, the film cements the core of its commentary to this point and the sympathy that it encourages spectators to

Chapter Three

feel toward the indigenous people. The intense and disturbing image of the naked indigenous woman extended on the rack and killed by priests crystallizes spectator condemnation of Spaniards. At this point the film begins to propose a possible release of the tension that it establishes by inspiring sympathy for, but not identification with the indigenous, and visual and linguistic alignment with, but condemnation of the Spaniards. The woman's husband, a Creole man, dies from shock when he sees his wife on the rack. Before she dies and he follows, however, the camera adopts his point of view. A medium close-up of him is followed by an eyeline match to a medium close-up of her on the rack, and then showing him from her perspective as he falls backward, dead. This rare sympathetic non-indigenous character—really, a repentant former abuser of indigenous people—and the alignment of spectator perspective with his and with that of his indigenous wife initiates more plainly what we might see as a gesture toward encouraging a broad, Mexican spectator identification—across the spectrum from European, mestizo, indigenous identity categories—generally with the oppressed indigenous people of the film, but allowing for identification with good non-indigenous people. So, this partial release of perspectival tension does not consist of a simple switch or inversion of alignment, but rather with the disruption and complication of established patterns of identifying.

As we have seen, *Nuevo mundo* clearly encourages viewers to sympathize with indigenous victims by way of the behavior of the Spanish characters. Other techniques seek to take full advantage of the inclination that the film attempts to inspire by solidifying spectator identification with them. One of the ways in which *Nuevo mundo* tries to shape the point of view and political disposition of spectators is through its play with language. Throughout the film, viewers are immersed in Nahuatl,[14] and in the opening scene, the language is not translated. Non-Nahuatl-speaking spectators are necessarily led to share the perspective of the colonizer, if not their ideology. In effect, spectators witness atrocities from the point of view of the perpetrators. Like a dissenting Spaniard, viewers are thus encouraged to take the acts personally, to couple shame with outrage. From another angle, the lack of subtitles de-familiarizes Mexico for spectators. Viewers who do not understand the native language are made to feel out of place. What is more, because Nahuatl shares the stage in this Mexican film, Spanish is partially de-centered and the linguistic hybridity of the region is emphasized.

Nuevo mundo later attempts to realign the troubled, destabilized point of view that it has up to this point sought to provoke in spectators. The film gives viewers access, at intervals, to the perspective of the indigenous people through, ironically, the language of the colonizers. Spanish-language subtitles of Nahuatl dialogue represent an invitation to join the conspiracy. The film thus confirms, reifies, and emphasizes an inferred shift in the point of view of spectators. It gradually entertains the viewers' inclination to see the Spaniard as the other. At the settlement that was the destination of the military and ecclesiastical party, one of the soldiers rapes an indigenous woman, which provokes an insurrectionist exchange in Nahuatl. The indigenous language is now translated for viewers. Indigenous men are speaking with what we might read as the viewer's transitional proxy, the sympathetically portrayed Creole man, whose indigenous wife was the one who was raped, and who later was tortured. In a subsequent scene, the alignment with an indigenous point of view culminates when spectators are made privy to the space and content in Nahuatl, of an insurrectionist conspiracy among only indigenous people.

The film generally exploits cinematic polyperspectivality.[15] As I have pointed out, the camera work contributes to the destabilization and realignment of spectators' point of view. At times we share the perspective of Spaniards, and at other times that of the indigenous characters. Viewers are taken into the midst of scenes solely populated by, or visually guided by, either one group or the other. At one point in the film, a group of indigenous people are burned at the stake.[16] As soldiers light the pyres, the camera displays the act from the perspective of the Spaniards. In a series of traveling medium long shots moving across the backs of the Europeans and showing the pyres in focus in the distance beyond them, cross cut with similar medium long shot displays of the faces of various groups of Europeans viewing the executions, spectators see the stakes and the people burning. The film's tactic here recalls the opening scene, which would provoke discomfort through the forced adoption of a despicable perspective.

Chapter Three

Another scene follows, and intersects with, the pattern of the film's alternating use of subtitles for the Nahuatl dialogue. A man, whom the church suspects of sculpting indigenous idols, is being tortured, stretched on the same round rack that killed the woman earlier. The camera encourages alignment with his point of view by showing him from above and behind, and framing his torturers below to either side. His arms are tied above his head and to the sides in a position and condition reminiscent of crucifixion. The priest is to the left, while an indigenous or mestizo interpreter, a male Malinche, a collaborator, is to the right. The translated words: "Tú lo hiciste. Tú le ayudaste al maestro don Manuel a lo menos. O tu compañero que se escapó" [47]. The man is then pulled tighter, closer to the camera, his agonized expression filling the screen, in intimate proximity to the spectators, who see the Spaniards beyond and from the same perspective as the tortured man. The shot reminds viewers of a comment that Manuel had made earlier; he suggested that the indigenous people of Mexico suffer like Christ—a comment in this context that distances Christ from Christianity/Spaniards—which is why he is able to capture the agony of Christ in his depictions of the figure. Under Spanish rule, Manuel had insisted, his companions provide a constant model for his art. In the shot of the man on the wheel, the tortured man responds to the Spaniards in Nahuatl. The interpreter begins to translate, and the priest says "¡Habla español!" ["Speak Spanish!"] as the man dies or passes out. This time the Nahuatl is not translated for the spectator, despite the camera's proposal that we sympathize, and even identify, with the native man, a dynamic that contributes to the tension of perspectives in the film. His dying words are lost on spectators, as they are lost on the Spaniards, which once again obliges viewers to hear through the ears of the Spaniards at the same time as they have been seeing through the eyes of the tortured indigenous man.

The camera work of the crucifixion scene models for viewers the appropriation of imagery—Christ on the cross—and its redeployment as a tool of discursive resistance—the condemnation of Christians on their own iconic terms. The film taps the symbolic power of Christ's martyrdom to infuse its own martyr with sway or to better dissect what it sees as the Church's hypocrisy. Within the context, then, of a sympathetic disposition toward reasonable indigenous characters who are mistreated, the film begins to display a nascent organized resistance among the indigenous population, and the quick response on the part of Spaniards to squelch that resistance. Up to this point, the film has envisioned an awestruck indigenous population basically powerless to challenge its oppression. Finally, the accumulation of martyrs, and the catalytic vengeance of the woman being raped (when she stabs and kills her attacker), lead to insurrection.

From early on in Retes's film, it is apparent that power struggles between natives and colonizers take place through icons. The film gradually and concurrently proposes that spectators locate social leverage in iconic domination. Shortly after the ecclesiastical party arrives at the hacienda, the sympathetic Creole man places religious imagery at the core of the intercultural conflict. He proposes that Spaniards accept the idols of the indigenous people, claiming that the faith, after all, is the same. This suggestion of religious universality recalls a theological assertion of Cabeza de Vaca, who seeks to convince his sixteenth-century readers that the native people with whom he has developed a relationship possess the same beliefs as Christians; they need only change the name they use to refer to their tripartite deity. This assertion was replayed again as one of the central tenets of *La otra conquista*. Despite its ubiquitousness, such an outlook on religious syncretism in colonial New Spain is inherently problematic, as it conveniently erases the form and specificity of indigenous beliefs and attempts to justify their forced conversion.

The scene in which the indigenous men gather to plan their insurrection culminates with a rally cry around religious imagery. The film shows here a united, proud, resistant indigenous population that insists on agency. Their plan, spoken in subtitled Nahuatl, articulates the battle for liberty in terms of a religious struggle, as the camera weaves its way behind carved idols to frame the group:

>   —Debemos enviar emisarios al sur y al norte; tenemos que unir a todas las tribus. Sólo unidos podemos vencer.
>   —Nuestra dulce señora no nos perdonaría si dejamos vivo al dios de los españoles.

Chapter Three

>—Con sus propias armas debemos acabarlos. Mis hombres están en espera de la señal.
>—Los míos también, pero necesitamos de todos los pueblos.
>—Los españoles destruirán nuestros dioses.
>—Primero muertos que vencidos.
>—El poder de los españoles está en sus armas pero nosotros tenemos la fe.
>—Venceremos si confiamos en la dulce señora. Que cada quien elija. [48]

Their brief exchange assembles various persuasive strategies that reinforce the symbolic role that the film assigns to this group of indigenous men: they are emblems of unity and resistance for all Mexicans. They model for viewers unified action. The film fortifies rhetorically the first speaker's call to arms with an allusion to the ubiquitous revolutionary exclamation: "¡El pueblo unido jamás será vencido!" ["The people united will never be defeated!"]. In 1976 this likely intertext seeks to inspire solidarity, among spectators who support projects such as the Cuban Revolution, with this indigenous group and the ideals that they stand for. The willingness of this native group to die for a cause enhances its inspirational revolutionary spirit. At the end of the conversation, all of the men grab both weapons and idols, two kinds of resistance. Their rebellion is expressed, in fact, in religious terms: they must attack not the colonizers, the followers of a god, but the god itself. If the Spaniards focus their aggression and domination through religion, this indigenous resistance responds in like fashion.

Nuevo mundo contrasts through parallel editing the explicit insurrection of this group with other, more subtle, strategies of resistance. The scene that follows the insurrection conspiracy takes place in the church, where a large party of indigenous people are shown worshipping at the Christian altar. One Spanish observer remarks on what appears to be a miraculous mass conversion, but another dissents. Viewers would likely suspect the hidden explanation for their behavior. Later, when the church is empty, the skeptic reveals what lies behind their devotion, as it were. He removes an idol that had been tucked away on the other side of the altar—a sign of subversive resistance, and also a possible allusion to the notion that Mexican religion can only be syncretic. The Catholic clergy reaches a conclusion similar to that of both the overt and covert resistance factions among the indigenous people: they must dominate and transform iconography (much as the film itself is attempting to do). Soon one of the priests will recruit the indigenous artist, Manuel, to create a new, and more palatable icon for the native population.

One of the priests, Fray Pedro, conceives his plan to convert the indigenous population by transforming their manifest religiosity. The priest compels Manuel, through an implication that he might accuse the artist of heresy, to invent and produce a new image of a Virgin that would help to influence the native population. With no choice in the matter, Manuel acquiesces. Fray Pedro begins by proposing a white nun as a model, but Manuel rejects the suggestion. In one sense, we might read Manuel's insistence as reserving a degree of agency and resistance even within his obliged collaboration with the enemy. Yet his rejection of the priest's idea ultimately results in strengthening the scheme. When the pair pass by an indigenous woman, the priest modifies his plan.[17] Fray Pedro corrals several women and displays them to Manuel behind bars. The priest and the painter pass along the lined up potential models and arrive at one who spits on Fray Pedro. She and Manuel converse in untranslated Nahuatl. Even at this late stage in the game, the film continues its pattern of translating Nahuatl only when all of those present understand the language. When one of the non-Nahuatl-speaking priests is present, spectators are periodically confronted with the point of view of the Spaniards. In this scene, the lack of subtitles perhaps highlights the secrecy of their conspiracy. The painter indicates the rebellious woman—someone who embodies physical and linguistic resistance—as his choice.

Spectators are given access to a later conversation that takes place between Manuel and the young woman. He explains to her that the image that they are creating will help them to survive. At this point Fray Pedro and Manuel bring into sharp focus the two main ways in which Guadalupe has been simultaneously and consistently used: as a vehicle of oppression and opposition. "Pronto llegará el día," Manuel tells her, "en que a los dioses lleguen las lágrimas de nuestros ojos. Que baje su justicia de un golpe sobre el mundo. Este cuadro será útil.

Chapter Three

Aunque nosotros vayamos a morir" [49]. He believes that the icon that he is creating for the Spaniards possesses a lasting and dormant seed of resistance. Indeed, the uniform conversion sought through the painting has the potential to backfire and instead rouse a disgruntled people into rebellion.

After Manuel produces the potentially persuasive image, Fray Pedro attempts to ensure its acceptance among the indigenous population. This time threatening to accuse the young model of heresy, Fray Pedro forces the painter to claim that it was to him that the Virgin portrayed in the painting appeared. Manuel travels among indigenous groups with the image held high and telling his story, with some success. It is only toward the end of the film, when his tale intersects most clearly with the story of Juan Diego as told in the *Nican mopohua*, that his discourse appears to take hold among the population. Up to this point the film has continued to alternate and in this way associate progressively more violent scenes of insurrection with the story of the fabrication of Guadalupe, at one point through a slow dissolve that begins with a close-up of Manuel's face and transitions to a traveling medium long shot of an armed indigenous man running through the woods. Manuel enters a packed Church and tells the story of the apparition, but exploits its cachet among indigenous and Spaniards to achieve various results of his design. His explains:

> Esta imagen apareció en mi celda, bañada por una luz más intensa que la del amanecer. Oí una voz más suave que la de la diosa de la muerte que me decía, "Sal de aquí y lleva este lienzo a mi pueblo." Y yo respondí, "Señora, la puerta está cerrada y yo no tengo palabras para describir tu hermosura." Y ella me dijo, "si quieres todas las puertas se abrirán." Caí de rodillas y recé. Al abrir los ojos la encontré a ella en mis pies. Fui a la puerta y la puerta estaba abierta. Volví a oír la voz y esta vez me dijo: "Manuel, tú, que eres conocido y respetado por todos, di a mi pueblo que Dios, conmovido de tanto sufrimiento, me manda para darles consuelo. Diles a mis queridos hijos que confíen en mí, porque soy carne de su carne, y sé como nadie de su desamparo infinito. Quiero oír sus problemas en oración para llorar con ellos. No hagan la guerra, porque morirán todos, indios y españoles, y así la gran misión de formar una nueva raza no será cumplida.

Reimagining Guadalupe

> Diles a los españoles que no quiero más violencia. Los hago responsables ante nuestro señor de toda su crueldad contra los míos. Demando que los vean como iguales porque todos somos hijos de Dios. Es mi voluntad que desde hoy todos, indios y españoles, sean un pueblo, un sólo pueblo, unidos por el amor hacia mí y hacia Jesús, nuestro señor." [50]

Manuel's discourse follows some of the *Nican mopohua*'s persuasive strategies. Just as the portrait of Guadalupe appeared miraculously on the gown of Juan Diego, Manuel attributes a divine genesis to the painting that he offers as proof of his experience. And to confirm the miraculous capabilities of his Virgin, he, like the *Nican mopohua*, recounts a simple miracle: the desire for doors to be opened produces that result. If this promise of the Virgin is realized, he hopes to convince his audience, all of her words should be trusted. With her authority established, he begins to make use of it. His discourse clearly aligns the Virgin with the indigenous people—whose suffering she feels and who claims them as the people of God—and not with the Spaniards. His first goal in his exploitation of the icon is to quell the rebellion, which he believes to be doomed. He also turns the Spanish religious icon against them, condemning their mistreatment of the indigenous people and demanding equal treatment. The Virgin wishes for the end of the violence because, if not, "la gran misión de formar una nueva raza no será cumplida." Manuel attempts, here, a conciliatory message—much like that presented much later in *La otra conquista*—a celebration of a cultural mestizaje whose center is Catholicism. He seems to recognize that the figure that he has helped to create is destined to hold an influential position in Mexican society. Given that, he tries, like these two Guadalupe films, at least to determine the direction of her discursive sway.

Yet *Nuevo mundo* is, in the end, rather pessimistic. Manuel appears to realize the futility of his subversive strategy, his attempt to invert the Spaniards' iconic weapon. At the end of his speech, he pauses, gets up and grabs the image in an evident move of open rebellion. Later indigenous people are seen burning statues of Virgins. But the resistance is indeed doomed; subsequent scenes show a subdued native population. Now many indigenous painters are shown copying the image that Manuel created. Mass production helps to anchor Guadalupe in the imagination of the population, yet the Spanish recognize that it would have more sway in the population if reinforced through other means. One of the priests makes a possible allusion to the *Nican mopohua* when he says that a text should accompany the image. And to help to ensure durability of the icon, all players in the charade are murdered. What remains, the film might imply, is the unanswered question of whether Manuel's prediction to the young model will be realized. Will the gods rise up aided by the image of the Virgin to smite the Spaniards? Is *Nuevo mundo* the fulfillment of that promise?

Retes's film focuses its energy on dismantling colonialist ideology. He deconstructs Guadalupe, and thus encourages a departure from her as a source of Mexicanness. After its unrelenting vilification of the Catholic Church and Spanish colonial government, *Nuevo mundo* leaves neither hero nor martyr among the indigenous cast, only the collective image of a populace coerced into complicity and on the road to domination and assimilation. The catalyst for their defeat was an indigenous turncoat, but one who himself was also deceived and manipulated. Still, Retes unequivocally privileges the resistant, liberationist indigenous characters and treats them as the only true Mexicans (though he leaves some room in this privileged space for sympathetic Creoles), a tack that unavoidably proffers them as a collective icon of an oppressed people. Even a Mexican audience that may conceive of itself primarily in mestizo terms is encouraged to see itself reflected in this indigenous group. Despite the destruction of Guadalupe, the mestizo icon par excellence, the film leaves viewers a broad iconic identity option.

Even as it undoes her, *Nuevo mundo* depends on Guadalupe's currency to evoke conceptions of Mexicanness, and the source for Retes's rendering of present-day Mexico remains the colonial past. A clear example of the anthropophagous pattern in Latin American film that I am describing, the film consumes Guadalupe entirely and attempts to absorb her representational promise. Yet in exchanging Guadalupe and forging his own, alternate (collective) indigenous/mestizo icon from the period of the conquest, the director perhaps plants the seed of the film's own disruption. His attack on Guadalupe depends on destabilizing the Church's efforts to forge and deploy icons through art and persuasion, strategies that are mirrored in his own film. *Nuevo mundo* both typifies and critiques efforts to embody the nation.

* * *

La otra conquista, in its turn, tells the story of an illegitimate child of Moctezuma, Topiltzin (later dubbed Tomás), and how he is taken captive by Spaniards and sent to a monastery for religious, cultural, and linguistic indoctrination.[18] The protagonist ultimately perishes when a life-sized statue of the Virgin Mary, whom he has from the beginning associated with the Aztec deity Tonantzin, falls and crushes him. The film proposes through this syncretic association—which it had earlier suggested through a conversation in which Topiltzin and a priest attempt to reconcile religious beliefs—an alternate birth of the figure of Guadalupe in Mexican society. The director of *La otra conquista*, Carrasco, has said in an interview that the title of the film refers to the spiritual conquest that was woven into the political conquest in Mexico in the sixteenth century (Interview 66).[19] His intention, he maintains, was to speculate about the period between Cortés's conquest of Tenochtitlán in 1521, and the apparition of the Virgin of Guadalupe in 1531, equivalently foundational moments for Mexico (Interview 66). In naming the film, Carrasco also sought to evoke the fact that the story focuses on an indigenous protagonist and tells a version of the conquest not traditionally included in the "official story." When asked about the originality of his approach to reimagining the colony, the director insists that the indigenous community that he portrays is creative, critical, and resistant, and seeks agency in the shaping of its destiny.[20] Carrasco says the following of his protagonist: "Topiltzin [es] un hijo natural del emperador, cuya 'otra conquista' tiene que ver con la identificación y apropiación que lleva a cabo de un icono de la Virgen María, para recuperar a su propia diosa madre, Tonantzin […] que en cierto modo es lo que sucedió en nuestro país con la Virgen de Guadalupe" ("Entrevista" n. pag.) [51]. In fact, such is the commonly held understanding of the syncretic origin of Guadalupe. Edmundo O'Gorman has famously articulated the view that in the middle

Chapter Three

of the sixteenth century the second archbishop of Mexico—who held his post from 1551 to 1572—founded the chapel dedicated to Guadalupe at Tepeyac, a place of worship for the indigenous goddess Tonantzin, in an attempt to inspire the devotion of the indigenous population and control them.[21] The maternal aspect of the deity helps to highlight the generative role of the syncretic figure, how from her may emerge an idea of Mexicanness. The film, then, directly and openly engages the genesis of Guadalupe. However, the explanation for her emergence—which *La otra conquista* offers in place of that told by the *Nican mopohua*—differs substantially from that of *Nuevo mundo*.

Unlike *Nuevo mundo*, which eases into foregrounding iconographic battles, *La otra conquista* immerses viewers in the negotiation of Amerindian and European icons from the beginning of the film. The appearance of the film's title sets the stage: an indigenous-looking icon—a stylized face with the tongue stuck out—is fused with a cross, likely emblematizing syncretism. The words "La otra conquista" overlay the images before they subside, leaving only the words. The cultural and religious struggles that gave rise to Mexico, this graphic design seems to imply, underlie modern arbitration of their aftermath in society. The film intends to give viewers access to those cultural palimpsests, and to ensure the success of its revelatory efforts. An introductory intertitle appears that summarizes the background of the action, a typical device of historical films. The nature of this image, however, seeks to authorize the film's message, by rooting it in (a simulacrum of) a textual source. The following words are written on a mock-up of an aged manuscript that combines words in Spanish with indigenous iconography: "En 1519 el conquistador español Hernán Cortés y su reducido ejército penetraron en Tenochtitlan [...] Al cabo de dos años, la civilización azteca [...] trataba de adaptarse a un nuevo mundo" [52]. With this technique, *La otra conquista*—like two contemporaneous Brazilian films, Lúcia Murat's *Brava Gente Brasileira* (2000) and Guel Arraes's *Caramuru: A invenção do Brasil* (2001)—attempts to ground persuasively its story in an invented intertext. The action of the film begins with a complementary foundation in history. The words "Templo Mayor Mayo de 1520" ["Templo Mayor, May 1520"]—a specific time and place—appear on the screen and imply a verifiable basis for the film.

Reimagining Guadalupe

This historically rooted juxtaposition of European and indigenous iconography is paralleled from the beginning of the film with polyperspectivality: spectators are alternately exposed to indigenous Mexican and European points of view. Following the opening scene, which depicts the indigenous protagonist as a lone survivor of a battle emerging in the rain from under a cadaver at the Templo Mayor in 1520, the film cuts to a bright, dry, intimate interior sequence showing an old priest, Fray Diego (1548, La Coruña), in a series of medium close-ups and close-ups, with two other men, in the moments before his death. At one point Fray Diego looks up, the camera following his eyeline to frame in a medium shot the two other men, and then cutting in a graphic match to the representation of what apparently is a memory of Fray Diego's: shadows on a wall depicting him and Topiltzin as the priest makes the sign of the cross over the indigenous man and finalizes his conversion to Christianity. These first sequences foreground an indigenous and then a European point of view, and then display in a visually abstract way, from a neutral or ambiguous standpoint, the convergence of the two constituencies through memory/shadow. In this way, the film initiates a complex relationship to perspective and identification, which it will parley to propose a plural as well as hybrid, and always inclusive, symbolic representation of Mexicanness.

The scene in which Fray Diego dies also emphasizes the centrality of iconography. It recruits a scrap from an indigenous painted manuscript as the catalyst for a flashback. One of the priest's companions finds a corner of an indigenous Mexican pictorial manuscript between the pages of one of Fray Diego's books. A close-up of the scrap transports viewers back to 1526 (a date flashed on the screen later indicates this), through a graphic match cut to an extreme close-up of that detail in the codex from which the scrap came. The camera pulls back and tilts up to show the back of a young indigenous man, Topiltzin, whom we learn later is one of Moctezuma's sons, and his view of the scene that he contemplates beyond and below. The man sits alone and paints atop a temple and looks out upon the aftermath of a battle, where apparently his compatriots were crushed by their enemy. His painting recounts the battle through pictographs. He narrates in Nahuatl voiceover that Spanish subtitles translate. Viewers are thus encouraged to identify with

Chapter Three

Topiltzin, as they are made privy to his private moment and are given access to his language. The voiceover, in a first-person plural that may act as an inclusive gesture toward spectators, locates agency in the iconographic preservation of indigenous memory: "[T]odo esto pasó con nosotros. Nosotros lo vimos. A nosotros nos tocó. Este fue nuestro destino. Pero al darle voz al papel, nuestra esencia vivirá" [53]. But the film implies that this cultural essence did not fare so well, as the scrap of paper that Fray Diego would hold years later was all that remained of this codex, which viewers see burned in a subsequent scene. If the manuscript itself represents resistance for the writer/painter, Topiltzin also models another kind of resistance by featuring in his images an indigenous man strangling a Spaniard. The voiceover continues to decode the pictographs: "Gran sol, ¿por qué nos has abandonado?" ["Great sun, why have you abandoned us?"]. A possible referent for Topiltzin's desperation, of course, is Jesus. The faith of the indigenous people of Mesoamerica is being put to the test. Topiltzin will indeed persevere in the face of terrible adversity. His determination establishes him as a spiritual paragon, an example, like Jesus, to be followed. His faith never wavers, yet it does take on a syncretic, universalist character. His advocacy for the convergence of beliefs soon begins to play itself out through the juxtaposition of indigenous and European icons.

Inside the temple, as Topiltzin continues to paint, his grandmother confirms the young man's characterization of the codex as preserver of a cultural essence, and takes the commentary into religious territory: "Tu códice es la palabra de nuestra gente. Es digno de nuestra Diosa Madre Tonantzin" [54]. Topiltzin expresses his desire to offer the codex to the goddess, and his frustration, along with that of his brother and grandmother, that there remains no suitable place to do so because of Spanish restrictions on their religious practice. In a subsequent scene, at the conclusion of a ceremony that entreats Tonantzin to guard the manuscript, the man conducting the ceremony hides it inside a statue of the goddess. Religious identity and cultural memory are intertwined here, mutually dependent. At this moment, the film represents a waning state in which this indigenous population is in control of their history and culture.

The scenes depicting the process leading up to this hiding of the codex have been intercut with the progress on foot of a

Spanish party that includes soldiers and a priest, Fray Diego, who lugs a large cross. After displaying again this procession, the film cuts back to the indigenous context, where they are preparing to sacrifice a young woman—an act that they realize and which confirms their beliefs. The two spaces converge—when Spanish soldiers and Fray Diego break into the temple shortly afterwards. The soldiers, despite protests by Fray Diego, kill several of the indigenous people there, which display of gratuitous cruelty, as in *Nuevo mundo*, likely inspires spectator sympathy for the victims, with whom, in *La otra conquista*, the audience has been generally encouraged to identify, even if the seeds have been planted for a somewhat broader spectrum of identification through a relatively positive exposure to Fray Diego. Topiltzin's brother betrays the location of the codex, and the Spaniards destroy both the statue and the codex, and with them what we might see as Topiltzin's dual strategy of survival through icons. The rest of the film, through Topiltzin, tries to imagine another strategic path that takes into account the Spanish cultural and iconographic hegemony that awaits the indigenous population.

Topiltzin is the first to collapse the iconography and related beliefs of his people and the Spaniards. The party of colonizers that enters the temple has been hauling not only a large cross, but also a life-sized sculpture of the Virgin Mary. After the Spaniards shatter the statue of Tonantzin, a series of shots cements the association of icons. A close-up of the face of the statue of Tonantzin is followed by a close-up of Topiltzin's face as he, face up on the ground, looks at her depiction and begs her forgiveness. At this point he looks up at Fray Diego, the camera sharing his point of view, and what is beyond the priest: the covered statue of Mary. A soldier uncovers what will emerge in the film as Tonantzin's blond analog. Topiltzin looks intently at the European rendering: from a close-up of his face, the camera cuts to a dolly-in of the statue that ends in a close-up and then alternates to a dolly-in of Topiltzin that frames once again his face in a close-up. The priest detects this charged moment of introspection and fusion, and what he perceives as his associated opportunity to proselytize. A shot of the priest's face implies his well-intentioned conviction, as his seductive catechism begins: "Mirad la Virgin. Esta hermosa mujer es María, la madre de Dios. La vuestra no es más que un puñado de piedras" [55]. Rather than seeing one or the other as an empty simulacrum, Topiltzin conceives the correspondence in divine characteristics of the two figures (motherhood), which represents the core of the film's message of spiritual universality (or perhaps its leveling of cultural distinctiveness). The filming of this scene, which shifts from shots of Tonantzin to the Virgin, conveys Topiltzin's intuition. When, later, the statue of the Virgin sits upon a hill and Topiltzin, now captive, looks upon her, he makes a decision and takes the first steps in his strategy of iconic revision. He runs up the hill and kneels before the statue, which convinces Fray Diego that Topiltzin has experienced a spontaneous change of heart. Actually, the film is rather ambiguous about the implications of the young man's actions. Perhaps it suggests either that Topiltzin considers Tonantzin to have simply adopted a new face, or that he postulates a shared referent for Tonantzin and the Virgin. In any event, Topiltzin's ostensible epiphany has no effect on his disposition toward the Spaniards, as he turns to Fray Diego, throws a rock at him, and makes his escape.

When finally the Spaniards recapture Topiltzin (due to another betrayal of his brother), he is brought before Hernán Cortés, where he meets Tecuichpo. Also a child of Moctezuma, she translates for the Spanish *conquistador*.[22] In a demonstration of oblique solidarity Tecuichpo speaks to him in Nahuatl that is translated for spectators but not for Cortés: "No digas nada, no hagas nada. No me juzgues por estar aquí" [56]. She collaborates, much like Malinche, with the enemy, yet she holds a position of influence within the colonial power structure. She thus models for Topiltzin an alternate, less overt, vehicle of resistance. In this instance, her small rebellion takes the form of covert communication. She wins one battle through her domination of signs, her control of the linguistic channel. Spectators are encouraged to identify with the pair because they are made part of the inside joke. Cortés responds to her resistance also, at first, in the territory of signs: when she tells the Spaniard Topiltzin's name, he calls her Doña Isabel and sentences her brother to a lashing, to the new name of Tomás, and to a Catholic education with priests. Later, Cortés takes his response to her resistance into a more palpable realm when he rapes Tecuichpo.

Fray Diego refuses to be present at the torture—rather, he looks on, concerned, from a window—which further imbues him with a sympathetic air that the film will exploit in conjunction with that of Topiltzin when the two later reconfigure their beliefs through the icon of the Virgin. The priest inverts the civilization/barbarism paradigm and voices the hypocrisy of a Church in collusion with the colonial power: "No soy responsable del barbarie que se comete en nombre del Dios nuestro" [57], he tells Tecuichpo as the torture is carried out. Earlier, in preparation for Topiltzin's punishment, the statue of the Virgin is placed in front of him, thus forcing him to contemplate the symbol of the religion that he is being compelled to adopt while he is whipped. The camera cuts in an eyeline match from the gaze of Topiltzin, who is framed in a medium close-up, to another medium close-up of the Virgin. The following image is of Topiltzin: a medium shot from the point of view of the Virgin whose hair and shoulder we see to the right of the screen, which suggests that she is looking at him, and guiding as well the spectators' perspective. At the close of the torture scene, Fray Diego arrives and embraces the broken, unconscious young man. The priest looks up and behind himself at the Virgin, and an eyeline match cut shows a close-up of her face as she sheds a tear for Topiltzin in an apparent reaction shot, which, in collusion with the suggestion that she is gazing at him, defies her inanimate state and suggests a miracle. The film thus suggests an alliance between the icon and whatever she represents (the Virgin Mary? Tonantzin?), and Topiltzin and what he represents (indigenous Mexico in the sixteenth century? All of Mexico in 1998?). At this point, *La otra conquista* contrasts sharply with *Nuevo mundo*. Retes's film does anticipate *La otra conquista* in that it proposes that the Virgin was the champion of the natives, yet it puts the proposal in the mouth of Manuel, who was obviously shaping his discourse strategically. *La otra conquista* depicts such a sympathy as real. In *La otra conquista*, as in other recent Mexican films about the colonial period, such as Nicolás Echevarría's 1991 *Cabeza de Vaca*, the supernatural reigns. The eyeline match cuts and the statue's tear in *La otra conquista* help to reify Topiltzin's beliefs.

During a break in the torture of Topiltzin, the camera travels in close-up past the somber faces of indigenous men and

Chapter Three

women, who look on, a shot that corresponds with one at the end of Rossoff's *Ave María* (1999), when the title character, who herself is associated with Tonantzin and the Virgin Mary, is burned at the stake for heresy. Topiltzin's treatment provokes in more than one member of the crowd a manifestation of resistance. His brother abandons finally his collaboration and comes forward to attempt to save Topiltzin, but he is beheaded. His only contribution, in the end, is martyrdom. Another says to the torturer in Nahuatl the following phrase that is translated for viewers of the film, "¡Tu sangre no vale nada!" [58]. The interpreter's translation recalls Tecuichpo's manipulation of signs: "Dice que vuestras palabras en nada responden a la imagen que tienen de la gran señora de piel blanca" [59]. He suggests here a core aspect of Topiltzin's beliefs: the problem lies not with Christianity, but with the Christians. This exchange seems to want to preserve the viability of the Virgin (even a white-skinned one) as a symbol for Mexico. In the final moments of Topiltzin's punishment, the image that the film has painted of the young man as a representative of a proud indigenous Mexico is reinforced through an allusion to Cuauhtémoc's torture. The camera cuts successively in close-ups to the torch on Topiltzin's feet, to Topiltzin's face, to the Virgin, and then back to his face, and again to his feet being burned. This Christian—and by now in the film, syncretic—icon has now born sympathetic witness to the mistreatment of indigenous Mexico.

Shortly after Topiltzin is taken to the monastery for his indoctrination, he and Tecuichpo essay another domination of signs. This time, however, they attempt to control official discourse in Spanish. She has pilfered a stamp of Cortés's signature and with it they sign a letter that they have written to the king. "Dulce venganza" ["Sweet vengeance"], translates the Spanish subtitle of what Tecuichpo says. Yet their efforts are in vain, as Fray Diego observes their machinations. When the priest arrives, he takes over the manipulation of signs, insisting that they stop speaking what he calls Mexican. In private, the pair fight back in two ways. First, Topiltzin sets aside the name with which the Spanish had clothed her (Isabel), referring to her as Tecuichpo. Additionally, the couple is shown in a slow long shot having sex. He comments that the survival of their blood depends on their intimate union. The film in this way suggests the continuity of the Mexican people and reinforces the symbolic privileging of the Aztecs. *La otra conquista* thus may advance a proposal of ethnic and/or racial preservation, rather than an acceptance, reconfiguration, or celebration of cultural or racial mestizaje, which punctuated the closing discourse of Manuel in *Nuevo mundo*. When Tecuichpo, imprisoned for forging the letter, reveals to Cortés that she carries a child that is not his, she repeats that this is her body, and this is her blood. Their act of procreation was an act of resistance that ensured for her a degree of agency and attempted to provoke the symbolic birth of a Mexico with indigenous identity at its center.

While the film suggests through the union of the siblings that Mexico of 1998 should conceive of itself as the imaginary descendents of this originary indigenous pair, it allows the survival of the syncretic Guadalupe, but revises her, through Topiltzin, as a proud synonym of Tonantzin. Topiltzin, toward the end of the film, is delirious with fever. He flashes back to the moment when the Spaniards entered the temple just after the sacrifice of the young woman. At one point in the dream-like sequence, the image of the white Virgin, in a medium shot, dissolves into that of Tonantzin. Topiltzin, in his delirium, collapses the two maternal divine symbols into one. He confirms his position, at a point in which he is not hallucinating, in a conversation with Fray Diego: "Ahí [en el templo] quedó hecho humo nuestra verdad de las cosas [. . .] En el fondo, compartimos la misma creencia, Fray Diego, aunque [venimos] de mundos tan distintos" [60]. Topiltzin reluctantly accepts that indigenous discourse and the power of their icons has begun to subside. His reaction is to harmonize the new symbols with his own beliefs. By proposing religious universalism, he preserves his pride and a path to long-term survival. He also reconfigures Guadalupe: rather than a European figure grafted with indigenous elements, he proposes that she can be considered, at her core, either indigenous or European; for him they are the same. He tries in this way to make her more malleable and palatable. He attempts, from another perspective, to de-colonize her. Later, Fray Diego coincides with Topiltzin's message, and thus fortifies it for those spectators who might also identify with this sympathetic Catholic figure. He says that "Esta hermosa mujer no es ni más ni menos verdadera que la vuestra. Lo que ahora

Chapter Three

importa es que ésta es la nueva palabra" [61]. Fray Diego's position is actually more radical. He emphasizes that whatever one's beliefs may be, they will have to accept this new symbol. But rather than suggesting that Tonantzin and the Virgin share the same referent, he implies that both of them are real.

The final segment of the film, which chronicles Topiltzin's bizarre death, combines his and Fray Diego's new conception of Guadalupe with the not entirely straightforward insinuation of Topiltzin (and by extension, native Mexico) as an indigenous Christ, who sacrifices himself for his people. When Topiltzin is caught trying to access the chapel where the statue of the Virgin is kept, guards carry him off toward the receding camera: each one has an arm and his legs are dragging behind him, suggesting with this composition the crucifixion of Jesus. In the climactic sequence of the film, Topiltzin replaces his Spanish frock with a loincloth. He sheds the signs of his transculturation and makes a final gesture of pride in native culture. Topiltzin sneaks into the chapel and removes the Virgin's crown. The camera frames in close-up the faces of the young man and the statue, who are facing each other and apparently gazing into each others' eyes. It then moves 180° around the back of her head to rest again on an image of their faces from the other side. The film in this way revises its vision of an originary pair: now it begins to imply a mestizo birth for Mexico. Topiltzin then pulls the statue through the window. In his final act, which the film once again accompanies with flashes of the Virgin and Tonantzin, he tries to dominate the icon, to take her with him and reconfigure her. But rather than represent the realization of this optimistic symbolic revision, the film instead reflects the tragic truncation of his symbolic scheme.

He and the statue fall backward from the window as he cries out the name of Tonantzin, and the statue—which now embodies both Tonantzin and the Virgin—crushes Topiltzin. Rather than killing the icon and replacing Guadalupe with a new mestizo emblem as in the case of *Nuevo mundo*, *La otra conquista* here represents a partial and mutual disintegration and absorption, but one that retains a white exterior. Topiltzin and the indigenous beliefs that he stands for are all but annihilated, but he attempts to take the European Virgin down with him. The Virgin, of course, who rises as the phoenix from the ashes, remains relatively intact. In her subsequent incarnation, the film would imply, she has adopted some of the qualities with which Topiltzin has earnestly attempted to infuse her through his association of the Virgin with Tonantzin.

Carrasco's film attributes the conception of the syncretic Guadalupe to indigenous rather than European authorship. Topiltzin's efforts to verbally and visually, through reason and symbolism, reconcile indigenous and European beliefs, imagines a degree of indigenous agency in mestizo conceptions of identity. The postulation of an alternate, indigenous invention of a Guadalupe-like figure promotes an appropriation and reconfiguration of this ingrained icon of Mexicanness. In endeavoring to achieve social harmony, in the end, the film maintains the essentially European character of Guadalupe (a Catholic icon, after all, and one represented by a European statue in the film). Her transformation lies in what *La otra conquista* does with Mexico's symbolic surrogate, Topiltzin: in addition to shifting the iconic authorship, his character posits religious universality. He is neither praying to Tonantzin through the Virgin Mary, nor has he replaced wholesale his god with another. He imagines a fusion, a perfect overlap. Mexico can be proud, in other words, of its indigenous heritage even while maintaining the status quo of European-dominated social and religious practices. The film, in this sense, attempts to come to terms with a social reality rather than proposing a substantive change.

After Topiltzin's death, the priest realizes a reciprocal syncretism. He demonstrates his own heart-felt linguistic, cultural, and religious acculturation by blessing Topiltzin in Nahuatl. Whereas *Nuevo mundo* offers no model of kind Spaniards, and only and almost grudgingly acknowledges the mestizo reality of Mexico, *La otra conquista* leaves viewers the option to imagine an egalitarian syncretism. This optimistic outlook on transculturation or cultural mestizaje de-centers Europe's role in the formula. On the one hand, in doing this, the film may be seen to sweep under the carpet the dominant and oppressive role that the (Catholic) Church and (Spanish) State did take in Mexico. However, on the other hand, the film's unequivocal depiction of the overall behavior of the colonizers brings this priest's gesture into clear relief. Thus, the priest's own alignment with Topiltzin's point of view may be understood as a proposal for spectators to follow his lead and rethink the nature and proportions of Mexican mestizo culture.

* * *

Both of the films, through iconography, alternate proposals for pride in indigenous culture with reconsiderations of mestizaje. For its part, however, *La otra conquista* does not offer a very consistent view of Guadalupe, and much less of Mexican identity.[23] But perhaps the film's ultimately unwieldy symbolic intricacy, whether intended or not, is what best reflects the complex, layered, irreducible Mexican imaginary. It does contribute nonetheless to a re-evaluation of the emergence of the powerful icon of identity that is the Virgin of Guadalupe. Carrasco's film recognizes the vitality of viewing Mexico through this cultural icon. If nothing else, *La otra conquista* centers the indigenous population of colonial Mexico within negotiations of the figure's cultural value and uncovers a strategy for all to embrace this ubiquitous icon. Carrasco characterizes his film as conciliatory, "una invitación al diálogo, a reflexionar sobre nuestros orígenes y a respetar nuestras diferencias" (Interview 66) [62]. *Nuevo mundo*, on the other hand, while perhaps not an invitation to dialogue, certainly is a catalyst for reflection. Its relatively more stable indictment of the conquest and its cultural, religious, political, and social aftermath disrupts inherited conceptions, and loosens the rooted icon within her place in the Mexican imaginary. The films coincide nonetheless in seeing their reformed Guadalupes as double-edged swords. In both films the indigenous protagonists manage to manipulate the meaning of Guadalupe—privately, in *La otra conquista* and publicly, in *Nuevo mundo*. Yet in both cases, the protagonists' deaths were a direct result of their involvement with her. Guadalupe thus possesses extraordinary promise to reform conceptions of identity, yet her consumption and digestion, these films would seem to imply, is sometimes a risky endeavor.

Chapter Four

Sor Juana Inés de la Cruz and the Retooling of a National Icon in *Ave María* (1999)

Eduardo Rossoff's film *Ave María* was released in May of 2000, just two months before the PRI,[1] after seventy years of uninterrupted rule, lost the presidential election to the Alianza por el Cambio (PAN-PVEM)[2] candidate, Vicente Fox. The film, which was partly financed by the former imperial power that *Ave María* condemns,[3] proposes a hybrid hero who clearly occupies iconic territory within the sphere of Mexicanness. Perhaps ironically, the creator of the script was a woman from the United States, Camille Thomasson.[4] Like so many other Mexican and Brazilian films of the twentieth century, Rossoff's film plainly and persuasively amplifies the contrapuntal resonance of the present and the colonial past, but in this case, the varied and international factors contributing to the production of the film exemplify a new, complex model of Latin American historical film, in which several and varied parties share their colonial sustenance. However, *Ave María*'s relationship with colonial literature is best characterized as grazing rather than eating. Rossoff's exemplifies an ever-more-prevalent sector of colonial films—a term I use to denote films treating the colonial period—films that establish loose or tenuous connections with written intertexts.

Curiously, *Ave María* invokes a seventeenth-century Creole icon in an attempt to inspire solidarity with the indigenous population of Mexico, and to shift mestizo conceptions of Mexican identity toward the indigenous side. The protagonist of Rossoff's film, María Inez, owes an obvious debt to the seventeenth-century poet who was awarded in her lifetime both international renown and the jealous, oppressive contempt of the Church for her lyrical and intellectual prowess: a prominent

Chapter Four

figure in Mexico even today, Sor Juana Inés de la Cruz. Nonetheless, *Ave María*'s reimagination of Sor Juana, María Inez, is not of European descent, but mestiza: her mother is indigenous and her father is Spanish. Over the course of the film she adjusts her cultural self-identification from European to indigenous. She suggestively comes to embody a proud fusion of the Spanish and Nahua cultures before she is burned at the stake for heresy.

María's resemblance to Sor Juana is especially transparent in the first half of the film, which depicts an exceedingly gifted young member of a religious community who inspires the envy of her peers and the wrath of the men who ostensibly hold sway over her destiny. The second half continues to draw on Sor Juana in cataloguing the genesis of María's iconicity, and finally attempts to footnote the seventeenth-century poet as the film follows María's defiant departure from the confines of the community in order to initiate a battle for the rights of Mexico's indigenous population. Perhaps surprisingly, Rossoff evades any claim of María's kinship with Sor Juana. In fact, the director makes no reference whatsoever to the nun-writer when quoted in reviews of the film. Nonetheless, the connection has been acknowledged in criticism about the film (e.g., Gransden 12; Barriga Chávez 10). Allusions to the famous figure and her writings, whether intended or not by the filmmaker, arguably open the door for spectators not only to re-view the film in light of the nun's writings, but also to reread the literature through the perspective of the film. The dynamic, which may help to explain the director's avoidance of associating María and Sor Juana, threatens to compromise the calculated instrumentalization of the past that I believe *Ave María* attempts to realize.

Ave María's particular open-ended intertextual relationship with the colonial period differs from the strict-seeming approach to adaptation of Humberto Mauro's 1937 *Descobrimento do Brasil*, or even the more transformational, but nonetheless still plot-grounded tack of Nicolás Echevarría's 1991 *Cabeza de Vaca* and Nelson Pereira dos Santos's 1971 *Como era gostoso o meu francês*. Rossoff's looser engagement with colonial intertexts is more aligned with, but nonetheless still dissimilar to Gabriel Retes and Salvador Carrasco's implicit confrontations with the *Nican mopohua* in their films, *Nuevo mundo*

(1976) and *La otra conquista* (1998), respectively. In these cases, the filmmakers' reconceptualizations of the emergence of the Virgin of Guadalupe gesture toward, but do not for the most part explicitly engage the Baroque Nahuatl text. Moreover, the *Nican mopohua* does not enjoy the same canonical position as the works of Sor Juana. Her writings, in a Mexican context, are always present, always poised to assert themselves as an active intertext.

Ave María elucidates thus how at times cinematic reconfigurations of the colony underscore the latent living state of colonial literature. By living state I refer to how readers, writers, directors, and viewers potentially converse not only with the aftermath of colonialism, but also directly with a literary and intellectual heritage from which part of that legacy derives. My reading of the adaptational strategies of most Latin American colonial films, including *Ave María*, holds that filmmakers avoid such engagements; rather than inciting viewers to review the record or to think critically about historiographical discourse, they attempt persuasively to adjust the etchings that colonial discourse has left on the popular imagination. This relationship between past and present is provocative in a special way, but also possibly unwieldy, in those films with a clear literary basis that retains a vigorous presence in society.

In this film, the past comes into focus through the lens of the present and the present through the lens of the past, old and new cultures coexisting in palimpsestic, syncretic flux. *Ave María* represents the latest layer pasted on Sor Juana. The points at which they come into contact allow Sor Juana to help *Ave María* forge a representative of Mexican identity, and enable Rossoff's film, in turn, to generate yet another permutation of Sor Juana's importance for Mexican culture. One of the issues that I address in this chapter is the role that Sor Juana plays in *Ave María* after it has diverged from her biography. Assuming that the film, in harnessing the persuasive value of allusions to Sor Juana, also risks provoking an on-going intertextual dialogue with the Baroque poet, what are the consequences of her lingering presence, and interactions with spectators, throughout the film? In other words, does the director successfully direct the exploitation of Sor Juana?

The intertextual fugue that I see played out between *Ave María* and Sor Juana[5] represents yet another of the means through

Chapter Four

which Latin American cinema has woven colonial texts into the question of identity. The ensuing pages trace Rossoff's dialogue with the biography of Sor Juana and the resulting reflection on and contribution to the ways in which Mexico imagines itself. More specifically, I look at *Ave María*'s interaction with Sor Juana in the construction of a national icon. I begin by considering how Rossoff re-forges and wields Sor Juana, and by addressing some of his possible motivations for doing so. In subsequent sections I examine: the ways in which the path and pitfalls leading to María's iconicity parallel the development of Sor Juana's own iconic status; the nature and complexity of the Mexican icon that María becomes; and, finally, some of the problematic implications of Rossoff's iconographic project.

Part of the depth and complexity of Sor Juana's irresistible if muted presence in *Ave María* is betrayed by a curious critical ambiguity with regard to the protagonist's name. The credits at the end of the film, the Internet Movie Database (www.imdb.org), The Latin American Video Archive (www.lavavideo.org), several reviewers, and Rossoff himself (Matamoros 34) call the protagonist simply María. The full name of the protagonist of *Ave María* is María Inez. That María's last name is Inez becomes apparent when one of the characters refers to her father by his last name: "Nadie fue tan eficaz como Inez a la hora de someter a los Indios"[6] [63]. However, many of the reviews of *Ave María*, in particular those that explicitly associate María with Sor Juana, refer to her as María *Inés* (e.g., Jorge Ayala Blanco, Ezequiel Barriga Chávez, Perla Ciuk, Patricia E. Dávalos).[7] The confusion likely stems from Sor Juana's undeniable presence in the film and the telling phonetic coincidence between María's last name, Inez, and part of Sor Juana's first name, Juana *Inés*, when the names are pronounced in Mexican Spanish.[8] The reviewers that expand the protagonist's first name from María to the inaccurate María Inés complete the connection that the director himself implied by giving her the surname Inez. It is worth noting that a review written in a cultural context not so saturated with Sor Juana, one that was printed after *Ave María*'s release at the 2000 Seattle International Film Festival, calls the protagonist María, and accurately reports her last name as Inez (Hartl M2).

In accordance with the critical tendency to name the protagonist of *Ave María* María Inés, and despite Rossoff's silence on the issue, as the film begins in 1659—which viewers learn when a date is flashed on the screen, a persuasive tactic that anchors the action to a concrete past[9]—it becomes clear that we are witnessing the development of a character intimately tied to Sor Juana, who lived from 1648(?)[10] to 1695. Those familiar with the writings of Sor Juana, Octavio Paz's famous book on the nun-writer, *Sor Juana Inés de la Cruz o las trampas de la fe*, or the film by Argentinean director María Luisa Bemberg, *Yo, la peor de todas*, immediately notice abundant clues relating María to the seventeenth-century writer.[11] Numerous biographical elements unequivocally connect the two figures. María, like Sor Juana, is a prodigiously intelligent woman. The film's protagonist, echoing the seventeenth-century writer's religious vocation, is close to taking her vows in a religious order. Both are remarkably attractive and notably enamor the men that surround them. The women deflect their advances, intellectually or spiritually transcending that category of social interaction. Drawing on *Yo, la peor de todas* for its familiarity—and in recognition of the fact that *Ave María*'s intertextual relationship with Sor Juana, to some degree, passes necessarily through Bemberg's film—I would ask the reader to recall, for example, the scene in which Bemberg's Sor Juana allows a man to kiss her, just once, for the intellectual value of the experience, and subsequently abandons even the semblance of heterosexual desire.[12] María's indifference toward men likewise derives, at least at first, from all-absorbing intellectual interests. (Later I will argue that María's apparent asexuality owes to the film's sanctification of María.)

Also reminiscent of the historical figure, *Ave María*'s protagonist is self-taught. Whereas Sor Juana's forte was verse, however, María instructs priests in a small religious community on cartography, and excels in botany and astronomy, as well.[13] She treasures her scientific instruments and the censored books (e.g., Galileo and Kepler) that an admirer sometimes smuggles to her, details clearly evocative of Sor Juana, especially as Bemberg represents her. María receives, for example, a telescope lens, her most valued object and one that plays a prominent role in the film.[14] She declares, upon receiving the gift, that she plans to map the nighttime sky of New Spain, which aids in marking her ability and ambition. Bemberg's Sor Juana, as well, relishes her "telescopio," in addition to the other objects that she lovingly enumerates: her "reloj solar," "espejo de obsidiana," "astrolabio," and "imanes" [64]. The explicit connection between the films, in sum, begs the viewer to read María in relation to Sor Juana. At the same time, as in the case of Mauro's use of intertitles or his detailed reproduction of scenes described by Caminha, Rossoff's insertion of the telescopic lens and his choice to have the film take place in precisely 1659, which attempt to anchor *Ave María* to the past through palpability and specificity, may signify an attempt to lend the film an air of veracity and authority. *Ave María* means to convince us that it faithfully revives a corner of seventeenth-century New Spain. Moreover, Rossoff silently demands that the viewer recognize the protagonist's debt to Sor Juana. By establishing a relationship between María and Sor Juana, Rossoff, one could argue, makes his character more readable to a Mexican audience than if the protagonist were entirely fictional. Just as the director pinpoints the film's chronology in order to place in the mind of the viewer the array of associations that the seventeenth century suggests, *Ave María*'s Sor Juana subtext asks viewers, from the moment that they see the connection, to read the film in terms of what they know about the famous nun, and to transfer Sor Juana's iconicity to María.

Notwithstanding the obvious parallels between Sor Juana and María, it is important to note that critics have compared *Ave María*'s protagonist to a number of other figures. Even those who associated her with Sor Juana did not limit themselves to that interpretation (e.g., Pardo 4). The diverse personages with which María has been associated indicate the protagonist's symbolic potential. After reading the review in which Pardo compares María to Joan of Arc, the viewer might expect to witness a hero and a martyr, a suggestion confirmed by another review that likens the protagonist to Braveheart. Given the film's title, as well as the fact that additional parallels have been drawn to Jesus and Saint Francis of Assisi, we might also expect a figure of profound religious importance. Tere López-Tarín, the actress who plays María, guides the divine interpretation of her character back into Mexican territory by portraying her as a combination of the Virgin of Guadalupe and the deity Coatlicue (Mendoza González 1).

A desire to promote a symbolically polyvalent María may help to explain some of the irony of Rossoff's silence on the issue of the protagonist's obvious grounding in Sor Juana. For example, we must ask if the director is an unwitting victim of the nun's cultural ubiquity, or if he evades reference to the nun to some purposeful end. Perhaps the director feared that pinning María explicitly to Sor Juana would limit the desired universality of the character or trap his protagonist in the shadow of such a colossal figure. Preserving a broad and plural appeal for the protagonist does appear to be paramount for Rossoff. Before the film's premiere, articles on the production and anticipated release of *Ave María* based their characterizations of the protagonist on how the director chose to characterize her in press conferences. For example, Patricia E. Dávalos, in an article dated after the film's release, compares the protagonist to Sor Juana, but her August 17, 1998 article, published before the film was completed, makes no such claim. And José Luis Gallegos quotes Rossoff explicitly relating María to Joan of Arc (4). More generally, the director primes an interpretation of the film by insisting that *Ave María* is really about feelings, desire, and values: "Me interesa contar una historia de sentimientos, de corazón, por ello traté de rodearme de buenos actores. Hay luchas en la película, pueblos saqueados y quemados, pero eso es parte de la historia, lo que me interesa es tocar al espectador con valores" (qtd. in Lazcano 2) [65]. Rossoff, from outside the text, hopes to delineate an interpretive path for the viewer of the film to follow.[15]

Part of Sor Juana's iconic flexibility also resides in her having been a resistant colonial intellectual, territory that is easy or tempting to mine politically. Accordingly, several interpretations of María and the message of *Ave María* place special emphasis on the film's commentary about the historical oppression of women. Tere López-Tarín argues that the film is "una forma de demostrar y enseñar al mundo entero la fortaleza y la inteligencia de muchas mujeres de esa época, que no pulieron su talento innato" (qtd. in Mendoza González 1) [66]. Jorge Ayala Blanco calls the film "un ensayo dramatizado sobre la condición de la mujer pensante de la Nueva España del siglo XVII" (100) [67], and puts the film at the center of the phenomenon that occupies this dissertation by characterizing *Ave María* as a "relectura femenina de la Otra Conquista que faltaba en la soberana trilogía *Retorno a Aztlán-Cabeza de Vaca-La otra conquista*" (100)[16] [68]. If the previous characterization corresponds precisely to Sor Juana,[17] the next one illustrates, yet again, that the poet's usefulness bends in diverse directions: Lorena Ríos Alfaro calls *Ave María* a "historia que se desarrolla en el siglo XVII sobre la leyenda de una valiente mujer que enfrenta el genocidio, la intolerancia religiosa, el racismo y el fanatismo" (24) [69]. Ríos Alfaro's comment adds the denunciation of injusticias to the protagonist's list of virtues. Ayala Blanco articulates Rossoff's conceivable universalizing goal, characterizing María as "hipotético / sintético / alegórico / emblemático" (100) [70], and suggesting, along with the director (Lazcano 2), that we should read the film in light of the present.[18] In Rossoff's words, "Creo que en determinadas épocas pasamos por crisis existenciales y posiblemente estamos atravesando por una de ellas: a todos nos interesa retomar los valores morales y éticas" (qtd. in Ramírez Hernández, "Ave María" 10) [71]; he goes on to say: "por desgracia, aún en nuestros días las diferencias entre unos y otros afectan gravemente nuestra existencia" (27) [72]. Mauricio Matamoros concurs with these allegorical interpretations of the film and generalizes, calling the colonial period an "espejo del prejuicio y la intolerancia en los tiempos modernos" (34) [73]. He asserts that protagonist and story are "metáforas del mundo actual que permiten acentuar problemas del presente, como el genocidio, el fanatismo, la intolerancia religiosa, el racismo, etcétera" (34)[19] [74].

Rossoff asks viewers explicitly to consider his film an allegory of the political present. The bellicose presence of colonial troops in María's mother's village, for example, would arguably remind viewers of Chiapas, for instance. Rossoff characterizes *Ave María* as "una historia que habla de la intolerancia, que habla de la represión de la mujer, que puede pasar en cualquier época, que sigue ocurriendo hoy en día desgraciadamente, que sigue existiendo mucha intolerancia hacia otras razas y otras creencias" (Ciuk, "Ave María" 30) [75]. The film constructs María as an icon of a diverse Mexican population, understood as a transhistorical body always underlying the territory's diverse procession of governments, from the sixteenth to the twentieth centuries. Hence, the intolerance shown toward her evokes the historical intolerance experienced by the indigenous and mestizo Mexican population at the hands of a predominantly Iberian Church and State. Rossoff's request that we associate the film with the present extends the representative value of María across time. We have to ask, then, what the director's effort to cast his film as an allegory of present-day oppression may have to say about the political situation in Mexico at the time that the film was released, in May of 2000. Rossoff himself makes the connection, as Manuel Monroy notes: "De hecho, Eduardo [Rossoff] calificó como interesante el ofrecer al público, *en estos tiempos preelectorales*, una historia así" (1; emphasis mine) [76]. Rossoff underscores in this comment the on-going need to valorize women in Mexican society; yet because of the film's overwhelming thematics of oppression, which derive from colonial governance, viewers who first read this review would be encouraged to read allegorically, in those pre-electoral times, the film's indictment of an oppressive and decadent governing body. Furthermore, in the final scene of the film, a suggestion to have a propagandistic portrait painted of a conveniently mestiza María in order to subdue indigenous rebellion is tied, at least in name, to a bumbling and opportunistic representative of colonial power. For that reason, the film could equally be construed as an accusation of hypocrisy directed at an official culture that had long rallied behind a mestizo ideal (at least in name).

Given the preceding connections, Rossoff's allegorical interpretation of his film evokes Sor Juana's *Neptuno alegórico* [*Allegorical Neptune*], which in 1680 offered counsel to the incoming viceroy. As did the *Neptuno alegórico*, *Ave María* may represent a word of advice for a future Mexican administration, providing an image of an ideal to which to aspire and, by way of contrast, the kind of government that must be avoided.[20] In fact, *Ave María* may mirror several elements of the *Neptuno*'s means for achieving its ends. Much as Rossoff revises the iconic poet, Sor Juana enlists the aid of the malleable mythological intertext

Chapter Four

of Neptune, molding it to form a versatile image: one that interleaves her own image with that of an ideal political present.[21]

As a result of his desire to cultivate an almost universally applicable political commentary, Rossoff comes close to losing his grasp on María, whose versatility threatens to spin out of control. The director insists that *Ave María* speaks to the present, but also insists that the tone of his film is not historical or conceptual,[22] an odd disclaimer that may stem from his apparent desire to sidestep any association of the protagonist with Sor Juana (Lazcano 2). Yet, in conflict with his effort to distance the film from a strictly historical interpretation, Rossoff promotes its desired universal appeal both by encouraging a reading of María as a global Mexican icon and by taking advantage of the allegorical value of a story about the historically anchored colonial period by saying that *Ave María* "construye una heroína mestiza de rasgos tan fuertes y contradictorios que por sí misma debe representar el conflicto espiritual y social del pueblo mexicano en la conquista" (Pardo 4) [77]. Once again, aided by the illusion of historical grounding that Sor Juana lends the film, Rossoff projects, as did Mauro with regard to Brazil, his own vision of the birth of Mexico, a nation that has tended to promote hybrid conceptions of identity. Rossoff, in another comment, says that the film represents a spiritual conflict, yet during the production he refers to *Ave María* as a provisional title because "[c]ontrario a lo que podría pensarse, la película no es sobre religión sino, fundamentalmente, sobre la intolerancia y la justicia" (Peguero, "*Ave María*, historia" 40)[23] [78].

The protagonist's iconicity is multifarious, yet her distinct symbolic referents invariably grow out of *Ave María*'s unique dependence on Sor Juana. The film's polytropic protagonist overflows with associations, just as the malleable Sor Juana easily adopts the shape of María. Indeed, the filmmaker was heir to Sor Juana's practiced pliability; over the course of the intervening centuries the literary figure has experienced, and sometimes even contributed to, her symbolic exploitation and the related, perhaps partially consequent, attainment of legendary status. One of the reviews of the film underscores María's inherited malleability by referring to her story as a "legend" (Ríos Alfaro 24); the flexible utility of legend recalls how Sor Juana herself primed her legacy for easy transformation. In sum, Sor Juana's tractability derives from the frequent historical reformulations of her persona that culminate in a kind of mythification and that inextricably place the poet in the public domain.[24]

Sor Juana's entrance into the plastic realm of myth issues in part from the battles of fashioning in which she herself participated. These skirmishes over the poet's symbolic significance helped to lay the foundation for *Ave María*'s reformulation of Sor Juana, in the most general sense of establishing her as a malleable Mexican icon, and in terms of the way that the character of María is developed in the film. Throughout *Ave María*, the protagonist's iconicity emerges as a result of struggles, by María and others (before and after her death), over her fame/notoriety. We find an antecedent for these dynamics of persona-fashioning in the biography and works of Sor Juana. Efforts to control the fate of the writer's persona often centered on her need to deflect praise.[25] Her attempt to ameliorate the repercussions of praise and her bid to recast her persona on her own terms (Echenberg 177) were pivotal motifs in Sor Juana's life and her poetry. Consider, for example, Romance #38, a response to a complimentary poem written for her by an aide to the Marquis de la Laguna.

The nun-writer's study in what might be viewed as productive anxiety clothed in false modesty culminates in the following way:

> Quien viere vuestro Romance,
> podrá decir lo que a Egipto,
> que una pirámide tal
> erigió para un mosquito [...] (1.111)[26] [79]

The foregoing verses drip with a humility that encapsulates the first layer of the poem's tack. However, the acute preoccupation with the dangers of praise that gives rise to Sor Juana's hyperbolic implementation of the modesty topos throughout this poem is best appreciated early on, in the opening verses of the text:

> [...] ¿Quién pensara
> que un pobre Romance mío,
> [...]
> merecía aquella ofensa
> que me hacéis, pues imagino
> que es vituperio, y no elogio,
> la alabanza en el indigno? (1.106) [80]

Chapter Four

In classic modest fashion, Sor Juana maintains that her acclaim is undeserved, yet her insistence on labeling the praise "ofensa" and "vituperio" may also underscore the imminent peril stemming from the nun-writer's snowballing renown exemplified by the poem to which Romance #38 responds. Sor Juana's chief tactic to counter the missive at first consists of zealously reciprocating the praise that has been bestowed on her poetry. She claims, for example, that her correspondent is exceedingly more deserving of acclaim than the poet herself (1.107). He is more deserving, in fact, than the greatest of the ancients, she claims (1.107). Sor Juana's favorable estimation of the man's verse goes on to mention scores of other presumably less worthy forefathers (e.g., Caesar, Ptolemy, Plato). Toward the end of the poem, Sor Juana extends her comparative enumeration of figures to celebrated *women*, and insists that she could comprehend her correspondent's praise if it applied to them (1.110–11). Throughout the poem and the three lists that Méndez Plancarte calls an "[e]numeración (sin orden y al azar) de grandes nombres en la Historia—o la Fábula—de los viejos Pueblos y de las Leyes" (1.414) [81], Sor Juana characteristically crafts the context of humility into a display of her encyclopedic knowledge. Moreover, in addition to casting herself as both ingenious and an intellectual, the progression of her comparisons—from ancient to modern and from men to women—each one more closely approximating the poet herself, makes more plausible the notion that the praise that she ostensibly rejects is actually deserved. As we have seen, Sor Juana follows the mention of ancient men with celebrated women from the past. Notably, however, the poet caps the list with the Duchess de Aveyro, contemporary of Sor Juana, who boldly (perhaps even gallantly) extends a bridge over the chasm that separates the nun-writer from possible justified renown by eclipsing the normally incomparable (except, of course, in the case of her correspondent) ancients.

From the battles to fashion her persona followed by the historical manipulation of her image that led to her legendary mythic status, Sor Juana emerges from her centuries-long symbolic sojourn primed for potential universal applicability. Such a quality could understandably have enticed Rossoff, for a universal articulation of Mexican identity is what he apparently sought through María. This film asks that Sor Juana once again submit herself to manipulation, a fictional reconfiguration of the writer grounded in modeling the very sort of battles of fashioning that gave rise to her symbolic flexibility. I would argue that this process of retransformation through which the Baroque poet passes in the film inculcates in María the lesson of iconic ductility. In order for a broad swath of the Mexican population to embrace her as a universal representative of identity, viewers must be able to fluently re-forge her. While it is precisely the malleability of *Ave María*'s protagonist that makes her such a versatile cultural icon, such qualities also make her potentially unmanageable.

The intertextual path that laces its way to and through Sor Juana helps to illustrate the intricacies of María's iconic development. Moreover, the compelling connections to the nun-writer may lead viewers to complement their reading of the film by finding and following links to Sor Juana's life and work. María, much like Sor Juana, becomes a national icon by passing through the stages of fame, notoriety, and finally martyrdom. Sor Juana's concerned interaction in poems such as Romance #51 characterizes the culmination of her reaction to external insistence on her fame.[27] Consider these lines of Romance #51—a response to the "matchless pens of Europe, whose praise only enhanced her works," as an editor's rubric reads—which we might see as a fatigued yet seasoned sequel to the biting lines of Romance #38:

> ¿Cuándo, Númenes divinos,
> dulcísimos Cisnes, cuándo
> merecieron mis descuidos
> ocupar vuestros cuidados?
> ¿De dónde a mí tanto elogio?
> ¿De dónde a mí encomio tanto?
> ¿Tánto pudo la distancia
> añadir a mi retrato?
> ¿De qué estatura me hacéis?
> ¿Qué Coloso habéis labrado,
> que desconoce la altura
> del original lo bajo? (1.158) [82]

Romance #51 may betray the anxiety associated with the devastating final slide of her renown into notoriety.[28]

Chapter Four

The writer's eventual fall from grace is largely tied to how Sor Juana becomes centrally embroiled in a famous feud between the upper levels of New Spain's ecclesiastical hierarchy, and her resulting clash with the misogynous Archbishop of Mexico. The episode takes place three years after the departure of the nun's protectors, the Marquis and Marquise de la Laguna,[29] and four years before her death. As is well-known, the Archbishop, Francisco Aguiar y Seijas, was an enemy of the Bishop of Puebla, Manuel Fernández de Santa Cruz, a longtime friend of Sor Juana's. In order conceivably to annoy the Archbishop, a professed admirer of the renowned Portuguese Jesuit, Antônio Vieira, and a Jesuit himself, the Bishop of Puebla requested from Sor Juana, and published without her consent, a critique of a famous sermon delivered years earlier by the Portuguese priest.[30] However, along with the nun's text, the *Carta Atenagórica* [*Letter Worthy of Athena*], the Bishop also included a letter criticizing her intellectual pursuits, penned by the Bishop but signed with the name Sor Filotea de la Cruz. The pendulum, for Sor Juana, had nearly completed the arc from praise to condemnation, from fame to infamy. She attempted to defend herself in the well-known *Respuesta a Sor Filotea* [*Reply to Sor Philothea*], which dates from 1691, a proto-feminist tour de force that nonetheless does little to postpone her defeat within the viceregal society.[31]

Similar to Sor Juana's damning acquisition of fame by means of beating men at their own game, as it were, with the *Carta Atenagórica*, *Ave María*'s María dangerously shines as her community's unchallenged intellectual superior, acting, for example, as professor of cartography for the priests. And paralleling the conflict with the religious hierarchy that results from Sor Juana's literary triumph, later in Rossoff's film we witness how the nefarious influence of recently arrived priests from Toledo turns the tables on María: the misogynous leader of the Spanish priests, humiliated by María for his ignorance and unfounded arrogance, accuses the protagonist of excessive pride. The same priest, Cuña, additionally expresses concern that her passion for the stars is greater than that which she feels for God. María responds to the accusations by asking another priest: "¿Es preferible el caos a la uniformidad impuesta por una mujer? ¿Es la inteligencia mi transgresión [...]?"[32] [83]. In the court proceeding that follows, María attempts to defend her dedication to scholarship, reminiscent of the *Respuesta*, to no avail. She is found guilty of pride and one of her envious fellow nuns even questions her chastity.[33]

As a result of the trial, María is forbidden—as Sor Juana once was—from pursuing intellectual activities, and enters a state of severe depression, an event that the film shows only after the protagonist confesses to one of the priests, Padre Miguel. María's descent and the incipient reconfiguration of her persona are evident in her shifting relationship with Padre Miguel. Where once the protagonist, clearly his and his peers' intellectual superior, defiantly asked if her intelligence was a sin, in this scene María is reduced to accepting as sinful her powerful intellect. In a final and doomed effort to preserve her scholarly work, she tells him: "No puedo vivir sin mi trabajo. Es como si alguien me hubiera arrancado el corazón, estoy vacía" [84]. At this point, the film intersects directly with *Yo, la peor de todas*. One of the signs of Sor Juana's downfall in Bemberg's film is the dark image of the nun on her knees, scrubbing floors. Rossoff, as well, portrays María's ultimate breakdown with a scene in which she scoops manure in a now defiled white dress while her books are being burned, which anticipates hyperbolically another floor-scrubbing scene. In *Ave María*'s version, a bleak, dim, interior, high-angle long shot moves toward the kneeling figure, which then cuts to a medium eye-level shot of her, and finally to indicate passage of time, to a long shot of her at night continuing to scour the floor.

Having represented the breaking of her spirit, Rossoff inserts a reference that refers specifically to a text written by Sor Juana, and not, as I've been reading it, to the text that is Sor Juana. Perhaps the director chooses to connect explicitly the film to Sor Juana's writing at this point in order to underscore the significance of the way that the film will soon diverge from the historical figure's story. Or perhaps, in order to reinforce the presentation of María as a national icon—which is beginning in earnest now, as the protagonist's fame feels its way through the purgatory of notoriety—the director takes apparent care here to concretize the connection between the protagonist and the existing cultural icon, Sor Juana.

I refer to the fact that after a spell of catatonic seclusion, María writes a repentant letter in her own blood. Those familiar with *Yo, la peor de todas* will recall a powerful scene toward the

Chapter Four

end of the film in which the Argentinean director's Sor Juana, also beaten by oppression, smashes her glasses into the palm of her hand and signs her name with blood to a public renunciation of her literary vocation. Both films recall document 409 from Sor Juana's complete works, "Protesta que, rubricada con su sangre, hizo de su fe y amor a Dios la Madre Juana Inés de la Cruz, al tiempo de abandonar los estudios humanos para proseguir, desembarazada de este afecto, en el camino de la perfección" [85]. In it, Sor Juana declares her current and eternal belief in God, the Trinity, the Virgin Mary, and affirms that she wants to die obedient to the Church. She ends the short text with the following words, "Y en señal de cuánto deseo derramar la sangre en defensa de estas verdades, lo firmo con ella, en cinco de marzo del año de mil seiscientos y noventa y cuatro" (4.519) [86]. That document, which dates from a year before her death, represents Sor Juana's response to the external efforts to reform her, to truncate her fame or revise the nature of it seen in her last poem, Romance #51. In another document, a petition presented to a religious tribunal at about the same time, Sor Juana repudiates her fame, calling herself the most ungrateful and unknown creature created by God's love.[34] Although her words clearly represent a defeat, we might choose to see Sor Juana's statements as continuing to participate in the development of her public image, as marking the moment in which Sor Juana takes an active role in capturing her notoriety and converting it into one of the seeds of her iconicity. Partly as a result of these two documents, Sor Juana moves toward becoming a spiritual mother of Mexico, an aspect of her persona that over the centuries will merge with her image as both a feminist intellectual and an acute and sensual poetic wit.

Although the blood-signed letter in Sor Juana's life and in Bemberg's film contributes to the ongoing iconicity of the nun-writer, it also constitutes an ending, as the act precedes her death. For its part, *Ave María* reformulates the signing and its connotations as a beginning, a fundamental turning point in the film. Bemberg's Sor Juana, like the author herself in the *Respuesta* and as opposed to María, does not give up when condemned, vowing to study "en el cielo, en la hierba, en la cocina" ["in the sky, in the grass, in the kitchen"]. However, María's early and total defeat underscores the importance and implications of her resurrection. Rossoff casts María's initial fame and then decline and fall—which, as we have seen, parallels many aspects of Sor Juana's life—as a prelude to a new phase in which her personal fame turned notoriety is consequently converted into public iconicity. What is more, the extent to which we see María as a rewriting of Sor Juana may improve the poet as a national icon. The letter marks the moment that immediately precedes María's discovery of a mystical connection to her indigenous roots, a revelation that constitutes the first step toward her spiritual leadership of her mother's people: María is the mestiza child of a powerful Spanish duke and a poor indigenous woman from a nearby village. Providing the viewer with a clear contrast, initially María denies or ignores her indigenous side, clinging to the Creole identity reminiscent of Sor Juana. Yet now María has begun to complete her progressive transformation into the syncretic icon that the film will christen the "Ray of Light."

Gregorio Gransden, one of the reviewers who connects the protagonist to the seventeenth-century nun, criticizes the filmmaker for what he sees as the fictional changes made to the life of Sor Juana. Gransden argues that Rossoff embellished her story in an unnecessary attempt to lend drama to the tale. In his generally negative review, Gransden writes, for example: "[N]o deja de complacer la lascivia del público con tomas, a menudo gratuitas, del escote de María o de su cuerpo desnudo" (12) [87]. While the nude scenes do merit some critical consideration, I believe that the film appropriates and then shapes Sor Juana not gratuitously or frivolously, but in order to enrich its commentary on national identity. The director attempts to enhance or expand Sor Juana's iconicity to make her into an ideal national representative.[35] As I have pointed out, Rossoff seeks to universalize Sor Juana by making her mestiza and having her embrace religious syncretism, elements central to the way in which Mexico has come to imagine itself. Furthermore, María develops the religious following of a messiah and, as a result, her death carries the force of martyrdom. The director borrows the best, as it were, from Sor Juana, such as her intellectual superiority and early feminism. At the same time, by making her mestiza, Rossoff fortifies Sor Juana's symbolic appeal through racial and religious markers more representative of the deeply

Chapter Four

rooted mestizo imaginary center of Mexicanness. *Ave María* constructs María as a dream, an ideal, the image of a painfully yet proudly born mestizo Mexico. With this, María finally begins to leave behind her dependence on Sor Juana for effectiveness. Or, from a complementary perspective, Sor Juana acquires in the later part of the film an indigenous connotation.

The letter that María writes with her own blood initiates her transformation into the Mexican icon that the film ultimately presents to viewers. Echoing the self-deprecating tone of Sor Juana's document 409, the text that María slips under the door of her cell reads, "Mi vida de pecado brota en mí como una enfermedad. Debo consumirme en ella hasta que la enfermedad se extinga. Debo arder hasta quedar vacía y limpia. Rezaré entonces" [88]. When she finally leaves the isolation of her cell, María makes a declaration that follows Sor Juana's, but adds a significant yet subtle dose of irony. In the following words directed to the head of her spiritual community, María participates in the redefinition of her public image under the guise of surrender: "Deseo darle las gracias. Veo claramente que Ud. ha sido el instrumento de Dios. Si no hubiera sido por Ud. no hubiera sufrido tanto. Y si no fuera por ese dolor yo nunca hubiera cambiado" [89]. The change to which she refers is a mystical, yet pagan epiphany.

From the ashes of her destruction, María is resurrected. Toward the end of her depressed seclusion, the protagonist has a mystical vision inspired by her indigenous grandmother, one that unequivocally incites her to defend her mother's village from the Spanish soldiers who are systematically and consciously attempting to wipe out the indigenous population by distributing disease-infested blankets. Just as the initial scenes of *Ave María* enlisted science, specifically the telescope lens, as a marker of both María's Europeanness and her close ties to Sor Juana, the film treats the indigenous vision in this sequence as a sign that María has left behind (or utterly reshaped) the famous nun.[36] The nudity that Gransden considers gratuitous appears following this dream-like sequence. Outside, after receiving her vision, the camera shoots María nude in two separate moments: in silhouette, at night, in an extreme long shot as she rids herself of her white dress, which follows the gaze of two nuns who see her through a window, and later, in a brief, shadowy montage of her making love to Padre Miguel in his own steamy dream sequence. *Ave María*, much like *Cabeza de Vaca* and *La otra conquista*, appears to entangle the mystically indigenous with sex in its portrayal of María, who will soon be treated as a divine figure within the indigenous community. Recalling one of Echevarría's and Pereira dos Santos's strategies, perhaps Rossoff hyperbolizes in this scene the exotic lure of the mystical vision by eroticizing a mestiza subject, and thereby attempts to laud indigenous identity through self-exoticism. Or the director may be risking—like Echevarría, I would argue—a typical Hollywood objectification of women in a ploy to sell his film, or to make it more accessible.[37]

Also reminiscent of Nicolás Echevarría's *Cabeza de Vaca*, Rossoff portrays María's mystical vision as real. For example, during María's vision sequence, disembodied whispers of "María" emanate from the dark, empty stone corridors. An extreme long shot shows her enter a resplendent beam of light; as she is magically illuminated, sound effects suggest that something (communication?) is taking place. After a few moments, María says, "Voy" ["I'm going"], and starts to walk off. At another point, the camera alternates shots of a religious statue with others of María lying face-down on the stone floor of the Church, limbs spread in the manner of Christ crucified, and brilliantly illuminated by a shaft of light descending inexplicably from a nighttime sky. As in Mauro's shot in *Descobrimento do Brasil* of the two indigenous men aboard the ship who, as a marker of their Christian indoctrination by the Portuguese, find themselves illuminated by a ray of light as Cabral puts them down to sleep, Rossoff relies on the religious connotations of light. Yet he transforms María's illumination into a symbol of syncretism by placing it within the context of an indigenous vision. Before the vision sequence, the director intensely illuminates María as she prays, as Mauro does with a praying Caminha as the Portuguese reach land. Later, the meaning of light is reconfigured, as María finds herself illuminated while receiving her mystical pagan invocation. This event marks the moment immediately before María leaves the Catholic community. When she says "Voy ... ," she responds to the call that she is receiving to go to her mother's village, and the light that illuminates her emanates from an indigenous spiritual source.

Chapter Four

Through the nuns that form part of María's religious community, as well, the director reinforces the treatment of the mystical as real at the same time that he clearly begins to suggest María's divinity. One of the nuns awakens in the night sensing a presence. Another calls out for María upon opening her eyes. The oldest one claims that the first thing that she did in the morning was to recite an "Ave María." At this moment the film's theme song begins. The chantlike repetition of the words "Ave María" accompanied by a close-up of María, shown from the side, praying with light bathing her face again weaves together the divine implications of the Christian and the indigenous.

A scene that takes place shortly after María's spiritual transformation spells out her new and powerful alliance with her indigenous roots. She has just left the leader of the religious community, Padre Serra, from whom she has bought her freedom with a large inheritance from her Spanish father. María requests that young Padre Miguel hear her confession. Her confession takes the following form: "Como Ud. sabe, regreso al pueblo de mi madre. Me arrepiento de haberlos abandonado por tanto tiempo. Y he adorado mi padre español[38] y he adorado el conquistador y el precio que mi madre tuvo que pagar. ¿Cómo puedo perdonarme?" [90]. Through a series of poignant reversals, María distances herself from Christianity and Spain and subtly wields a recently acquired confidence and power. Immediately prior to this scene, for example, María has kissed the hand of the leader of the religious order. Here, the young priest offers María the same act of reverence. And here, María gives Padre Miguel her ideological (not religious) confession, and refuses absolution for the sins committed against her people.

At the end of the scene, however, María switches roles, and she hears the priest's confession. Though Padre Miguel's confession takes the form of a declaration of love, María quickly shifts the tone of the dialogue, making it once again political, by advising the priest on how he might also contribute to the well-being of the indigenous population of Mexico. Rossoff visually fixes the reversal of roles through suggestive play with the confessional curtain and close-up shot/reverse shots that display the confessions from both perspectives. In an earlier confession scene, María still resides fully within an Occidental ideological sphere, as the film indicates by means of the closed curtain, which confirms the chasm that separates her from Padre Miguel. In the second, transformational confession scene María reifies her iconoclasm and newly assumed power by pushing aside the veil that separates her from the priest when she nudges Miguel's confession in a political direction (just as he moved the curtain when he confessed his love). The film suggests in this way her effortless symbolic dissolution of the oppressive power dynamic represented by the symbol of the confessional curtain.[39]

Through the confessional scene, Rossoff demonstrates the shift in the definition of María's identity. By embracing her indigenous side and rejecting her Spanish heritage, María finally and unequivocally sheds Sor Juana or, perhaps more accurately, attempts to enact the final transformation of the poet into a universalized representative of a modern, postcolonial Mexico. María casts herself as something of a reformed *malinche* figure who goes through a mystical, religious conversion in order to locate her identity primarily in indigenous Mexico. María begins to approximate the kind of Mexican icon that she will become. By infusing her with authority, the film also anticipates the position of power that she will hold within the indigenous community.

Following Padre Miguel's confession to her, María leaves to be with her mother's people and, upon arriving at their village, she begins to negotiate, through language, her new identity. As María enters the village, her grandmother, who had called her to the village in the vision, approaches and speaks to her granddaughter. María must confess her inability to understand the language, thus establishing her grandmother as a marker of the protagonist's initial ethnic distance from her people. In a miraculously (or magically) short period of time, María masters the language of her mother's people, a feat that resembles Sor Juana's claims of learning Latin in twenty lessons. This coincidence, I might add, exposes Sor Juana's latent influence on the characterization of María within the film. María's linguistic proficiency may be seen as applying a lesson learned from Sor Juana to this crucial moment in her syncretic transmutation: much as Sor Juana models malleability by gliding into the slightly dissimilar shape of María, Rossoff's protagonist shifts

Chapter Four

linguistically with swift pliability. Read from a different angle, María's learning curve smacks of supernatural intervention, or may even imply a racial predisposition to language acquisition, as if the recognition of María's indigenous ancestry awakens a genetic memory of her maternal tongue. Much as the uttering of words in an indigenous language marked the culmination of Cabeza de Vaca's assimilation in *Cabeza de Vaca*, after learning the language, María confirms that she is mestiza and that she belongs to the people rather than they belonging to her, thus completing her condemnation of the Spanish ideology that she previously embraced.[40]

María wastes no time in incurring the wrath of both the Church and the State. En route to her mother's village, she initiates her doom by saving an indigenous woman from a Spanish soldier who is raping her. And shortly after reaching her mother's people, María confronts more soldiers who arrive and attempt, as I mentioned above, to distribute tainted blankets to indigenous communities in order to exterminate them. With regard to the Church, María provokes, and soon receives, its condemnation by encouraging an extreme brand of syncretism. María's second and final defeat at the hands of the Catholic Church is sparked once again by the Spaniard, Padre Cuña. The villainous priest travels to the center of María's spiritual realm in search of the entire population of nuns, who have abandoned the community in order to follow, along with the indigenous population of the village, the guidance of María. To his horror, Cuña finds Catholic crosses placed on an indigenous pyramid and the nuns showing deference only to María. One of the nuns had earlier gone so far as to revel in María's lesson that Jesus and Quetzalcoatl are one and the same. Cuña departs flustered and irate, and promises María's imminent and utter destruction.

By this point in the film, María has risen to the status of a religious icon. Like Álvar Núñez in *Naufragios*, María has attracted a vast following among the indigenous population. Her influence extends, as well, to relatively marginal members of Creole society, her fellow nuns, who have overwhelmingly converted to her cause. María seals her deification when she replaces the role of the priest for the nuns who have joined her. One of the nuns, Adelina, asks María to hear her confession. María responds that only a priest can do that, but the young nun insists that she will only confess to María. The viewer, who up to this point has principally witnessed a profound but not worshipful reverence paid to María within the village, realizes that she has been elevated to the status of a god when two new priests arrive from Spain and tell of the word spreading throughout the land about María. They say that the *indios* asked them if they had come to work for Tonaneyotl; characters in the film translate the name as Rayo de Luz and explain that the appellation applies to María Inez. The director once again syncretizes the religious connotation of light and illumination by giving María the name Tonaneyotl. And it is through this name that Rossoff most explicitly proposes that María embodies a fusion of the Virgin Mary and the Aztec deity Tonantzin. The nuns claim that "Dios hace su labor a través de María Inez" [91], arguably linking her again to Jesus. In retrospect, María's apparent asexuality, her indifference to Daniel's and Padre Miguel's declarations of love, anticipates her role as a religious icon: a god's love must be universal, for all of its subjects. The peoples' (indigenous, mestiza, and Creole) acceptance of María's divinity, of her religious iconicity, acts as a suggestion to the viewer to interpret the character in a similar way.

Little time passes before the law apprehends María and throws her into the stockade to await her fate. Padre Cuña accuses María of telling the people that she is divine, thereby acknowledging the widespread belief in her divinity. After being raped,[41] María is burned at the stake under the solemn and pained gazes of her indigenous followers and the nuns, which the film records through medium shots and medium close-ups of María engulfed in flames that alternate with medium close-ups and close-ups of the reactions of her followers. Later she is declared a martyr by Padre Miguel and María's friend and onetime suitor, Daniel. Martyrdom seals María's iconicity and traps it in religious territory.[42] María has come to represent mestizo Mexico and here, Christ-like, sacrifices herself on its behalf and for its future. As I suggested while discussing María's indigenous awakening during the dream sequence, I believe that Rossoff fortifies María's association with the Virgin Mary by additionally tying her to Christ.[43] It is worth noting that in the "Ejercicios devotos para los nueve días antes de la purísima Encarnación del Hijo de Dios" [92], Sor Juana, as if in anticipation of Rossoff's conflation of the Christian figures, draws on Sor María de Agreda's (1602–65) biography of the Virgin Mary.[45] In a way then, Sor Juana anticipates her role in *Ave María*'s recasting—in the person of a transformed Sor Juana, María—of the Virgin Mary as the central religious and national figure of Mexican identity.[45]

In using the term *icon* throughout the chapter, I have had in mind the three main shades of its meaning, as defined by *Webster's Third New International Dictionary*: "1. a usually pictorial representation [...] 2. a sacred image venerated in churches and homes of Eastern Christianity depicting Christ, the Virgin Mary, a saint, or some other religious subject [...] 3. *in philosophy of language and semiotics:* a sign (as a straight line on a map) that signifies by virtue of sharing a property with what it represents (as a straight road)" (1121). All three aspects of iconicity—pictorial representation, venerated sacred image, and semiotic sign—have found their way into the preceding discussion. Up to this point, we have observed the preliminary stages of María's iconic development: I have traced the thread of María's construction, for example, along the weave of the confessional veil by means of which she declares her alliance with the indigenous Mexican population that she will soon represent, and through the coarse cloth of the disease-ridden blankets that set María on the path leading to her martyrdom. In other words, we have already seen María as "religious icon," but not before we established how she became an "icon" in the semiotic sense: how she came to embody (to represent with her body) the Mexican people, principally by means of realizing (in both senses of the word) the cultural and political potential of her mestiza heritage.

Now I will turn to a pivotal scene at the end of the film that adds another layer of complexity to the manipulation of iconicity in *Ave María*, a scene in which a visiting priest suggests to friends of María that a portrait be painted of the martyred protagonist. In this concluding discussion, I take steps to unravel and problematize the film's reflection on how images are used in the construction of iconicity and commentaries on how nations are imagined. In these final pages of the chapter, I go about unpacking the complexities of the icon that the film offers by considering the crucial role of image in how Rossoff asks the viewer to imagine the nation and its population.

The painting of María intends to display a religious and cultural icon, an image that will appropriate, transform, and finally nationalize what has become, at the same time but from different perspectives, the protagonist's fame and notoriety. *Ave María*'s final scene establishes painting or, more generally, visual representation, as the space in which personal fame, or even notoriety, intersects with national identity. Be it intentionally or unintentionally, this scene draws attention to and lays bare the film's own attempt to create an icon of and for the Mexican people. As in the campfire scene in *Cabeza de Vaca*, the closing moment of *Ave María* offers viewers a metafictional microcosm of the film itself. Whether or not he intends it, Rossoff is giving viewers clues to assist in untying the potentially knotted message of the film and its dialogue with Sor Juana. Much as the film has been inevitably in dialogue with Sor Juana, here it enters into a conversation with itself. As a result, my analysis of this final scene collects moments from throughout the film that only here achieve full relevance and resonance.

Little time has passed since María's martyrdom was carried out by the powers of the Colony. Because of her death, she has become an example not only of unity among the oppressed but also of resistance. Her unjust demise has provoked an air of unrest among the indigenous subjects of colonial rule. As the final scene of the film commences, several of María's followers—Christians who have adopted her cause—gather in mourning at the monastery. A Church leader arrives to evaluate the fallout from María's execution. The protagonist's followers regard the representative of a vilified Church with skepticism and contempt (e.g., in a medium reaction shot in which one of the men shakes his head after a comment made by the priest). Because the film has encouraged sympathy toward and identification with this group—they attempted, for example, to prevent the execution of the film's heroine—spectators are here urged to view the old priest through their suspicious eyes.

As the action of the portrait scene progresses, viewers observe how María's friends astutely manage the interaction with the old priest. They determine the fate of the protagonist's legacy and then demonstrate how it might be interpreted and put to use both within and outside the film. Upon the priest's arrival in the final scene, the followers tell the old man that the indigenous people insist that "María vive" ["María lives"], that she continues to live in all of them. The intimation of María's spiritual proliferation and the consequential implication of her divinity finds corroboration in a previous scene. On the day before her execution, María makes a telling comment to Cuña, when he accuses her of claiming to be a god. She patiently explains to him that "Dios vive en cada uno de nosotros" ["God lives in each one of us"], a declaration that lingers and, in this final scene, links up with the group's announcement of a miracle. Though María's comment deflects the notion that she possesses a supernatural aspect, nonetheless it meshes with her followers' later insistence on her divinity. As if to anticipate her friends' theology, María expands her explanation to Cuña by insisting, in a characteristically iconoclastic reversal, that God speaks to her. María goes on to say, "Escucho la voz de ella" [93], transforming God into a woman, and further priming the interpretation that she is a divine offspring, like Jesus.

In the portrait scene, the miraculous nature of the group's claim of María's continued presence begins to inspire the wrinkled cleric. The priest succumbs to the enticement of the film's underlying assumption of María's iconic usefulness and convenient pliability. Upon hearing of María's perpetual life, he exclaims that this miracle should be represented in a portrait based on the likeness of the white European face of Margarita (presented as the princess of Spain). María's friends, still sculptors and would-be marketers of their friend's image, as I will show, nonetheless ensure that María's malleable figure not return to the Creole shape that it once held (when she so liberally shared traits with Sor Juana), as the priest manifestly desires. Her followers point out that she was mestiza, a revelation that elicits the horrified response from the sour-faced Church official of "¿!Mestiza!?", which sparks recollection of a previous scene. A conversation early in the film between Padre Cuña and another priest anticipates and again, inasmuch as it lingers in the mind of the viewer, broadens the significance of the film's last scene. Cuña complains about María, crying out with disgust, "¡Ella es mestiza!" [94], to which his companion, who has known María much longer, explains that her biracial heritage stems from the fact that her father was most efficient in subduing indigenous people, implying that her conception resulted if not from rape, at least from coercion. Besides providing some connotational texture for the exclamation of the old priest in the final scene, this early conversation also serves to associate him with the nefarious Cuña. In the portrait scene, María's disciples go on to spell out that mestiza means "un símbolo de la unión pacífica entre España y el Nuevo Mundo" [95], a notion that the old priest receives with enthusiasm: "¡Sublime idea!" ["Sublime idea!"]. He wishes to quell potential rebellion, to subdue the indigenous population through María and her now powerful and potentially useful image.

By means of the portrait, the priest plans to enlist and enlarge María's iconicity, to perpetuate, one might say, her own father's oppressive ideology. *Ave María* represents the Church in the person of the old priest who commits to the propagandistic plan not premeditatedly but in the heat of the moment. In fact, the film leads the viewer to wonder who actually is the agent of the proposal of the portrait, the priest or the group of María's followers, who seem to steer both the events of the scene and the interpretation of those events. The old priest seeks to incorporate María into the staid tradition of Catholic iconography, enlisting a powerful marker of her Mexicanness, her mestizaje, as a means to perpetuate the colonial status quo. But the group manipulates the implications of the priest's plan. Their insistence that María's image reflect her mestiza identity actually reconfigures the religiosity of the portrait. Under the very nose of the would-be ecclesiastical schemer, they support the portrait but manage to mute its Christianity because they, along with viewers of the film, recognize that María's mestizaje has come clearly to signify her syncretic or, even better, her hybrid religion.

From another perspective, as well, María's followers cast the painting as a mutually beneficial endeavor at the same time that they chip away at Christianity. Referring to the possible popular uprising, the group insists that "sólo el amor puede curar las heridas de este lugar" [96]. The old priest asks, "¿El amor a Dios?" and one of María's followers concludes, "No, padre, simplemente el amor" [97]. Once again, an aspect of the portrait scene invokes and invigorates an earlier moment. At the

Chapter Four

beginning of the film, a conversation between María and Daniel anticipates the tactic at work in the film's final scene. Looking at a telescope that her friend has just given her, a María still immersed in European ideology says, "Es un milagro" ["It is a miracle"]. Daniel previews her departure from the Church and her companions' secularization of the priest's question in the final scene by responding, "No, María. Es pura ciencia" [98].

In the culminating portrait scene of *Ave María*, if we follow the lead of a knowing smile shared by the nun and one of her companions, a monk—which the camera shows in medium close-up shot/reverse shots of the two—when the old priest agrees that it is a sublime idea to paint a mestiza María, we as viewers should interpret and embrace María as a representative of racial and national unity. María's followers do so, despite the cynical motives that the old priest may have for so enthusiastically adopting the plan to capture and distribute María's likeness. As we have seen, he first suggests having a portrait painted of María as a pure-blooded Spaniard and later agrees that it is a sublime idea to paint her as a mestiza, which, in a sense, resembles what Rossoff has done to Sor Juana. By finally accepting and even encouraging the portrait—slightly redefined but still caught up in the oppressive power structure of the colony—María's followers seem to indicate that no matter who advances what they consider to be a valuable national icon, it is valuable nonetheless. The group seems to conceive of the painting in terms of how it will promote peace and establish a mestiza as an official representative of the nation. María's followers are treating their martyred leader as an ideal to which all Mexicans should aspire, and venerating her planned portrait as they would a religious icon. An attempt to cure the wounds caused by the cruelty of the conquering Spanish and to counter the univocal nature of the colonial enterprise, the painting serves to privilege mestizaje. Broadly conceived, the group may also be thinking—like those who carry out what I call anthropophagous adaptations of colonial films—that if an icon is going to have sway in society in any event, they should attempt to take control of it and transform it according to their design. In this particular instance, one could ask if the apparent motives for the portrait (or the film) are entirely unproblematic. We should take into consideration at what cost the group will realize its iconographic orchestration. Reminiscent of Manuel's compromise in *Nuevo mundo*—he hoped, in the end, to put a stop to the devastating indigenous losses deriving from their rebellion by inspiring unity through the syncretic image that he had been forced to paint of the Virgin—the portrait, for all of its potential good, carries with it a concomitant perpetuation of social hierarchy. In order to keep itself in power, a governing body co-opts the fame of a loved representative of the people. Yet María's disciples appear to accept the compromise.

The problematic issue of who is the agent of the iconic fashioning in *Ave María* remains unresolved. Among the characters, *Ave María* apparently presents María as the agent of her own iconicity. For example, we have seen how the film gives the impression that María controls the fashioning of her own image in the confessional scene. The same impression results from a scene that takes place shortly before her execution. One of her companions goes to María's cell and pleads with her to accept an attempt to free her. María refuses the help, insisting that no popular rebellion take place on her behalf and thereby sealing her fate and intensifying the significance of her martyrdom. María's refusal may be seen as an act of self-representation, a resistance to external (male) control of her person, and thus ultimately another step in the nun's cultivation of her own image. María makes sure that she will be remembered as a self-sacrificing deity. However, as we have already seen, those participating in planning her portrait take up where María left off, filling the silence she left with their own voices. The old priest and friends of María are complicit in determining the definition of her legacy and the medium through which it will be propagated.

It is worth noting a complicating factor in the implications of the portrait scene. One of María's followers, Daniel, receives the priest's initial enthusiasm for the mestiza portrait of María with a disappointed shake of his head. His dissenting gesture may act as another cue for the viewer, a suggestion that we not give the priest the benefit of the doubt. When the camera cuts sympathetically to Daniel shaking his head, does the director wittingly or unwittingly undermine his own project? Because the portrait resembles the film, an interpretation of the portrait's implications may act as a key to the interpretation of *Ave*

María. We should consider whether or not Rossoff, in creating and shaping María, is paralleling the act of the old priest. The answer perhaps hinges on the viewer's interpretation. Such problematic ambiguities do, however, complicate the film's seemingly straightforward ideology. Daniel at first condemns the priest's attempt to appropriate María's iconicity by shaking his head. Yet, in the end, he and María's other followers approve of her calculated representation in the portrait. The same, of course, could be said about the film: like María's followers, Rossoff creates and deploys a cultural icon through visual representation.

As it happens, throughout the film Daniel plays a central role in shaping María and suggesting her interpretation, and thus his gesture carries especial, and complicating, weight. Earlier, we saw how he sets María on the path that she will take away from Christianity. The film seems to attribute the very core and impetus for María's ultimate iconic value to this man. Daniel effectively frames and guides the interpretation of *Ave María* for the viewer. As the film opens, a narrative voice-over makes the following claim: "Ella no era diferente de ti o de mí, al menos, al principio"[46] [99]. This veiled prediction of the discovery of María's divinity acquires new significance after we pause to replay the second and final voice-over with which the film closes. As the camera shows a silent, contemplative, narrator riding slowly away, we hear the following words: "Y así pasan los años para nosotros. A mí me toca narrar la historia, a ustedes, decidir" [100]. At this final moment of the film we realize that the entire story that we have just witnessed has been filtered through Daniel's perspective, that he has crafted the image of María that we possess. Rather than predicting what María will represent, he in fact creates her iconic transformation. The English subtitles underscore Daniel's agency: "And so the years go by. This story is *mine* to tell. And yours to decide" (emphasis mine). Because Rossoff insists that *Ave María* acts out perpetual injustices, Daniel's first statement, "Y así pasan los años para nosotros," emphasizes that he embodies the director's perspective. *Ave María* appears to posit a mestiza and syncretic essence of Mexican identity. It censures colonial oppression of the indigenous population, but proposes a hybrid protector and a sympathetic Creole voice of denunciation, Daniel.

Moreover, the dynamic between María and Daniel parallels the interaction of the screenplay's author, Camille Thomasson, with the director of the fim, Rossoff. The film credits Thomasson exclusively for the screenplay. However, review articles on the film reveal the extensive filtering that her work experienced at the hand of the director, who carried out more than a year of his own research for the film. The director insists that Thomasson, from Corpus Christi, is "como una mexicana de Texas y conoce muy bien nuestra cultura" (Peguero, "*Ave María* no será" n. pag.) [101]. Nevertheless, Rossoff, in the end, decides how to construct María and guide our interpretation of her.

Daniel's second statement, "A mí me toca narrar la historia, a ustedes, decidir," concludes with an invitation to participate, if not in the formation of the film's Mexican icon, at least in its interpretation. Tere López-Tarín, in representing María as if on her behalf, accepts the invitation and provides an interpretive model. She captures a degree of control over her own character, calling María a combination of Guadalupe and Coatlicue. López-Tarín's act of attaching an associative label to her character for viewers before the film's release faintly echoes how Sor Juana maintains a hand in the interpretation of a portrait of her by attaching to it a poem that begins, "A tus manos me traslada / la que mi original es" (1.102) [102]. In contrast to the way in which Daniel's voice overlays María's and acts as the caption for her image, Sor Juana's poem accompanying the portrait preserves her voice. She provides her own voice-over for the icon.

Sor Juana's intertextual presence in *Ave María*, unacknowledged by Rossoff, widens the space opened by Tere López-Tarín's comment. By means of the inevitable dialogue into which the film enters with Sor Juana, the poet may dispute the director's attempted domineering voice. Both outside the film and within it (in particular, the portrait scene), Sor Juana's poetry retains a broad and indisputable influence over the formation and interpretation of María. The writer continues, in *Ave María*, to fashion not only herself, but also her symbolic progeny. Hence, I think it is appropriate to offer Sor Juana the last word in the dialogue that I have been tracing. I would invite the reader to incorporate the poet's Sonnet #145 into our

Chapter Four

conversation. In reference to a portrait of her, Sor Juana's sonnet denounces the deceptive nature of painting:

> Este, que ves, engaño colorido,
> que del arte ostentando los primores,
> con falsos silogismos de colores
> es cauteloso engaño del sentido;
>
> éste, en quien la lisonja ha pretendido
> excusar de los años los horrores,
> y venciendo del tiempo los rigores
> triunfar de la vejez y del olvido,
>
> es un vano artificio del cuidado,
> es una flor al viento delicada,
> es un resguardo inútil para el hado:
>
> es una necia diligencia errada,
> es un afán caduco y, bien mirado,
> es cadáver, es polvo, es sombra, es nada. (1.277) [103]

With the words of her famous poem, Sor Juana Inés de la Cruz has interjected a final comment into the conversation. Perhaps in the present context we can understand Sor Juana's intertext to be urging us to exercise caution with regard to *Ave María*. The painting to which Sor Juana refers and its cinematic counterparts—the portrait in *Ave María* and the film itself—deceive before fading. Indeed, let us accept the poet's invitation to adopt a skeptical stance not only in our interpretation of María Inez, the national icon that Rossoff has offered us, but also with regard to how Mexico has—with this film and throughout the history of the nation—appropriated the writer's fame for its own use. Manufactured icons may revel in transitory autonomy, yet the poet's voice endures, and with it the sinuous image that Sor Juana indefatigably continues to fashion.

Chapter Five

Inverted Captivities and Imagined Adaptations in *Brave Gente Brasileira* (2000) and *Caramuru: A Invenção do Brasil* (2001)

Brava Gente Brasileira (2000), directed by Lúcia Murat, weaves a fictional story that stems from a historical event: an indigenous rebellion that takes place in 1778 in the Brazilian region of Mato Grosso do Sul. The "Notas de produção" ["Production Notes"] emphasize the film's historical basis, thus authorizing, like Humberto Mauro's 1937 *Descobrimento do Brasil*, the message of the movie: "Este filme se propõe a trabalhar em cima de um fato verídico ocorrido em Mato Grosso do Sul, na região do Pantanal, em 1778" (n. pag.) [104]. The "Making of ..." segment of the DVD's extras complements this externally applied air of fidelity by pointing out that the actors who play the eighteenth-century Guaicuru tribe are actually their descendants, the Kadiwéu. Among the motives for this decision would also appear to be the benefit of concretely tying past to present. The narrative of the film itself reinforces these efforts to suggest accuracy and contemporary relevance. As *Brava Gente* draws to a close, it buttresses its extratextual endorsements with a hyperbolic, but unfounded, example of the based-on-a-true-story device. A modern-day elder Kadiwéu woman is shown reading the contrived eighteenth-century textual basis for the story told by the film: *Viagem Filosófica à Capitania do Mato Grosso*, by Diogo de Castro e Albuquerque, who is one of the protagonists of the film.[1] *Brava Gente* thus implies that it has faithfully relayed the events described by a person that the film suggests was the real eighteenth-century author and illustrator of the book being held centuries later by the old Kadiwéu woman.

The book—a new, modern edition of what was presumably written by Diogo toward the end of the eighteenth century, which viewers see in a close-up—is held open for a moment to

Chapter Five

a page with a portrait of the film's other main character, Ánote, a high-ranking member of the Guaicuru. The film attempts to reify its grounded-in-history ploy through the correspondence between the portrait in the book and the actress who plays her, which viewers would not fail to recognize, since the film had earlier shown Diogo making the initial sketch of this illustration for his *Viagem Filosófica,* and later, toward the end of the film, an interior shot of Diogo and Ánote's room shows variations of this very painting pinned to the wall. Immediately after this closing scene of the film, an intertitle appears and indicates the historical basis of the events conceived by *Brava Gente*: "Em 1793, doze anos depois do massacre do forte, os Gauicuru firmaram um acordo de paz com o império Português. De seus descendentes, apenas sobreviveram os Kadiwéu. Cerca de mil vivem hoje numa reserva no Mato Grosso do Sul" [105]. The film here suggests the present-day relevance for the story by revealing the connection between the people depicted in the film and the surviving Kadiwéu. The final, spoken declaration of the modern Kadiwéu woman who is looking at Diogo's book, which follows a period of chanting, complements the connection between the film and present-day Brazil. The Portuguese subtitles translate her concluding words in this way: "Assim termina o nosso antigo canto de guerra. Ainda posso cantar outras histórias ... boas e ruins, do Guaicuru. Mas são histórias de hoje, histórias das guerras de hoje" [106].

The story that Diogo's apocryphal text tells, and that *Brava Gente* attempts to authorize through these various means, begins when members of a Portuguese military outpost break a peace treaty and massacre several people from Ánote's tribe. She is soon raped and taken captive by the murdering soldiers. The film, in broad terms, traces the development of the relationship between Ánote and her rapist, Diogo, the Portuguese intellectual newly arrived from Coimbra. In the end, the Guaicuru seek revenge for the massacre and carry out an attack, summarily defeating the Portuguese. Notably, at the beginning of the film, when the party, led by the cruel soldier born in Brazil (principally of European descent, but with an indigenous ancestor), Capitão Pedro, first returns to the fort after Ánote's rape, the officer in charge criticizes having taken indigenous people captive: Ánote and a light-skinned boy, Januya, who the European characters in the film believe had been taken captive by the Guaicuru years before. However, the film implies that his critique derives from a concern for how the act will compromise a peace treaty with the Guaicuru. Regardless of the commander's motives, the irony of his condemnation of individual captivity stands out: the Portuguese colonial enterprise is attempting to hold captive and, in a sense, acculturate the entire indigenous population (later, for example, the same commander expresses frustration that the indigenous people refuse to become civilized and build houses made out of wood). His discouragement of indigenous captivity also underscores how *Brava Gente* is inverting the more common tale of European captivity, much like other "colonial films" such as Eduardo Rossoff's 1999 *Ave María* and Salvador Carrasco's 1998 *La otra conquista*.

Brava Gente, in effect, cannibalizes the traditional captivity tale—as re-envisioned in films like Pereira dos Santos's 1971 *Como era gostoso o meu francês* and Echevarría's 1991 *Cabeza de Vaca*—primarily by portraying captive indigenous characters who attempt, but ultimately and valiantly fail, in the spirit of martyrdom, to resist being force-fed European ideology. While retellings of European captivity often focus on willing, fascinated, or respectful assimilation of the European into indigenous culture, *Brava Gente*, like *La otra conquista*, portrays indigenous captives who resist efforts to acculturate them. Both of these films show indigenous protagonists reverse processes of transculturation through which they have passed and resolutely reassume, in the end, indigenous culture practices. In *La otra conquista*, Topiltzin changes out of European clothes before his final confrontation with the statue of the Virgin Mary which leads to his death. In *Brava Gente*, the defiance of (or tactical exploitation of) assimilation and the reconfirmation of indigenous culture—from which the characters of the film only drifted slightly, either by force or need for survival—can be seen in several ways. I'll sketch a few of the salient reversals: (1) After Pedro's efforts to indoctrinate Januya into European culture, in part by teaching him to shoot a gun, and Christian culture, in part symbolized by covering the boy in bright white cloth, reminiscent of the mass scene in Mauro's 1937 *Descobrimento do Brasil* when the indigenous woman is covered, the boy removes the white shirt, exposing the decorative markings of Guaicuru on his body, and kills a Portuguese man, which provokes Pedro to execute the boy.[2] (2) Ánote, who becomes pregnant by Diogo, and lives with the Portuguese man throughout the gestation, in what Diogo seems to perceive as contentedness, kills the infant once it is born, which Portuguese characters in the film explain is accepted in Guaicuru culture, as a woman is only allowed one child so that the tribe can stay mobile. (3) During the battle at the fort at the end of the film, in which the Guaicuru defeat the Portuguese, an indigenous soldier cuts off the ear of the most despicable of the European soldiers, Pedro, which represents a return to the Guaicuru custom; viewers learn that up until this point the Guaicuru had begun cutting off hands rather than ears because Portuguese had done that to living Guaicuru earlier. The film makes clear in the final moments that these acts of resistance were merely battles won in a war lost, but that they still may retain symbolic value for present-day Brazil.

Brava Gente finds expressive potential in the inversion of the already suggestive tale of European captivity, in which the roles of the conquest are reversed and the captive European minority must assimilate into indigenous society. The film not only reappropriates and reconfigures tales of European captivity, but also amplifies the potential for modifying conceptions of identity by treating the indigenous culture as the benchmark. Instead of consuming the captivity tale in the way that *Cabeza de Vaca* and *Como era gostoso o meu francês* do, Murat's film attempts to individualize and energize what generally took place: the oppression and destruction of entire indigenous populations. By showing an indigenous, multifaceted, protagonist to be a captive *per se* and not a collective under hopeless domination, *Brava Gente* elevates the indigenous characters into the sympathetic category of the exception, which is normally occupied by Europeans in such narratives.

Not only do the indigenous characters fight assimilation in *Brava Gente*, but also a somewhat sympathetic European character, Diogo, respectfully adopts some aspects of the culture of their indigenous captives, which enhances the complexity of the film's proposals for spectator sympathy and identification, which I'll discuss below. This is also the case in *Ave María* and *La otra conquista.* In *Ave María,* several of the nuns embrace

María's brand of syncretism; in *La otra conquista,* the priest in charge of Topiltzin's captivity in the end recognizes, while surprisingly speaking Náhuatl, the validity of Aztec religion. In *Brava Gente,* after a scene in a cave that shows consensual sex between Diogo and Ánote, he—not captive, but apparently captivated—allows her to paint his face in the style of his prisoner's tribe, which the audience realizes only when the two are shown returning to the fort. The conversation in the cave leading up to Ánote's decorating Diogo's face helps to plant a seed of spectator identification with the Guaicuru. In general, *Brava Gente* shows the Guaicuru to be civilized, reasonable, and logical, and the Portuguese to be sadistic, savage, and absurd, which urges viewers to feel a cultural and ideological alignment with the indigenous people, despite the language barrier maintained by the lack of subtitles when the Guaicuru speak.[3] The scene in which Diogo asks Ánote why she paints her face helps to advance these oppositions. His reaction, in Portuguese, to her explanation indicates to spectators the nature of that logic: "Eu sou macaco ... porque tenho pelos ... e tu pintas-te porque não tens ... porque é gente" [107]. The Portuguese man, who is beginning to learn Ánote's language, understands her explanation, and muses in this way about the irony, from his perspective, of her inversion of his cultural premises. Diogo, convinced, endorses the rationality of her explanation. Their interaction creates a space for the sense of indigenous cultural practices to be underscored, and to controvert assumptions of European cultural superiority.

Shortly after Ánote paints Diogo's face, he expands the implications of this symbolic act of collusion with indigenous resistance to the hegemony of European culture. When a priest admonishes him for eating meat on a Saturday, Diogo rolls his eyes to underscore what he sees as the unreasonable conventionality or illogic of certain Christian conventions. The priest then accuses him of living in sin, to which Diogo responds, "Aqui também é difícil saber exatamente o que é ou não é pecado" [108]. He insists that the Bible does not anticipate life among these "selvagens" ["savages"]. While he fails to dispute the categorization of Amerindians as savages, he does, based on his experiences with the natives of the region, question the universal applicability of the guiding principles of Christianity.

Chapter Five

The Portuguese Diogo helps to expose, from a perspective aligned with that of native Brazilians, the cultural oppression that results from the Portuguese colonial presence. Notwithstanding Diogo's distinction as the least detestable European character vis-à-vis the Guaicuru, it is worth noting that his use of the word *selvagens* is not an isolated indication of Eurocentrism, paternalism, or cruelty on his part, which spectators saw clearly in the early rape scene. For example, near the end of the film, at an outdoor mass, the camera shows an emotional Diogo, in a close-up of his face, praying out loud, and promising God that his child will be Christian, and will combine his abilities with her purity. Also, when Diogo finds Ánote after she has killed the infant, he beats her and calls her an animal.[4]

Much like Gabriel Retes's 1976 film *Nuevo mundo*, Murat recognizes a difference between viewer sympathy with the Guaicuru and identification with them. Diogo's marked imperfections enhance the film's unequivocal suggestion that viewers sympathize, if not yet identify, with the indigenous people portrayed in the film. *Brava Gente* makes clear that the Portuguese are cruel, and that the Guaicuru are innocent victims of colonialist practices. Capitão Pedro is the chief vehicle for the communication of Portuguese wickedness. Examples of Pedro's barbarism abound in the film. Most notably, it is he who carries out an early massacre of a group of Guaicuru; survivors of the initial clash are all executed, except for Januya and Ánote, whom Diogo asks to be spared. Such acts quickly propose that viewers feel sympathy for the Guaicuru and revulsion toward the Portuguese. The dynamics of identification, however, are another matter.

Though clearly imperfect himself as well, Diogo acts as the viewer's inevitable temporary proxy, in spite of his nefarious acts and the fact that he is not Brazilian (unlike the film's presumed audience). The film bolsters its partial endorsement of Diogo's perspective by taking steps to encourage increasing degrees of identification with the character, partly through his embrace of indigenous culture. *Brava Gente* attempts partially to attenuate spectator condemnation of Diogo by showing that he regrets responding to the pressure of the Brazilian soldiers for him to prove his manhood by raping her. After a period of rejecting Diogo's attempts to begin a romantic relationship with her, she is apparently, and surprisingly, won over by the Portuguese man's comic charm. The film exploits this initial, clearly somewhat tense and uncomfortable spectator alignment with Diogo, to encourage a gradual transfer of identification to the indigenous characters. Diogo by degrees lends us access, as he gains it, to the culture of Ánote, who comes to take (or share) his privileged place as the character with whom viewers might identify.

These narrative aspects of spectator positioning, and repositioning to identify with the Guaicuru, are reinforced visually and linguistically. Spectators who do not understand the language of the Guaicuru, wherever their sympathies may lie, are initially forced linguistically into adopting the perspective of the European, Diogo.

When, for instance, the film gives spectators access to a meeting in which indigenous men plan for war against the Portuguese, it does not supply translations in subtitles for their words, which places spectators in the ignorant position of a (hidden) Portuguese observer. However, their access to this private moment—and others, such as the opening sequence of the film, and when the Guaicuru grieve following the slaughter of the people by the soldiers—anticipates the film's ultimate convergence of sympathy and identification. Indeed, visually (as opposed to linguistically) the film is polyperspectival from the beginning: viewers are given access to a number of private moments of both the Guaicuru and the Portuguese, and perceive a variety of events from each perspective. Nonetheless, during scenes that give access to European-dominated spaces, the camera also sometimes privileges visually Diogo's point of view, and consequently aligns viewers with him. The eventual reform of Diogo's initially sexualizing visual perspective, which the camera follows, accompanies and aids the film's effort to encourage identification with the Guaicuru. In an early scene, one of the first of sketches of Diogo that viewers see, shortly before he rapes Ánote, is of naked women of African descent from the Brazilian coast (a comment by Capitão Pedro lends the drawing sexual connotations). Also, when Diogo sees a young indigenous woman, early on, the camera follows

Chapter Five

his eyeline to a close-up of her face, which subsequently tilts down to frame her breasts. The reaction shot of Diogo's face reveals transfixion and then the initial hint of a smile. As the film progresses, Diogo's gaze loses this objectifying quality. As a result, the relatively clear opposition between indigenous and European visual perspectives in the film is somewhat compromised, as this privileged character revises the way that he looks at the other culture.

The ever-narrowing distance between spectators and the Guaicuru that the film has maintained through language, and has gradually reduced, as in *Nuevo mundo*, through privileged access to Guaicuru spaces and shared point of view, begins to dissipate when Diogo questions Ánote about their missing infant in her language. Though viewers are not given a translation for his words, the linguistic boundary maintained up to this point, which retains a certain distance between the Guaicuru and viewers who do not understand their language, is blurred by the film's protagonist, with whom viewers are visually and (to a limited extent) ideologically encouraged to identify, displaying access to that linguistic realm. Finally, the barrier potentially disappears entirely at the end of the film when the words of the elderly Kadiwéu woman reading Diogo's apocryphal book are translated by the subtitles: if the DVD's Portuguese subtitle option is turned on, the film translates into Portuguese the last segment of what the modern Kadiwéu woman has been saying (initially, her words were in the form of a chanted song); if the subtitles are turned off, nothing that she says is translated. Thus, if the subtitles are on, spectators' perspectives are, in this way, fully fused with that of this woman. The film suggests, through potential access to her words and the intertitle following the old woman's monologue that summarizes the fate of the Guaicuru and the survival today of a few of their descendants, the Kadiwéu, that we also consider ourselves descendants of the Guaicuru. In addition to delaying identification with the Guaicuru, the lack of Portuguese subtitles for their language, except for that possibility in these last moments, may challenge the notion that Portuguese, today, should be considered the default, natural, mode of communication in Brazil. By extension, the descendents of Europeans, should not necessarily occupy a central position in conceptions of identity. *Brava Gente* thus reinforces its overall de-centering of the Portuguese contribution to Brazilian conceptions of identity.

Within the context of this proposal that spectators accept and even champion an indigenous point of view, *Brava Gente* models resistance. Resistance to cultural domination, an essential element in *Brava Gente*'s exploitation of indigenous captivity, takes the ultimate form of the attack on the fort. However, the film anticipates this climactic rebellion from more than one angle. I'll now return to two acts of resistance that I synthesized earlier: Ánote's infanticide and Januya's martyrdom. Within the space allowed her, Ánote is shown to fight assimilation into the society of her captors. As we have seen, after Ánote has apparently forgiven Diogo for raping her and they begin an ostensibly happy union, she eventually becomes pregnant, and Diogo expresses his conviction that their child will take the best from both worlds. Diogo's point of view suggests that the two of them have become a metaphor of a peaceful, harmonious, and proudly *mestiço* Brazilian nation. Yet this well-ingrained Brazilian foundational myth is powerfully debunked when Diogo arrives home after Ánote has given birth. In that moment, Diogo discovers that she has killed their offspring. The character likely relinquishes whatever sympathy he may have accrued among spectators up to this point by hitting her and accusing her of barbarism.

The film complements Ánote's resistance to assimilation and the implications of her acts and her relationship with Diogo vis-à-vis Brazilian identity largely through another Guaicuru character, Januya. If Ánote helps to undermine Brazil's most pervasive foundational myth, Januya may model for spectators a person of European descent embracing an ideal of identity centered on indigenous culture. When Ánote is taken captive, the soldiers detain as well a young, light-skinned, European-looking boy, who has presumably been taken captive as an infant and raised among the Guaicuru.[5] The presence of this character alludes to the traditional tale of European captivity among indigenous peoples. Januya takes the relative de-centering of European culture typical to the captivity tale to another level. Not only has he been fully assimilated, he has no desire to reenter European society and covertly resists his captivity and the assimilation that goes with it, most strikingly through

Chapter Five

his final act of killing the Portuguese man, which I described above.

Ánote's decision to kill her baby can be seen as one of resistance to being absorbed into the Portuguese cultural and genetic pool. More broadly understood, the act implies that she will not abide cultural erasure through the process of miscegenation. The film thus offers an alternative model of identity for Brazil, one that repudiates the long tradition of conceiving of identity in terms of the unproblematic union of diverse racial constituencies, and instead promotes pride in indigenous culture that resists European hegemony. In the aftermath of his condemnation of Ánote, Diogo reflects in voiceover on his experience in Brazil: "A colônia não pode ser mais que um momento passageiro nas nossas vidas, uma aprendizagem difícil e tortuosa" [109]. His comment evokes the film's own examination of Brazilian identity through a return to a traumatic moment in the nation's colonial past, one that may be seen as particularly slippery or fleeting for its fictionality. By the same token, his words are an apt way to conceptualize the project of Latin American colonial films in general: they facilitate a brief passage through the colony in order to offer scattered and, ideally, fresh and insightful glimpses of the past, the present, and of identity.

As in the cases of *Ave María* and *La otra conquista*, *Brava Gente* harnesses the persuasive potential of the captivity tale in order to transform a general rule into poignant specificity. However, and importantly, all three of the films also tap the powerful and intertwined benefits of the retellings of captivity tales being "based on a (more or less) true story." Whereas *Ave María* ties itself loosely to Sor Juana and foregrounds in the action the production of a seventeenth-century (apocryphal) portrait of the protagonist, *La otra conquista* showcases shots of the protagonist painting a doomed (and also apocryphal) pictographical manuscript that records the tragic moment that he is experiencing and would, if not burned by the Spaniards, act as the memory of the Aztecs. And *Brava Gente* fortifies the rhetorical force of its inverted captivity by inventing, even more explicitly than the other two films, a chief intertext for its story, and by tying the past concretely to the present. What I term anthropophagous adaptation—a consumptive approach to source texts that Murat's film shares with the other mentioned

Inverted Captivities and Imagined Adaptations

films—is altered here. *Brava Gente* effectively dominates and transforms an imagined, but emblematic source text. What is key, however, is that we observe the film's attempted indigenous subject position consuming a non-existent European text about a suppressed reality, which is transformed into an expression of indigenous identity. By way of its abstraction of adaptational tactics, *Brava Gente* cannibalizes the very concept of the captivity tale, taking advantage of it at the same time that it turns it around.

Guel Arraes's *Caramuru: A Invenção do Brasil* (2001) represents the other side of the same esthetic and strategic cinematic coin as *Brava Gente*. This disparate but complementary reinvention of Portuguese and indigenous interactions set in the sixteenth-century also authoritatively invents an intertext and inverts, albeit in an erotic and jocular setting, the tale of captivity. *Caramuru*—directed by Arraes and co-written by him and Jorge Furtado—is a comedic, cinematic rendering of the oft-revisited, historically rooted tale of the sixteenth-century Portuguese man, Diogo Álvares, and his relationship with the Tupinambá princess Paraguaçu. The film is a re-edited version of a miniseries for TV Globo—a branch of the Brazilian media conglomerate Rede Globo. The pared-down film extracts from the miniseries a no-less-ludic documentary with which the narrative portion was interspersed for television broadcast.[6]

Caramuru's version of the legendary couple's liaison begins in Portugal, with a young Portuguese painter, Diogo Álvares, who is duped into committing espionage and condemned to be exiled from European civilization. He is sent on a voyage that ends in shipwreck near the coast of Brazil, several days before the 1500 arrival of Pedro Álvares Cabral—a convenient chronology, as the film locates the birth of the nation in this story. After paddling to shore in a makeshift raft, Diogo collapses, and later awakes to meet a captivating Tupinambá princess, Paraguaçu, and her equally enchanting sister, Moema. At first, the castaway's captivity appears metaphorical, deriving from the sexual allure of the two sisters, who insist on sharing Diogo's affection. Soon thereafter, however, it becomes clear that he truly suffers a captive state and that his projected destiny, like that of Jean in Nelson Pereira dos Santos's 1971 classic, *Como era gostoso o meu francês*, is to be eaten by the tribe. But unlike

151

Chapter Five

Pereira dos Santos's luckless Frenchman, Diogo stumbles upon his salvation when he finds a firearm, the discharge of which inspires the awe of those who would consume him. As a result, the man is able to modify the nature of his incorporation: dubbed Caramuru,[7] he is absorbed into the political body of Tupinambá society as its head/chief. Our Portuguese protagonist later travels with Paraguaçu to Europe, where they marry. Upon their triumphant return to Brazil, the couple reinitiates its love triangle with Moema.

In contrast with *Brava Gente*, *Caramuru* generally replays the standard tale of captivity, channelling the productive appeal of this narrative tradition in terms of thinking about identity. However, the film also represents a reversal of the thrust of other cinematic recollections of European captivity in the Americas. Compared to films like *Cabeza de Vaca* and *Como era gostoso*, *Caramuru* reverts to the European subject position embodied by the typical colonial-era captivity tale, despite an early gesture at polyperspectivity.[8] Notwithstanding *Caramuru*'s perpetuation, rather than critical transformation, of the broad lines of colonial narratives of captivity, the film stands out for its anthropophagous approach to adaptation. In fact, I read *Caramuru* as a neo-anthropophagous text in several respects. I evaluate here the film's intervention on this long-standing Brazilian cultural trope, and how it, consistent with tradition, exploits assorted cultural cannibalistic tactics in order to re-invent Brazil. It is cannibalistic—according to the definition conceived and developed within Brazilian Modernism in the 1920s, which was famously articulated in Oswald de Andrade's 1928 "Manifesto antropófago"—in that it consumes and processes diverse cultural manifestations to realize strategic objectives.[9] Much like the anthropophagous texts of Brazilian Modernism, *Caramuru* uses humor to reconfigure a foundational amalgam of history, fiction, and legend into a revised commentary on the nation.

Very little is known for sure about the historical figure of Diogo Álvares/Caramuru, and any conjecture must derive from a reconciliation of sometimes conflicting versions relayed by early modern historiographical texts. Nonetheless, we know enough to distinguish with some certainty between the plot elements of the film that appear to be rooted in fact—e.g., Diogo became the leader of the Tupinambá in the region in which he landed; he traveled to France with Paraguaçu and married her there—and the plot elements that appear to diverge from fact and that either build on preceding fictionalizations or offer original revisions to the story—e.g., the love triangle with Paraguaçu's sister, Moema; Diogo as painter-turned-spy who arrives in Brazil before Cabral.

Janaína Amado, in her article "Mythic Origins: Caramuru and the Founding of Brazil," sifts through the intermingled categories of historical fiction and historiography—which similarly organize the information at hand to varied ends— in order to deduce probable historical facts and, even more importantly, to study how and why the story of Diogo/Caramuru has been retold and exploited as a foundational fiction of Brazil as either colony or eventual nation.[10] Her analysis of erudite and popular sources from the sixteenth to the twentieth centuries extracts an outline of the historical figure.[11] Notable among the sources is the influential eighteenth-century epic poem by José de Santa Rita Durão, *Caramuru: Poema épico do descobrimento da Bahia*, one of the most canonical intertexts for this sixteenth-century historical-event-turned-legend, and one that exposes and reinforces the dominant tendency in sources treating Caramuru: the permeability of fiction and history (Amado 802). Possibly of noble birth, Diogo Álvares was Portuguese—perhaps from the town of Viana do Castelo—and likely arrived, shipwrecked, in Brazil in the first decades of the sixteenth century (Amado 783).[12] He made his home in Bahia for several decades, was in contact with the Portuguese, learned the language and culture of the indigenous people of the region, "and evidence shows that he had children with either the 'many indigenous women' attributed to him by certain chroniclers, or with Paraguaçu" (Amado 783–84).

In Amado's evaluation, Simão de Vasconcellos's seventeenth-century *Chronica da Companhia de Jesu do Estado do Brasil* is the earliest source that synthesizes the key plot elements generally present in both historiographical and intentionally fictional versions of the story:

> [T]he voyage from Portugal, the shipwreck, the shot fired in the air, the respect of the Indians, the name Caramuru, Paraguaçu's love, the trip to France, the envy of the women who

> remained in Brazil, the baptism and the marriage, the return to Brazil, the shipwreck of the Spanish vessel, Paraguaçu's vision [of what would be dubbed our Lady of Grace (791)], the descendants of Caramuru, his support of the Portuguese authorities in their relations with the Indians. (792)

As the summary of the film's plot that I included above makes clear, Arraes's *Caramuru* incorporates many of these components into the variant that it presents of Diogo Álvares and his time in Brazil. Nevertheless, *Caramuru* predictably and always ludically tweaks, substantially modifies, or eliminates some of the standard features of the story. The film clearly suggests Paraguaçu's love for Diogo/Caramuru, but attributes her even greater preoccupation with the health of the love triangle that she shares with her sister Moema, a plot element with some relationship to Durão's eighteenth-century epic poem.[13] Likewise, Paraguaçu's baptism in France remains, but only implied through a fleeting reference in the dialogue to her new Christian name—a surprise for Paraguaçu—in the moments before the couple take their vows. A more substantial modification consists of the fact that whereas earlier versions of the story of Caramuru and Paraguaçu tended to emphasize the couple's foundational status through references to offspring, *Caramuru*'s affective union of Caramuru and Paraguaçu (and Moema) is unproductive, their symbolic progeny—the Brazilian population—only implied. Typically, texts treating Caramuru and Paraguaçu as a Brazilian myth of origin emphasize the couple's children, thus painting them as parents of the nation (Amado 786). Additionally, while previous accounts emphasize Brazil as a subset of Portugal (Amado 786), *Caramuru* is steadfast in its Brazilianness. The film does articulate its commentary on identity loosely within these customary, transatlantic parameters, but inverts the inclusive equation to which Amado refers, representing a Portugal esthetically dominated by Brazil, generally caricaturizing the Portuguese characters other than Diogo/Caramuru, much in the way that Carla Camurati's parodic historical feature, *Carlota Joaquina, Princesa do Brazil* (2001), does.[14] What is more, if the conventional core plot tended to underscore Caramuru's "support of the Portuguese authorities in their relations with the Indians" (Amado 792), the film focuses on the period before such purported long-time collaboration gets underway—excluding as well Paraguaçu's religious vision and Caramuru's aid to shipwrecked Spaniards—and carefully develops an initial portrayal of its protagonist as powerless and alienated within the Portuguese political sphere, a tactic that reinforces an association of Caramuru principally with Brazil. Beyond modifications or truncations of the standard story, the film indulges in several concrete historical revisions, such as Diogo Álvares as painter, which I mentioned earlier, an add-on, which I will discuss in more detail below, that facilitates both the plot flow and the rhetoric of the film. The cinematic production grounds much of the restyled significance with which it infuses the story of Diogo/Caramuru and Paraguaçu in, on the one hand, such alterations to certain established features of the tale and, on the other, the maintenance and stressing of distinct features.

Globo's cinematic fictionalization of this European/Amerindian encounter consumes the corpus that has collaborated in absorbing Caramuru and Paraguaçu into the national imaginary, and contributes to that already somewhat anthropophagous body of texts.[15] However, the film intensifies the cannibalistic dynamic inherent in any tale retold. In addition to sampling and distinctively digesting the intertexts about the couple,[16] *Caramuru* adds liberally to its feast from other sources. In its effort to reshape present-day popular impressions of the foundational fusion of history and fiction and, by extension, of Brazilian history and identity, the film also draws on diverse cultural texts that have nothing directly to do with the tale and on ingrained stereotypes of Brazilianness. Notwithstanding the film's sundry referents, however, *Caramuru* implies a single source of nourishment for its version of the story, the significance of which tactic I will address later: an invented primary source-text that the film purports was written by Paraguaçu and illustrated by Diogo/Caramuru.

This film, or more specifically, the DVD version of this film, is cannibalistic in another sense as well, in that it consumes a powerful late twentieth-century aspect of Brazilian visual culture: television.[17] The 2001 film *Caramuru*, which is a shortened version of a miniseries that was broadcast the previous year, in a sense absorbs and effectively integrates into cinema esthetic qualities from the popular and influential medium of

Chapter Five

television.[18] This millennial cinematic engagement of the aftermath of Andrade's "Manifesto antropófago" within Brazilian culture is reinforced thematically, as the protagonist, destined to be consumed in an anthropophagic ceremony, ends up being sexually "consumed" by the two indigenous princesses, Paraguaçu and her sister Moema (the verb *comer* in Brazilian Portuguese facilitates this wordplay, as it denotes both the act of eating and sexual consumption).

In broad terms, *Caramuru* attempts to reinvent Brazil by modifying in a less-than-critical way the nation's traditional happy *mestiço* myth of origins. In addition to excluding, as Robert Stam has observed with regard to the earlier miniseries version, the role played by Africans in the emergence of conceptions of Brazilianness ("Cabral" 208), the film reshapes Brazil's multi-racial creation myth by lending it a two-fold veneer of what might be seen by some spectators as playfully illicit or at least unconventional: cannibalism and ménage à trois. *Caramuru* argues that Brazil emerges from a sex triangle in which a European man and two Amerindian women "eat" and subsequently incorporate part of the other. The text on the back of the DVD clearly associates the provocative sexual arrangement with an explanation of the nature of Brazilian identity: "A invenção de um pais chamado Brasil" begins in Portugal and continues in Brazil, where Caramuru finds himself "vivendo então o primeiro triângulo amoroso da história do Brasil" (n. pag.) [110]. *Caramuru* allegorizes the genesis of the Brazilian nation, then, through the representation of an unorthodix sexual dynamic. Such an explanation for Brazilianness, of course, tends to perpetuate the stereotype of an eroticized, savage, submissive, female Brazil; a fertile ground, in large part, for male fantasies.[19] Of course, at the same time, *Caramuru* partially subverts such an exoticizing fantasy through the depiction of Caramuru's realization that he is not entirely in control, that his rather convenient arrangement is merely an aperitif to the meal in which he is intended to be the main dish. The film attempts to anticipate and mollify with humor reactions to its potentially polemical vision of national inauguration, a strategy that the marketing machine of *Caramuru* tries to signal and sell. The insert of the DVD characterizes as "lúdica e bem-humorada" its reinvention of the story of Caramuru and Paraguaçu, and emphasizes the way that the tale—"uma das histórias mais remotas do imáginario popular brasileiro" (n. pag.)—continues to contribute to imagining Brazil[20] [111].

In order to parse *Caramuru*'s proposed Brazilian self-image, I take as the object of this study the DVD version of the film, rather than the broadcasted miniseries ("A Invenção do Brasil"), the 35 mm theatrical version of the film, or even the VHS of *Caramuru* that was released shortly after the film was in theaters, for two principal reasons. First, the DVD is the media through which the film will with most frequency continue to be viewed. Second, the design and options of the DVD compound and help to expose certain intertextual layers latent in the film, in particular as a result of the availability of the documentary portions of the miniseries, and the spectator's ability to intersperse the viewing of the film with sections of the documentary by clicking on a green parrot that periodically appears on the screen.[21] In contrast to the DVD, both the cinematic and VHS versions of the film contain only the continuous, fictional narrative.

In the remaining pages, I examine *Caramuru*'s diverse and provocative cinematic return to anthropophagy, a cultural trope that enjoyed a heyday in *Cinema Novo*, through such films as Joaquim Pedro de Andrade's *Macunaíma* (1969) and Nelson Pereira dos Santos's *Como era gostoso o meu francês* (1971). In general, I examine how the 2001 *Caramuru* consumes and transforms texts and I consider the effectiveness of what we can loosely call the film's adaptational strategies. However, in lieu of comparing *Caramuru* in detail to preceding iterations of the story of Diogo/Caramuru and Paraguaçu, I opt to focus on certain salient instances of intertextuality and key visual and conceptual "cannibalistic" tactics employed by the DVD, such as how *Caramuru* abstracts or stylizes its own cinematographic images through a cartoon-like (or watercolor-like) filter, a central element in the film's integral suggestion that it has principally adapted an inscrutably faithful source text— one produced by the players themselves, Paraguaçu (author) and Caramuru (illustrator), and which viewers may or may not know, is fictional. Notwithstanding the film's self-authorizing insinuation that it adapts what in reality is an apocryphal text, *Caramuru* is not an adaptation, per se, of any single source, as we have seen. Rather, it draws on and refashions a fusion of diverse, and always somewhat diverging, versions of the story that have survived from the sixteenth century on, in historiography, fiction, and the popular imaginary, and, importantly, liberally incorporates into its revision of this long-standing allegory of Brazilianness various other intertexts and concepts of Brazilian identity. Additionally, I look at several ways in which the DVD deploys and fortifies its multi-pronged anthropophagous strategy. I analyze, for example, how Globo packages and presents its digestion of this foundational Brazilian legend. I study specifically, as well, the interface between spectators and the DVD, and the ways in which the DVD's cannibalization of various media—its fusion of television, documentary filmmaking, animation, and hyperlink—may influence readings of the film and its commentary on the nation.[22] Of particular interest is the film's distinctive oscillation between exposing and veiling its adaptational devices: how it authorizes its consumption at the same time that it encourages spectators to understand such processes. Overall, this analysis seeks to uncover and explain how *Caramuru* demonstrates that anthropophagy—and, we might extrapolate, anthropophagous adaptation in general—remains a vital means to re-evaluate identity in Brazil.

Caramuru introduces its two-fold conceptualization of anthropophagy through a cinematic reference, an acknowledgment of one of the intertexts that it has consumed. Soon after the protagonist who will come to be known as Caramuru is shipwrecked off the coast of Brazil, the camera parodically engages a moment in *Como era gostoso* that reifies the anthropophagic theme of that film, and in so doing helps to expose the anthropophagous nature of this film and of cinematic adaptation, or intertextuality, in general.[23] The first shot of the female protagonist Paraguaçu mirrors one of the French captive Jean's assigned Tupinambá wife, Seboipep, at the end of Pereira dos Santos's film: in both films viewers are shown an extreme close-up of the eyes of the indigenous woman. In the case of the 1971 film, what the framing of this fractional shot alludes to by conspicuous exclusion is the shocking act of eating the roasted Frenchman. *Caramuru* makes it clear that the protagonist consumes not human flesh, but merely a piece of fruit. While in Pereira dos Santos's film Seboipep's mouth remains hidden at the end of the shot before the director cuts to an image of something else, in *Caramuru* the shot of the woman's eyes is followed by a cut to a close-up of Paraguaçu's hand picking a piece of starfruit, and then to a close-up, from the side, of her hand and face as she takes a bite. *Como era gostoso* reinforces through its concluding shot the shock, mystery, and exoticism with which it has infused the topic of cannibalism. *Caramuru*, in contrast, provokes a cultural expectation of cannibalism through the image and couples that association into its consistent sensual portrayal of Paraguaçu. Later, when it is revealed to Caramuru that he is to be eaten, the filmmakers once again cite Pereira dos Santos:[24] just as Seboipep merges the two meanings of *comer* by biting Jean's neck—the body part that she eats at the end of the film—Moema and Paraguaçu each playfully bite at the neck of their European captive as they explain to him his fate.

The same dual anthropophagous implications of the *comer* as literal flesh eating or sexual consumption re-emerges when Paraguaçu and Caramuru—as the king of Brazil—are later in Paris. Caramuru emphasizes to the French noblewoman, Isabelle, that he was under unusual stress in the New World in order to explain why he did not keep the promise that he made before departing Europe to be faithful. When he culminates the list of hardships with the allusion to cannibalism—"Quase fui comido" ["I was almost eaten"]—Isabelle glances guiltily away from Caramuru toward the camera as she says, "Eu também!" ["Me too!"], a statement that evokes the figurative, sexual meaning of *comer*. And moments later, when she and Caramuru are interrupted in a kiss by the appearance of Paraguaçu, Isabelle extends her hand to be kissed. In an act that literalizes the proposal of cultural cannibalism for Brazilians to consolidate power by consuming the other, the Tupinambá woman inverts the class-inflected European custom of kissing the hand of a social superior, as well as the sexual possession of Caramuru by Isabelle, by biting forcefully into the flesh of Isabelle's hand.

In both allusions to *Como era gostoso* to which I refer above, *Caramuru* de-centers the literal variant of *comer*, underscoring instead in its evocation and playful transformation of Pereira dos Santos's film the sexual implications of the scenes.

Chapter Five

Although the ritual practice of cannibalism among the Tupinambá plays a limited thematic role in *Caramuru*, by way of these two concrete references the film generally establishes a productive analogy with *Como era gostoso*. Even taking into account the shift in what is signified by *Caramuru*'s revisions of these moments, rather than enacting a parody, I would argue that the filmmaker attempts to provoke an esthetic and even conceptual alliance with Pereira dos Santos's influential film, which employs anthropophagy as central motif and fundamental adaptational inspiration in its re-evaluation of Brazil's past and present. *Caramuru*'s brief allusions to *Como era gostoso* efficiently achieve several results: generally, they locate *Caramuru* within the context of anthropophagous Brazilian cinema; more specifically, they conjure the powerful and multiple implications of cannibalism in the earlier film; and, at the same time, the resignified references advance *Caramuru*'s own, and distinct, revision of Brazilianness.

Como era gostoso undoubtedly helps to nourish *Caramuru*, but the primary intertext of the film as seen in theaters in 2001 is, of course, "A Invenção do Brasil," the television miniseries from the previous year. While the Rede Globo miniseries interpolated sequences of a complementary documentary with the dramatic narrative, the Globo Filmes cinematic version streamlined the story, leaving only the dramatic re-creation of the legend of Caramuru and Paraguaçu.[25] Despite director Guel Arraes's declared predilection for docudrama (Biaggio 8), he has indicated his reluctance to bring the genre to the big screen. In a review of the film, Carlos Alberto Mattos comments on the TV-to-film transformation and articulates one of the consequences of feeding on small-screen culture. He writes that Arraes's way of telling stories, "em ritmo de tagarelice alucinada, não deixa tempo para respirar nem para olhar paisagens. Está de olho num público que talvez não ligue mesmo para isso, educado que está na velocidade de apreensão e na indiferença à reflexão" (7)[26] [112]. The cinematic iteration of the dual-genre, two-and-a-half-hour-long miniseries reflects qualities often found in the world of sound bites and sitcoms: the result is swift and flashy, with a complementary captivating soundtrack by popular musician Lenine.

Inverted Captivities and Imagined Adaptations

The DVD later absorbed and digested the previous two versions, creating a hybrid by reuniting through hyperlinks the documentary with the stripped-down visual recounting, and adding, as is often the case with DVDs, various other elements, such as a "Making of …," footage of opening nights in different cities, trailers, a synopsis, and a textual discussion of the film and its production. The reincorporation of the documentary is flexible: spectators may watch it from beginning to end, whereas the miniseries presented it in sections; or they may view the theater-version of the film with periodic and optional interruptions of the documentary (when the parrot appears during the viewing, one can click on it and see a section of the documentary). While the parrot option is an engaging and often thought-provoking element, the interruptions are sometimes tenuously justified, and the result of watching the film in this way can be a choppy experience, a possibility of which Arraes expressed awareness in relation to the transposition of the miniseries "Caramuru" to the medium of film. When *Caramuru* was projected in theaters, it included only the narrative portion of the miniseries, a format retained in the subsequent VHS version of the product.[27] This aspect of the TV-film-DVD metamorphosis may imply a stance on cinematic adaptations and their reception, even if the texts adapted are two earlier versions of the final product: as the DVD offers to be a malleable collage, *Caramuru* may be seen to propose, not unlike Julio Cortázar's *Rayuela*, a dialogical—rather than one-way—interface with spectators.

A closer look at *Caramuru*'s relationship with source-texts contributes to illustrating the film's complex relationship with both the past and the present. Generally, the film tends to leave spectators with the impression that historical representations, and their evaluation by viewers, are in flux and negotiable. In the DVD's "Making of …" documentary, director Arraes says that he wants to break with the idea of "fidelidade histórica" ["historical fidelity"] (n. pag.).[28] Arraes's declared intention is manifest, for example, in the film's outlandish wardrobe, the soundtrack drawn from the present,[29] the robust, varied, stylized, and expressive color scheme—brought to the story by artistic director Lia Renha, wardrobe designer Cao Albuquerque, and cinematographer Félix Monti—and the speech patterns of the would-be Tupinambá sisters—which Arraes has called "'*macunaimês*,' com expressões da Bahia, do Sul, do Nordeste"[30] (n. pag.) [113].[31] These qualities conspire to offer viewers a comedic vision of the past that seems light, open-ended, and adaptable—one that liberally interacts with earlier versions of the story and even allows for modulation through the participation of spectators.

Yet the film's apparently and declaredly laissez-faire approach to cinematic adaptation has a notable obverse. In general, viewers are faced with strategies that attempt to manipulate and determine, both textually and extra-textually, interpretations of the legend of Caramuru and Paraguaçu and its relevance for turn-of-the-millennium Brazil. The film and its marketing apparatus take a firm grip on what the Caramuru-Paraguaçu legend signifies, and refuse to let go. The production company of *Caramuru* seems to be careful to endorse the film's transformation of the foundational legend. One article that appeared in *O Globo,* the newspaper branch of the media corporation, several days before the November 2001 release of the film, compares this version to the earlier miniseries and characterizes its interpretation of the past as a "ficcionalização bem-humorada" ["good-humored fictionalization"] (Biaggio 8). This endorsement is followed two days later, after the 120 copies of the film are being shown in theaters, by the conglomerate's unequivocal championing of the film: "[É] um filme bacana, não vai decepcionar quem for assisti-lo. Faz com competência e absoluta coerência a transposição de um produto televisivo para a tela grande" (Almeida 7) [114]. The *O Globo* review celebrates the film's pop appeal and the skill with which it adapts the miniseries, and goes on to declare that the entire product carries "o selo de qualidade da Globo" ["Globo's seal of quality"] (Almeida 7).[32] What is more, the same review also characterizes in favorable terms the ideological implications of the film, calling it "uma bem-humorada definição da gênesis da moral brasileira" (Almeida 7)[33] [115]. As we will see, these code words of "ludic" and "good-humored" appear repeatedly in diverse contexts, though chiefly in Globo products, suggesting at least a tacit marketing accord among branches of the corporation to guide interpretations of the film.[34]

Inverted Captivities and Imagined Adaptations

Globo promoted the film in its newspaper on various fronts. Several days later in the technology section of the paper, another article touts *Caramuru*'s use of HDTV, comparing this aspect of the film to *Star Wars II*, a product not only of Hollywood, but also of the famously cutting-edge special effects company founded by George Lucas (Monteiro n. pag.). The article goes on to detail several of the advanced techniques employed by the filmmakers, and makes sure to highlight the disparity between the development of Globo and that of Brazil: "E dá-lhe tecnologia. Toda a criação do filme usou a alta tecnologia, mas na hora da projeção tudo é transmitido de forma analógica, já que o Brasil não tem sequer uma sala de projeção digital" (Monteiro n. pag.) [116].

Globo's endorsement of the film and its vision of Brazil continues to resonate. On the web page of the Brazilian Embassy in Washington, DC, the September 2005 "Calendar of Events" advertises a showing at the Brazilian-American Cultural Institute of *Caramuru*, funded by TAM Brazilian Airlines. The plot summary included divulges a reading that augments the interpretation suggested by the DVD's box cover: "Love blossoms between [Caramuru and Paraguaçu] and is enlivened by the arrival of Paraguaçu's sister, Moema [...], who makes clear her intention to not be left out of the fun. The formation of the first love triangle in modern Brazilian history is quickly sanctioned by the girl's father—Tupinambá chief, Itaparica" (n. pag.). The use of the words "enlivened" and "fun," as well as its winking, almost proud insistence that the father has sanctioned what today may seem more prurient or at least titillatingly unconventional, indicate the anonymous commentary's complicit perspective toward *Caramuru*'s version of this foundational moment in the history of Brazil.

Even more than the theatrical version, the DVD brings into clear relief the conflict between innocent and humorous irreverence and thorough endorsement of a stereotypical view of Brazilianness. While the film claims lack of historical fidelity, it also seeks to authorize its version of the past and how it informs present-day conceptions of identity. The design of the DVD picks up where *O Globo* left off in the authorization of *Caramuru*. As I have discussed, the plot summary of the film on the back cover of the DVD—the first words through which

Chapter Five

viewers, since the DVD's release in 2002, are introduced to the film—highlights the idea of nation as construction, as an invention realized through the building blocks of legend, or of nation as capable of nourishing itself perpetually on legend. What remains unstated, but permeates this production and its packaging, is the participation of the film in helping us to digest this crafted version of the tale. One of the DVD's special features is a section called "Apresentação" ["Presentation"], an explanation of the production of the film that manages to model for spectators an interpretation of the film. There is a short paragraph at the end of this textual section that crystallizes the film's relaxed and forgiving perspective on its discourse. The film, it says, "aborda de forma bem-humorada, lúdica e sensual o encontro de dois mundos e as muitas possibilidades de trocas afetivas e culturais" (n. pag.) [117]. This apologetic comment finds its complementary converse earlier, in a passage that appears in both the liner notes of the DVD and the "Apresentação" section of the extras in which the text extols the investigative rigor of the filmmakers and the ability of their own resuscitation of a foundational story set in sixteenth-century Brazil to explain, and even invent (or, rather, reinvent) Brazilian culture: "Para inventar o Brasil. Guel Arraes e Jorge Furtado pesquisaram as inúmeras influências que fazem parte da história do país—de Macunaíma, o texto de Camões, e somaram rigor com irreverência, humor com afeto, confronto com leveza em uma comédia histórica, focalizando a origem de alguns dos bons e maus costumes desta terra" (n. pag.) [118]. In addition to highlighting the film's wide-ranging anthropophagous methodology, these comments encourage viewers of the DVD to see investigative rigor underlying the humor and stylization of the narrative portion of the film. Of course, it is worth noting that the references emphasized in the quotation—in particular Mário de Andrade's *Macunaíma*, which will be discussed in more detail below—can hardly be considered primary historiographical sources (although Andrade did archival and ethnographic research before writing the novel). However, the cultural impact of such somewhat historically engaged cultural texts do punctuate Brazil's past and present, and the filmmakers proudly exploit these and other lingering influences in their ravenous rewriting of Brazil's past.

As the previously referenced components of the marketing apparatus of *Caramuru* make clear, proposed readings tend to fuse affirmations of mere playfulness with authorizations of the film's commentary on history and identity. Globo would seem to be hedging its bet, if you will, through such ostensibly contradictory claims. At the same time as the unified advocates of *Caramuru* suggest that the film be valued as a rigorously researched representation of Brazil's past or as a valid vehicle to define the nature and trace the origins of present-day Brazilian mores, the message of the marketing apparatus anticipates critiques that would point to a less-than-serious or inexact portrayal of the past by pointing out that the film's approach to representing history is all in good fun, and as such, spectators should not take it too seriously. However, these apparently diverging interpretive proposals conveniently collaborate and reveal the dual approach through which *Caramuru* realizes its re-invention of Brazil. The film and its marketing apparatus allow a reading of the film as a simple comedy unconcerned with historical fidelity, but simultaneously attempt to inspire faith in the film's portrayal of Brazil. Comedy is the sugar that coats the pill. In the end, being "good-humored" in no way excludes an influential articulation of Brazilian history and identity. On the contrary, the "ludic" tone of *Caramuru*'s inevitably serious portrayal of Brazilianness enhances the film's potential to impact spectator perceptions. Indeed, the film's style emerges from TV Globo esthetics and coincides with that of the hyper-popular Brazilian soap operas, which have a long tradition of treating serious, often historical, subjects in ways that appeal to a vast public (e.g., TV Globo's own 1976 "Escrava Isaura").[35]

One key component of *Caramuru*'s serious playfulness is the DVD's "[D]ocumentário interativo" ["Interactive Documentary"] (n. pag.). The back cover of the DVD calls attention to and authorizes the parrot-option, pointing out that the bird "levará você a uma incrível aventura pela história narrada por Marco Nanini" (n. pag.) [119]. If the spectator clicks the parrot each time it appears, and watches all of the associated documentary sections, the DVD approximates the original TV broadcast of the miniseries, which alternated the narrative with the documentary. The parrot-led documentary reinforces the fact that the film already encourages spectators to share Caramuru's

165

Chapter Five

perspective and empathize with him: we, like Caramuru, are adventurers discovering the New World, and the exotic wildlife of Brazil is our complicit, Malinche-like guide, an accomplice of our exploration through what the "Apresentação" of the DVD calls the "paraíso tropical que era o Brasil à época de seu descobrimento" (n. pag.) [120]. The documentary and its (rather Eurocentric) extratextual endorsement, then, seek in part to persuade viewers to accept a particular perspective on the past and the present by offering an entertaining, yet purportedly trustworthy account. The film's use of humor, it should be noted, exemplifies the varied and indirect tactics of persuasion enacted by the documentary: on the one hand it may be interpreted as confirming the less-than-serious attitude with regard to cinematic historiography, while on the other hand it may be seen to help seduce viewers into suspending a critical perspective.

While the documentary does seek carefully to guide our interpretation, the hyperlink option on the DVD to interpolate the film with the documentary also contributes, as I have suggested, to creating an open-ended, dialogical, feel to the interface of viewer and film. The nature of the interface may in fact encourage viewers to remain more actively engaged. The parrot's appearance is rather fleeting, which obliges spectators who have chosen this interactive option to pay close attention and keep their hand near the mouse or remote control. If they are interested in the documentary's interjections, they cannot allow themselves entirely to become lost in or lulled by the film's narration. Such an awareness deriving from the punctuation of the film by the appearance of the green bird, combined with the varied content of the documentary sequences, may tend to lead viewers to pause and reflect more on what they are seeing in the narrative portions of the film. Moreover, by implicating spectators in the process, the DVD may be attempting to make more transparent and malleable the nature of its adaptational anthropophagy. They are led to share and appreciate the perspective of the filmmakers, for viewers can choose the extent to which the film cannibalizes the documentary, and can therefore determine, in part, the dynamics of their own absorption of the material of the DVD.

Inverted Captivities and Imagined Adaptations

Caramuru is exemplary of a new technology-driven trend in cinematic production, distribution, and consumption. Websites on which national and international consumers can purchase in DVD-format very recent films have facilitated the distribution of Latin American cinema. Not only is there an increased opportunity for films to reach a broader audience and for a longer period of time, the very nature of the cultural and political projects carried out by the films has shifted, theoretically, along with the change in the interface between viewers and filmmakers. Specifically, the enhanced control over the viewing experience that spectators now enjoy can affect their understanding of films.[36] Moreover, corresponding to the international interest in the production of historical films—a great many Latin American films about the colonial period, since the beginning of the 1990s, have been international co-productions—this new streamlined online distribution carries national concerns into an international arena, and invites a broad range of spectators to share in the feast of historical retrospection.[37]

When viewers of the *Caramuru* DVD do choose to sample the documentary snacks that the parrot brings, they enter a world of information presented through a variety of media. One of the chief tools of the documentary is animation, which the cover-design of the DVD anticipates through a comic-like collage of photographs of the protagonists with word balloons that indicate the actors' names, as well as those of the director and writers. The cover complements small, dark photographic images of three of the supporting actors—Tonico Pereira, Debora Bloch, and Luís Melo—with larger cartoon-like versions of fragments of their faces.

The first parrot of the film/documentary option takes viewers to an explanation of the fifteenth-century Portuguese exploration of the coast of Africa. The narrator appears in period costume in the upper corner of a colorful, ancient-looking map, an animated part of the document. The effect of "bringing to life"—animation derives from the Latin *anima*, or "soul"—history, or of incorporating it into the present, is bolstered by the visualization, through a video-game motif, of a Portuguese ship traveling down the African coast.[38] As it advances, large pixels of the ocean disappear before it: as the Portuguese "win

Chapter Five

the game," points are racked up at the bottom of the screen. It is immediately after this scene that the documentary draws the analogy between Vasco da Gama and Neil Armstrong. One aspect of the visual realization of the comparison illustrates, like the video game, the methods by which the documentary digests the past. As the scratchy recording of Neil Armstrong announcing the "giant leap for mankind" plays, viewers see within a moonscape collage a cut-out of a familiar painted image of the European explorer in a long shot—modified only by the presence of a bubble-shaped space helmet—hopping toward the camera. *Caramuru*'s strategy in this moment of the historical documentary seeks to make comprehensible, through a goofy analogy, a distant event. At the same time, however, the conflation of disparate historical moments here indirectly echoes the film's assertions that the past and the present should be treated as inseparable, and that license exists not only to evoke history in order to underscore that inevitable continuum, but also to take control of the dynamic, to irreverently devour a colonized past and incorporate it into the present.

Another example of the potential effectiveness of the parrot surfaces in the moment in which Caramuru first encounters the Tupinambás. The documentary option of the DVD here offers short and frequent interventions that help to subvert the initial and lasting Eurocentric perspective on the "discovery." Clicking on the bird produces not only a list of indigenous groups that emphasizes the heterogeneity of the native population of Brazil; it also, at another moment, juxtaposes European cultural assumptions with those of the Tupinambás.[39] When viewers are returned to the narration of the film, the camera allows them to shift slightly from sharing the visual perspective of the protagonist, Caramuru, to that of the Tupinambás, who cease to pursue the young painter and focus on something above and beyond him, out to sea. After a quick series of shot/reverse shots—of the group from Caramuru's perspective, and a cowering Caramuru from theirs—the camera follows what the group's attention is focused on and cuts, but only Caramuru looks, to an extreme long shot of a dozen Portuguese ships: the fleet of Pedro Álvares Cabral.

The DVD documentary and the cover design coincide with—more specifically, preview, reflect, and reinforce—*Caramuru*'s relationship with the past. Animation and cartoon—often the vehicles of caricature and parody—epitomize the film's tendency to stylize, and underscore the potential malleability of any raw materials derived from history. Even more than history, however, legend and myth lend themselves to such reshapings. The DVD version of *Caramuru* re-shapes this well-seasoned shape-shifter, Caramuru, in part through devices such as cartoon and animation. These techniques evoke the imagination of the viewers and ask them to suspend disbelief and fill in the gaps, participate in the re-creation, and consequently take ownership of the concretization of the legend and all that it implies about Brazilianness.

Carlos Alberto Mattos makes reference to what I would call the cartoon-like, or stylized, quality of the main characters of the narrative itself, and ties their nature in the film to a Brazilianness personified by the figure of Macunaíma, a primary touchstone of the film identified as well, as we saw earlier, by director Arraes and the DVD's "Apresentação" section. Mattos writes: "Todos têm aquela falsa pompa típica de personagens de teatro infantil, embora no contexto prevaleçam a malícia e o comentário antropológico. O Brasil inventado por Guel Arraes é um Brasil de gibi juvenil, cheio de subtextos irônicos sobre o caráter (falta de?) macunaímico que se convencionou agregar à imagem dos brasileiros: preguiçosos, espertos, sensuais, expansivos, etc." (7) [121]. A central figure of anthropophagy-as-cultural-strategy in twentieth-century Brazil, the character Macunaíma was created in *modernista* Mário de Andrade's 1928 novel, *Macunaíma, o herói sem nenhum caráter* [*Macunaíma*], and revived in Joaquim Pedro de Andrade's 1969 film, *Macunaíma*, a cinematic adaptation of the earlier written text that anticipates, in its portrayal of the protagonist, *Caramuru*'s cartoonish representational techniques.[40]

Mattos's, Arraes's, and the DVD's references to Macunaíma emphasize the place of *Caramuru* within the broad context of anthropophagous cultural production in Brazil, and underscore, as I have signaled, how the filmmakers have cannibalized diverse source texts. Arraes insists that *Caramuru* "teve por base os modernistas, e Macunaíma talvez tenha sido a grande luz para a nossa criação. Não quanto à trama ou o personagem mas em relação ao olhar que lança sobre o Brasil" (n. pag.) [122].

Chapter Five

Specifically, Arraes points to Macunaíma in reference to the conception of the film's Tupinambá characters and the analogy that *Caramuru* proposes with present-day Brazilians; he adds: it was Macunaíma "que orientou o projeto, e ele é índio e vira branco e é brasileiro. Por mais que se diga que descendemos de índios, brancos e negros, se colocássemos uma índia para fazer o papel de mocinha em um filme ou seriado de TV, ela seria vista com olhar estrangeiro. Assim, as índias do filme são quase garotas de praia, mas funcionando como índias de época" (n. pag.) [123]. Arraes's articulation of Macunaíma's influence helps to explain the liberal fusion of diverse identities in the design of the Tupinambá characters of *Caramuru*. This often anachronistic amalgam of social markers attempts to articulate an abstracted, tongue-in-cheek summary of modern-day Brazilianness, which the cartoon device helps to highlight. Like Mário de Andrade's novel, although in different ways, Arraes's film points to *mestiçagem* as the origin of Brazilian national identity, and cannibalism as a unifying concept. The film's conflation of contemporary, culturally hybrid Brazilians and indigenous cannibals suggests that viewers should embrace anthropophagy, at least as a cultural strategy.

The film's use of language, exemplified by the scene in which Paraguaçu first encounters Caramuru, contributes to this anthropophagous comment on identity. She speaks a modern-sounding Brazilian Portuguese (rather than Tupi), which the film ironically opposes, in a moment of linguistic exaggeration, to the incomprehensible mock-Continental Portuguese of Caramuru. The film, through humor, thus celebrates Brazilian Portuguese, treating it—in a way clearly not meant to be taken seriously—as natural and always present. Although it playfully suggests that Brazilians uniquely speak authentic Portuguese, the film exhibits here a real, proud understanding of the result of centuries of linguistic anthropophagy.

Beginning with the title sequence, and periodically throughout the film, *Caramuru* employs the same use of cartoon as the cover of the DVD. The title sequence buttresses the theme of morphing or transformation of the past that the design of the DVD cover employs. The credits gradually materialize over an abstraction of what appears to be a sixteenth-century manuscript. The visual effect is of a palimpsest: the filmmakers

Inverted Captivities and Imagined Adaptations

and cast, the design suggests, overlay and modify—or devour and digest—the past. The opening of the film culminates in the cartoonish, morphing esthetic anticipated on the DVD's cover and alluded to in the title sequence. Spectators see alternating images of Paraguaçu and Diogo/Caramuru—each alone in their separate spaces across the Atlantic and each contemplating the nocturnal sky—and hear an introductory voiceover narration, which ends with this commentary about Caramuru and Paraguaçu: "Vai-se tornar Rei do Brazil. A história dos dois juntos vai virar lenda" [124]. These words accompany a brief image of Paraguaçu's hand-written and illustrated book—the film's false source text—opened to a place that seems to record these first moments of the narrative portion of the film: the images of them in the book are cartoon-like snapshots of scenes just represented of the two: contemplative, alone, and separated by the ocean. The film declares they will become legendary, but also exploits the implication of a faithful textual basis for the story. Later, the stylizing device suggests that Caramuru possessed an (anachronistically) ethnographic eye. His paintings of people from Paraguaçu's village imply the exactitude and faithful durability of an eyewitness perspective. They are slightly blurred freeze-frames of people performing everyday duties, that would presumably be used later to illustrate Paraguaçu's book.

Much later, when Paraguaçu begins to write her book during the trip back from Europe, her words accompany an animated version of the now-familiar cartoon-like freeze-frames. Viewers see in this form a summary of the film's key moments, as recalled by Paraguaçu, through brief cartoonish clips. What follows is Paraguaçu's autobiographical synopsis of the action of the film up to that point:

> No fundo da mata virgem, o céu incendiou-se de araras vermelhas.[41] Depois fez um silêncio tão grande que alguma coisa estava pra acontecer. Eu ainda nem sabia que ia topar com o Diogo, mas tinha me enfeitada toda ... pintando o rosto ... e os distintivos [a word coined in the film to denote *seios*] com semente de urucum. Fiquei muito linda! Naquela tarde brincamos até mais não ... E conhecemos que o paraíso existia. Sendo o paraíso bem ali ... onde a gente estava ... mas o destino de Diogo era virar herói de nossa gente. E de repente, correu pelo mato uma notícia de assombro! Caramuru, o filho

Chapter Five

> de Trovão, desceu do céu para ser "Rei dos Tupinambás!" Ele Rei, eu sua Rainha, descobrimos as terras além do mar. Beijamos ... casamos ... e escrevemos nosso nome no livro! Agora o navio vai de novo, atravessando o mar ... e eu vou atravessando um livro novo com esses sucedidos que vocês acabaram de ouvir. E, por fim, o navio e o livro vão trazendo a gente de volta, até a praia onde essa história toda começou. [125]

In addition to reinforcing the device by which the film suggests that it has diligently consumed a sixteenth-century text, Paraguaçu's writing reveals aspects of the film's somewhat inconstant commentary on the nation. To wit, her references to the "virgin forest" and "paradise" demonstrate the adoption of a European worldview,[42] yet the way in which she describes their trip to Paris in terms of overseas discovery de-centers the traditional Eurocentric perspective on the encounter.

In *Caramuru*'s final scenes, the film confirms that it has adapted an imaginary source text written by Paraguaçu and illustrated by Caramuru. This influential moment merges two of the ways that the film, through the issue of adaptation/transformation, intersects with anthropophagy. When Caramuru and Paraguaçu return to Brazil, laden with the latest European fashions for the whole tribe, Paraguaçu excitedly recounts her adventures to her sister, Moema. Besides outfitting her in new clothing and explaining her new role as "amante" ["lover"] since Caramuru is now married—Moema feels encouraged when she learns that her main duties will be sexual—Paraguaçu reveals her most treasured possession: the autobiographical tale that she has written.

Paraguaçu opens the book and begins to read, once again allowing viewers access to the film's fictional main intertext. She describes the aftermath of their arrival:

> O nosso pai e seus guerreiros gostaram foi muito das roupas da francesa. E quando iam pra guerra só se vestiam com elas. E ficavam mais valentes ainda! O quadro que Diogo fez de Moema foi pra Europa! Ganhou fama e nossa praia encheu de gente querendo casar com ela. Mas Moema desejava ser esposa não. Amante só o que ela queria ser. Diogo me ensinou a amar ... e eu ensinei ele a querer bem ... [126]

Inverted Captivities and Imagined Adaptations

While she is reading, the film represents through action everything that she describes. This explicit and authorizing correspondence between the words of a film's purported source text and the action of the film recalls one of the chief persuasive devices in *Descobrimento do Brasil*, Humberto Mauro's 1937 adaptation of Pêro Vaz de Caminha's 1500 letter of discovery. The intertextual relationship with Mauro's film and the coincidence of adaptational strategies are underscored during *Caramuru*'s documentary scenes. When the narrator reiterates the long-standing metaphor that calls Caminha's letter Brazil's "certidão de nascimento" ["birth certificate"], wavy words from the letter stream across the screen, and the film re-enacts the moment of arrival that the text describes: "[N]este dia, ao entardecer, avistamos terra, primeiramente um monte muito alto e redondo e outras serras baixas ao sul e planícies com grandes arvoredos" [127]. The subsequent images, accompanied by continued reading from the letter, are brief clips from *Descobrimento do Brasil* that relay Mauro's version of the first moments of Portuguese-Amerindian encounter.

At the end of the enactment of each scene that Paraguaçu's book describes, the characters are frozen and stylized, like the supporting cast on the cover of the DVD. By freezing the characters in cartoon, the film may be seen either to concretize its own version of Brazil's birth, or perhaps to propose that the characters are once again now poised to re-enter the malleable realm of legend, or even, simply, to poke fun at "serious" historiography by laying bare its necessarily limited correspondence to reality. Viewers may choose to consume this stuff of history and fiction and incorporate them, re-morphed, into their own ever-changing conception of Brazilian identity. In this sense, the film would both model and facilitate its brand of cannibalism.

When the film reaches the moment when Paraguaçu proclaims that Caramuru taught her to love, the camera shows a close-up of the book propped on her leg as she writes. The viewer can see, upside down, the image of the same words that she is saying, and the blank page that sits below the latest line that she is writing. *Caramuru* suggests here that what remains of the film is what remains for her to write. The camera recedes and tilts up to show the whole of the kneeling Paraguaçu as well

Chapter Five

as the legs of Caramuru as he approaches from behind while she writes: "E fomos felizes agora ... que é melhor que pra sempre ..." The following dialogue in which the couple discuss how to end the text ensues:

> Caramuru: Ficou pronto?
> Paraguaçu: Quase quase.
> C: E como é que termina?
> P: A gente se beija ... e fim.
> C: Original!
> P: Só falta escrever.
> C: Espera! Não é a nossa história?
> P: É.
> C: Então primeiro a gente beija ... depois você escreve.
> [128]

Caramuru is concerned with the faithful, all-encompassing correspondence between Paraguaçu's text and the reality that it attempts to represent. Until they decide what the end of the story is and actually take that action, he insists, she cannot write the last lines of her tale. Caramuru's naïveté about the potential for unmitigated fidelity in historiographical discourse is certainly intended to be a device of comic relief. Nonetheless, by suggesting its own strict adherence to a textual source, the film also reveals an inclination to authorize through adaptation. However, the entire dialogue that we hear in this scene, of course, is not recorded by Paraguaçu, which perhaps inadvertently exposes the absurdity of the film's suggestion of exact correspondence between text and film, and thus potentially compromises the device.

Just as the dialogue between Caramuru and Paraguaçu ends and they prepare to kiss, the voice of the film's narrator, which has punctuated not only the documentary but also the narrative portion of the film, returns, and qualifies the film's implication that it has exactingly adapted a source text written by Paraguaçu and illustrated by Caramuru. He says: "A história de Caramuru e Paraguaçu é baseada em fatos reais, e também em outras histórias, em parte reais, em parte inventadas. É verdade que eles se casaram na França. É verdade que eles viveram no Brasil. E é verdade que eles viraram lenda"[43] [129]. His full-disclosure comments recall the tone of the documentary. Here

Inverted Captivities and Imagined Adaptations

the narrator indirectly disclaims the fidelity that the image of the book in the film powerfully suggests. Nonetheless he, and the film generally, try to inspire spectators' confidence in the project of the film. As the narrator has been speaking, the camera has been pulling back from a medium shot of the couple kissing to a long shot of the two. It is in the moment that the narrator says that they became a legend that the film fixes the couple in the act of their embrace, while carrying their visual stylization to a new level. Viewers see the blurry, abstracted image as if through wavy glass. The camera then moves back a bit more and exposes a frame that surrounds the image, as well as its nature: the portrait is apparently a watercolor illustration by Caramuru on the final page of the text on which Paraguaçu is writing "Fim." The voice of the narrator reappears to provide a "historical" summary of the future that awaits the two reality-based figures, Caramuru and Paraguaçu. Though the film is careful to admit that its version of the two is legendary and fictionalized, the dose of historical authority at its conclusion attempts, in my evaluation, to make this cannibalization of the past, and what it means for the present, easier to swallow. *Caramuru*'s meticulously executed but declaredly non-rigorous historical re-creation—ironic though that may seem—reflects the nature of legend: how a historical blur eventually crystallizes and becomes lodged in a collective imagination. And perhaps the precise nature of the film's lack of historical rigor brings to the surface a quality that to differing degrees exists in any historiography—whether it be written or cinematic, based on legend or on hard statistical data—that the historiographical text inevitably reflects the present in which it was produced. And *Caramuru* certainly ensures that spectators recognize that it is talking about modern-day Brazil.[44]

As we have seen, *Caramuru* enacts a varied return to anthropophagy. The DVD version of the film's sundry and sometimes innovative strategies for cannibalizing history and cultural texts are deployed in an effort to present the filmmakers' vision of Brazil. The anthropophagous devices that *Caramuru* uses, such as the imaginary source, the exploitation of a television esthetic, and the cartoon-like stylization, help to reify and authorize the filmmakers' reading of the story of Caramuru and Paraguaçu and to imprint it on the context of the present. *Caramuru*'s

Chapter Five

heterogeneous box of tools at times approaches a conception of the text/spectator interface that would appear to encourage viewers to intervene actively in the reinvention of Brazil. However, far more than an aid in empowering spectators to achieve a critical distance vis-à-vis history and legend, these are particularly well-equipped means to take control of both the consumption of the past and the reception of this transformation. Overall, these devices serve to bolster the way that the film attempts to persuade viewers to embrace its reinvention of Brazil, which at times gestures at critiquing a colonialist, Eurocentric discourse, but, in general, leaves such discourse firmly intact. Similarly, the film's use of humor is two-sided. Guel Arraes and Jorge Furtado, as well as Globo's marketing apparatus as seen, for instance, in the DVD's "Apresentação" and the film reviews in *O Globo*, characterize this vision as comedic and irreverent, an unrepentant departure from (the always ultimately vain attempt at) historical accuracy. However, while the genre of comedy may help to digest the past by making it more fun and familiar, it also conspires to ensure the re-absorption of a stereotypically eroticized and exoticized Brazil that is symbolized primarily through the union of Portuguese men and indigenous women.

Caramuru and *Brava Gente* tweak the dynamics of anthropophagous adaptations. The use of imagined sources inverts the equation. What is incorporated and transformed is not, as with other cinematic adaptations of colonial literature in Latin America, the persistent voice of the colonizer that not only survives in the archive, but also inevitably continues to echo in the imagination. What is incorporated and transformed in these films is rather an inherently malleable imaginary stand-in. Viewers access this surrogate in *Caramuru* through a paternalistically guided collaboration, but one nonetheless in the hands of an indigenous woman. *Brava Gente*, for its part, also exposes us to its apocryphal sources through the hands and voice of an indigenous woman, but its invertion of the formula is distinct. Despite their differences, both *Brava Gente* and *Caramuru* separately converge on a fertile formula for addressing issues of identity: they take advantage of the flexibility of fiction at the same time that they gesture toward a textual grounding, and exploit the appeal of a national literary or historiographical source.

Epilogue
The Unwieldy Dynamics of Anthropophagous Adaptations

The final scene of Eduardo Rossoff's *Ave María* uncovers a risk inherent in anthropophagous adaptations. This case, like several others covered in this book, involves the cinematic reconstruction of a national icon. The film's protagonist, María Inez (a mestiza transmutation of Sor Juana), has rallied the population against the injustices perpetrated by the colonial apparatus and, for her actions, has been burned at the stake. In the aftermath of her martyrdom, the film depicts a leader of the Catholic Church cynically planning to commission a painting of María as the embodiment of the Mexican people. The priest intends to propagate what promises to be a resonant image, thereby making use of María as a revised and influential representative of identity. Specifically, the Church hopes to smother the flame of resentment and dampen the spark of rebellion among the indigenous, mestizo, and even Creole populations of New Spain. Through his attempted instrumentalization of María's portrait, Rossoff essays a critique of creating and deploying an icon in order to shape attitudes in and about society. It is not hard to see a correspondence between the portrait and his own film. At the culminating moment of the director's transformation of Sor Juana into a stylized Mexican representative, a ploy designed to expose the core of colonial tyranny, Rossoff disrupts his own iconizing by analogy. By criticizing what amounts to a simulacrum of his own project, the director unwittingly undermines his argument. Nicolás Echevarría's *Cabeza de Vaca* similarly suffers the rebellion of its own critical devises; rather than iconizing in an effort to condemn the same tactic in colonialist hands, Echevarría's film exoticizes as a means to critique the perspective of the colonizer.

Epilogue

Whatever the filmmakers' intentions, anthropophagous adaptations, by seeking the persuasive retooling and reuse of influential colonial-era icons of identity—rather than promoting an intertextual dialogue or a critical outlook on historiography—risk unfavorable comparison to the imaginary legacy of colonialism that many of the films censure. The dual nature of myth—its promise and its peril—creates a second potentially destabilizing byproduct of filmmakers' efforts to take complete control of a colonial intertext and fashion it into a focused commentary on identity. The very myth that invites reshaping at the same time threatens to revert rapidly to the amorphous state, a forgotten iteration among an amalgam of variants. In addition to bringing to light the self-sabotaging potential of the films, *Ave María*'s portrait scene makes explicit the occasionally disruptive and always influential past manipulations of the stories that the directors cinematically revisit. Each of the Latin American filmmakers studied herein taps the legendary status and affiliated wealth of the tales and figures that they revive in order to offer the viewer a new national icon. However, the iconizing process proves slippery. The evasiveness lies in the negotiation of the layers of myth and legend through which the filmmakers must access their colonial source. Any new film about Columbus, for instance, dialogues just as much or more with the figure's existence in the popular imagination as with his texts. These anthropophagous adaptations interface with still-powerful tenets of identity in Latin America precisely because of that power. Yet in the process of revising an enticingly malleable myth, they create a product that likewise invites reshaping. Such is the case with *Nuevo mundo* and *La otra conquista*'s intervention on the textual life of the Virgin of Guadalupe.

A third facet of the precarious dynamics of anthropophagous adaptations involves the defective attempt of some films to take a firm enough hold of their colonial source and compel it to convey the film's thesis. The films' disparate dialogues are often punctuated with captivating, yet potentially disruptive intertextual interjections. In reanimating inveterate icons the directors inevitably invite into their conversation a multiplicity of voices. The directors each aim seamlessly to take over and transform the mark left by colonial literature, and to persuade the cinematic audience of their transformation. By means of their adaptational tactics they hope to assume an unassailable control over the textual source, thereby promoting a particular interpretation of the stories that they retell. However, despite the filmmakers' best efforts, their projects contain potential disruptions that risk rendering their assertions unmanageable. Two examples of potentially unmaneuverable intertextual interjections, *Caramuru: A Invenção do Brasil*, and *Ave María*, are the variety of media incorporated into the former, and the latter's invitation to reread Sor Juana. Such intertextual intrusions may mitigate control over the texts and confound the desire to delimit readings of the films. At the same time, they also may enrich or productively complicate the cinematic projects. Indeed, whether or not they intend it, some of the filmmakers allow an ambiguity and interpretive plurality that derives from relinquishing a degree of control over the films' cannibalization of the past. In general, however, these anthropophagous adaptations attempt convincingly to remake the past in a mold that the specific contexts of production inspire. Latin American cinematic efforts to overhaul the legacy of colonial literature—unwieldy though such endeavors may be—continue to leave their mark on the ways in which identity is understood.

Appendix
English Translations

Each English translation is keyed to a passage in the text by its number, which corresponds to the number in brackets in the text. The translations in brackets below are mine.

Chapter One
Re-creating Caminha: The Earnest Adaptation of Brazil's Letter of Discovery in
Descobrimento do Brasil (1937)

1   "They seem to me people of such innocence that, if one could understand them and they us, they would soon be Christians, because they do not have or understand any belief, as it appears [...] [A]nd furthermore, Our Lord gave them fine bodies and good faces as to good men; and He who brought us here, I believe, did not do so without purpose. And consequently, Your Highness, since you so much desire to increase the Holy Catholic Faith, ought to look after their salvation, and it will please God that, with little effort, this will be accomplished" (29).

2   [arrived in a land that he newly discovered],
    [people naked as in their first innocence, docile and peaceful];
    [because it is very convenient and necessary for the navigation to India]

3   "And then they stretched themselves out on their backs on the carpet to sleep without taking any care to cover their privy parts, which were not circumcised, and the hair on them was well shaved and arranged. The captain ordered pillows to be put under the head of each one, and he with the headdress took sufficient pains not to disarrange it. A mantle was thrown over them, and they permitted it and lay at rest and slept" (13).

Translations to Pages 24–29

4   [I attempted to narrate the event as if I were a reporter filming on Cabral's ship.]

5   [gentleness of an affectionate mother],
[slaveringly condescending smile]
[an expression of beatitude that belies the deeds that they were carrying out in Africa and Asia and finally in this hemisphere].

6   [The discoverers scour the virgin forest in search of wood for the cross.]

7   "new shirts and red hats and two rosaries of white bone" (14).
"From thence the other two youths departed and we never saw them again" (15).

8   "And then many began to arrive; and [...] took some kegs [...] and filled them" (14).

9   "The other two whom the captain had on the ships, and to whom he gave what has already been mentioned, did not appear again, from which I infer that they are bestial people and o very little knowledge; and for this reason they are so timid. Yet withal they are well cared for and very clean, and in this it seems to me that they are rather like birds or wild animals, to which the air gives better feathers and better hair than to tame ones. And their bodies are so clean and so fat and so beautiful that they could not be more so" (23).

10 "many of them, dancing and diverting themselves" (21).

"Mestre João encounters, with his astrolabe, 17°S Latitude [...] Diogo Dias [...] began to dance amoung them [...] making [...] a remarkable leap" (21–22).

11 "[...] on the other side of the river were many of them, dancing and diverting themselves before one another, without taking each other by the hand, and they did it well. Then Diogo Dias, who was revenue officer of Sacavem, crossed the river. He is an agreeable and pleasure-loving man, and he took with him one of our bagpipe players and his bagpipe, and began to dance among them, taking them by the hands, and they were delighted and laughed an accompanied him very well to the sound of the pipe. After they had danced he went along the level ground, making

many light turns and a remarkable leap which astonished them, and they laughed and enjoyed themselves greatly. And although he reassured and flattered them a great deal with this, they soon became sullen like wild men and went away upstream" (21–22).

12 "she did not think to spread it much to cover herself" (32).

13 "their privy parts [were] so high, so closed, and so free from hair that we felt no shame"

"her lack of shame [was] so charming, that many women of our land seeing such attractions, would be ashamed that theirs were not like hers" (16).

14 "We interpreted this so, because we wished to" (13).

15 [Intellectual collaboration and historical verification]

16 [we sighted the islands]; [we continued our journey]

17 [... April 21, we came across some signs of land.]

18 [glory of the Church and Portugal!]
[Long live Portugal!]

19 [an almost documentary description of the adventure],

20 [the intention of the creators of the best Brazilian film was not to denigrate the invader; it was to improve him, to lend him qualities that he did not have.]

21 [[t]o educate is to aid citizens in acquiring habits that have significance in the society in which they live [...] [I]ndividuals cannot educate themselves alone. Individuals can instruct themselves alone, but educating themselves alone is impossible.]

22 [Brazil is good because it doesn't make racial distinctions. Because it doesn't have prejudice based on color, nor on religion.]

23 [Today, there is only one Brazil! There is only one flag! There is only one Leader! This is why the Brazil of today is different from the Brazil of yesterday. This is why now we can affirm, with joy and patriotic enthusiasm, that BRAZIL IS GOOD.]

Translations to Pages 41–54

24 [the protection of the national historical and artistic patrimony], [stands out for its special significance]

25 [Recalling great historical deeds in a pleasant, picturesque, or even anecdotal way constitutes without a doubt a useful service to popular culture and to the improvement of the civic spirit of the masses [...] [W]e attempt here to convey patriotic lessons with a constructive meaning, notions and lessons that can become fixed without effort in the memory of all people, young and old.]

26 [Pero Vaz de Caminha's letter, the first document written about Brazilian lands, is a hymn to the beauty of primitive Brazil's savage nature and exuberance. Brazilians did not have, for many long years, a vision so acute as that of Cabral's prophetic scribe.]

27 [it can be said that no government had yet comprehended our necessities nor appreciated the importance of this problem, as did President Getulio Vargas.]

28 [an environment of near cultural reciprocity that resulted in the maximum utilization of the values and experiences of the backward peoples by the advanced one]

29 [Not even contact and mixture with indigenous or adventitious races made us as different from our overseas grandparents as sometimes we would like to be [...] We can say that from there came the current form of our culture; the rest was material that conformed badly or well to that form.]

30 [the most Christian of the modern colonizers in their relations with peoples considered inferior]

Chapter Two
Exoticizing the Nation in *Cabeza de Vaca* (1991) and *Como era gostoso o meu francês* (1971)

31 [There are many sequences that seem to be filmed by a documentary filmmaker from 1530.]

32 "The women cover their private parts with grass and straw" (106).

[They do not want to become pregnant, to avoid their breasts becoming flabby after giving birth, for they very much prize their breasts, which are very nice.]

[very beautiful bodies and very good faces, their hair short and thick, almost like the silky tail of a horse.]

33   [That was my passion: the Indians and above all, not indigenous issues at the level of ethnography or folklore, but rather mysticism and the technique to reach ecstasy. That was my obsession.]

34   "And the others dried the flesh of the ones who died, and the last to die was Sotomayor; and Esquivel dried his flesh and, by eating it, survived until the first day of March" (58).

35   "[A]nd their hunger [is] so great that they eat spiders and ants' eggs and worms and lizards and salamanders and snakes, and vipers such as kill the men that they bite; and they eat earth and wood and everything they can lay their hands on, and dung of deer and other things I will not mention; and I firmly believe that if there were stones in that land they would eat them" (61).

36   "they tried to make us into medicine men, without examining us or asking for credentials, for they cure illnesses by blowing on the sick person, and by blowing and using their hands they cast the illness out of him" (49).

37   "And seeing our resistance, one Indian told me that I did not know what I was talking about when I said that what he knew would be of no use to me, for stones and other things that grow in the fields have virtue, and by using a hot stone and passing it over the stomach he could cure and take away pain; and we, who were superior men, surely had even greater virtue and power" (49).

38   "all of us became medicine men, though I was paramount among us in daring and in attempting any sort of cure" (73).

39   "Our Lord, and His mercy, willed that as soon as we made the sign of the cross over them, all those for whom we prayed told the others that they were well and healthy" (50).

40 "Then the people offered us many prickly pears, for they had heard of us, and how we cured folk, and the marvels that Our Lord did by our hands" (66–67).

41 [the mysterious white and bearded man who arrives from the East]

42 [Because I am more human than you!]

43 [effort to involve spectators]

Chapter Three:
Reimagining Guadalupe in *Nuevo mundo* (1976) and *La otra conquista* (1998)

44 [We want to underscore the present-day relevance of these themes, the continuity of the issues covered by the film, given that the process of *mestizaje* and syncretism—and the violence implicit in said processes—does not pertain only to the past or to a moment in Mexico's history over which we have prevailed. I hope that *La otra conquista* contributes to the dialogue about a current reality of which all we Mexicans are part.]

45 [in an absolutely sincere and respectful way, in the sense that this film does not attempt to be the definitive version or the "new history" of the post-Conquista.]

46 [He asks why you are going to judge them, and says that you should leave them in peace.]
[Why are they abandoning the villages?]

47 [You did it. At very least, you helped Master Don Manuel, or your companion who escaped.]

48 [—We should send emissaries to the South and to the North; we have to unite all of the tribes. Only united can we triumph.
—Our sweet Lady would not forgive us if we leave the god of the Spaniards alive.
—With their own weapons we should finish them off. My men are awaiting the signal.
—Mine too, but we need all of the villages.
—The Spaniards will destroy our gods.

Translations to Pages 94–98

—We will die before being defeated.
—The power of the Spaniards is in their weaponry, but we have faith.
—We will triumph if we trust the sweet Lady. Each person should choose.]

49 [Soon the day will come in which the tears from our eyes reach the gods. May their justice descend swiftly on the world. This painting will be useful. Even if we are going to die.]

50 [This image appeared in my cell, bathed in a light brighter than the sunrise. I heard a voice softer than that of the goddess of death which said to me, "Leave here and take this canvas to my people." And I responded, "My Lady, the door is closed and I have no words to describe your beauty." And she said to me, "If you want all of the doors will open." I fell to my knees and prayed. When I opened my eyes I found her at my feet. I went to the door and the door was open. Again I heard the voice and this time it said to me: "Manuel, you, who are known and respected by all, tell my people that God, moved by so much suffering, has commanded me to give them consolation. Tell my beloved children to trust me, because I am flesh of their flesh, and I know better than anyone of their infinite neglect. I want to hear their problems in their prayers so that I might cry with them. Tell them to not make war, for all will die, Indians and Spaniards, and if that happens the great mission of forming a new race will not be realized. Tell the Spaniards that I do not want more violence. I hold them responsible before our Lord for all of their cruelty toward my people. I demand that the Spaniards see them as equals, for all of us are children of God. It is my will that from today on everyone, Indians and Spaniards, be one people, a single people, united by love for me and for Jesus, our Lord.]

51 [Topiltzin [is] a natural son of the emperor; his "other conquest" has to do with the identification and appropriation that he carries out with respect to an icon of the Virgin Mary, in order to recover his own mother goddess, Tonantzin [...], which in a certain sense is what happened in our country with the Virgin of Guadalupe.]

52 [In 1519 the Conquistador Hernán Cortés and his diminished army penetrated Tenochtitlán [...] After two years, Aztec civilization [...] was trying to adapt to a new world.]

53 [All of this happened to us. We saw it. It came our way. This was our destiny. But by giving voice to the paper, our essence will live.]

54 [Your codex is the word of our people. It is worthy of our Mother Goddess Tonantzin.]

55 [Look at the Virgin. This beautiful woman is Mary, the mother of God. Yours is no more than a fistful of stones.]

56 [Don't say anything. Don't do anything. Don't judge me for being here.]

57 [I'm not responsible for the barbarism that is committed in the name of our God.]

58 [Your blood is worth nothing!]

59 [He says that your words in no way correspond to the image that they have of the great lady with white skin.]

60 [There [in the temple] our truth went up in smoke. [...] In the end, we share the same belief, Fray Diego, though [we came] from different worlds.]

61 [This beautiful woman is no more or less real than yours. What matters now is that this is the new truth.]

62 [an invitation to dialogue, to reflect on our origins and respect our differences]

Chapter Four:
Sor Juana Inés de la Cruz and
the Retooling of a National Icon in *Ave María* (1999)

63 [No one was more effective than Inez when it came to subjugating the Indians.]

64 [telescope, sundial, obsidian mirror, astrolabe, magnets]

65 [I'm interested in telling a story of feelings, of the heart, and for that reason I tried to surround myself with good actors. There

are battles in the film, villages plundered and burned, but that is part of history. What interests me is touching the spectator with values.]

66 [a form of showing and teaching the whole world about the fortitude and intelligence of many women of that era who did not polish their innate talent]

67 [a dramatic essay on the condition of thinking women of New Spain in the seventeenth century]

68 [feminine rereading of the Other Conquest that was lacking in the superb trilogy *Retorno a Aztlán-Cabeza de Vaca-La otra conquista*]

69 [story that takes place in the seventeenth century about the legend of a valiant woman who takes on genocide, religious intolerance, racism, and fanaticism]

70 [hypothetical / synthetic / allegorical / emblematic]

71 [I think that in certain eras we experience existential crises, and we may be passing through one of them now: we are all interested in recovering moral and ethical values.]

72 [sadly, even in our time differences between people gravely affect our existence.]

73 [mirror of prejudice and intolerance in modern times]

74 [metaphors of the world of today that make it possible to accentuate problems of the present, like genocide, fanaticism, religious intolerance, racism, etc.]

75 [a story that speaks to us of intolerance, that speaks of the repression of women, that could take place in any era, that unfortunately continues happening today; there continues to exist much intolerance toward other races and beliefs.]

76 [In fact, Eduardo [Rossoff] characterizing as interesting the presentation to the public, *in these pre-electoral times*, of this kind of story.]

Translations to Pages 118–125

77 [constructs a mestiza heroine of such strong and contradictory features that on her own she represents the spiritual and social conflict of the Mexican people during the Conquest]

78 [[c]ontrary to what one might think, the film is not about religion; rather it is fundamentally about intolerance and injustice.]

79 [Whoever might see your ballad could say what they said about Egypt: that such a pyramid was built for a mosquito.]

80 [Who would think that a poor ballad of mine would deserve your insult, for it seems to me that any praise applied to the unworthy is affront, and not applause?]

81 [[e]numeration (without order and randomly) of great names from the history of, or fables about, ancient peoples and from laws]

82 "When, divine geniuses, / O sweetest swans, tell me when / my trifles ever deserved / to occupy your attention? / Why such praise of me? / How explain such panegyrics? / Has distance really the power / to magnify my likeness? / What view can you have of my stature, / to go and build a Colossus / whose lofty height ignores / the poor original's lowness?" (103).

83 [Is chaos preferable to order imposed by a woman? Is intelligence my transgression?]

84 [I cannot live without my work. It is as if someone has ripped out my heart. I am empty.]

85 [Oath that Mother Juana Inés de la Cruz made, signed with her blood, of her faith and love for God, upon abandoning nonreligious studies in order to pursue, free from this affection, the path of perfection]

86 [And as a sign of how much I desire to spill my blood in defense of these truths, I sign with it, on this 5th day of March of the year 1794.]

87 [Shots, often gratuitous, of María's cleavage or her naked body do not fail to satisfy the lasciviousness of the audience.]

Translations to Pages 126–139

88 [My life of sin wells up in me like a sickness. I should consume myself in it until the sickness is extinguished. I should burn until I am empty and clean. Then I will pray.]

89 [I want to thank you. I see clearly that you have been the instrument of God. If it had not been for you I would not have suffered so much. And if it weren't for that pain I never would have changed.]

90 [As you know, I am returning to my mother's village. I regret having abandoned them for so long. And I have adored my Spanish father and I have adored the Conquistador and the price my mother had to pay. How can I forgive myself?]

91 [God does his work through María Inez.]

92 [Devout exercises for the nine days before the supremely pure Incarnation of the Son of God]

93 [I hear her voice.]

94 [She is a *mestiza*.]

95 [a symbol of the peaceful union between Spain and the New World.]

96 [only love can cure the wounds of this place.]

97 [Love for God?
No, father, just love.]

98 [No, María. It's pure science.]

99 [She was no different from you or me, at least not at first.]

100 [And so the years pass for us. It is for me to tell the story, and for you to decide.]

101 [like a Mexican from Texas and knows our culture very well]

102 "My original, a woman, / sends me on to you" (63).

191

103 "These lying pigments facing you, / with every charm brush can supply / set up false premises of color / to lead astray the unwary eye. / Here, against ghastly tolls of time, / bland flattery has staked a claim, / defying the power of passing years / to wipe out memory and name. / And here, in this hollow artifice— / frail blossom hanging on the wind, / vain pleading in a foolish cause, / poor shield against what fate has wrought— / all efforts fail and in the end / a body goes to dust, to shade, to naught" (95).

Chapter Five:
Inverted Captivities and Imagined Adaptations in *Brave Gente Brasileira* (2000) and *Caramuru: A Invenção do Brasil* (2001)

104 [This film sets out to build on a real event that occurred in Mato Grosso do Sul, in the region of the Pantanal, in 1778.]

105 [In 1793, twelve years after the massacre at the fort, the Guaicuru signed a peace treaty with the Portuguese empire. Of their descendents, only the Kadiwéu survived. Close to 1,000 live today on a reservation in Mato Grosso do Sul.]

106 [That is the way our ancient war song ends. I can sing other stories of the Guaicuru as well ... good ones and bad ones. But they are today's stories, stories of the wars of today.]

107 [I am a monkey ... because I have body hair ... and you paint your skin because you don't have it ... because you are a person.]

108 [Here it's also difficult to know exactly what is or isn't a sin.]

109 [The colony cannot be more than a passing moment in our lives, a difficult and tortuous lesson.]

110 [The invention of a country called Brazil]
[experiencing at that moment the first love triangle in Brazilian history]

111 [ludic and good-humored]
[one of the most remote stories of the popular Brazilian imaginary]

112 [in a chattery, hallucinatory rhythm, leaves no time to breathe or look at landscapes. He has his eye on an audience that perhaps isn't even interested in that, educated as it is by perceptive velocity and indifference to reflection.]

113 ["*macunaimês*," with expressions from Bahia, the South, the Northeast]

114 [[I]t is a cool film. It won't disappoint those who go see it. It transposes the product made for television to the big screen with competence and absolute coherence.]

115 [a good-humored definition of the genesis of Brazilian morals]

116 [And bring on the technology! Advanced technology was used throughout the entire creation of the film, but at the time of projection everything was transmitted in analog, since Brazil does not have even one digital-projection theater.]

117 [*Caramuru: The Invention of Brazil* treats the encounter of two worlds and the many possibilities of affective and cultural exchange in a good-humored, ludic and sensual way.]

118 [To invent Brazil. Guel Arraes and Jorge Furtado researched the innumerable influences that are part of the history of the country—from Macunaíma to Camões's [...] [*Lusíadas* (*The Lusiads*)]—and blended rigor with irreverence, humor with affection, confrontation with lightness, in a historical comedy, focusing on the origin of some of the good and bad customs of this land.]

119 [will take you on an incredible adventure through history narrated by Marco Nanini]

120 [tropical paradise that Brazil was at the time of its discovery]

121 [They all have that affected ostentation typical of characters in children's theater, though in this context malice and anthropological commentary prevail. The Brazil invented by Guel Arraes is a children's-comic-book Brazil, full of ironic subtexts about the (lack of?) Macunaimic character that became

Translations to Pages 169–172

conventional to incorporate into the image of Brazilians: lazy, clever, sensual, effusive, etc.]

122 [had the [Brazilian] Modernists as a base, and Macunaíma has perhaps been the great inspiration ["a grande luz," literally, "great light"] for our creation. Not in terms of the plot or the character, but rather in relation to the gaze it casts on Brazil.]

123 [oriented the project, and he is an Indian who turns white and is Brazilian. No matter how much we say that we descend from Indians, whites and blacks, if we used an Indian to play the part of the female protagonist in a film or a TV series, she would be seen with a foreign gaze. Hence the film's Indians are almost beach babes, but in the role of period Indians.]

124 [He will become King of Brazil. The story of the two together will become legend.]

125 [In the heart of the virgin forest, the sky ignited with red macaws. Then there was a silence so large that something was going to happen. I didn't yet know that I was going to cross paths with Diogo, but I had adorned myself completely ... painting my face ... and my breasts with annatto seed. I was very beautiful! That afternoon we played until we couldn't anymore ... And we came to know that paradise exists. Paradise was right there ... where we were ... but Diogo's destiny was to become a hero of our people. And suddenly, amazing news spread through the land! Caramuru, the son of Thunder, descended from the sky to be "King of the Tupinambás!" He being King, and I his Queen, we discovered the lands beyond the sea. We kissed ... We got married ... and we wrote our name in the book! Now the ship is on its way once again, traversing the sea ... And I am traversing a new book with these events that you have just heard. And, finally, the ship and the book are taking us back, all the way to the beach where this story began.]

126 [Our father and his warriors really liked the French clothes. And when they went into battle those were the only clothes they would wear. And they became even more courageous! The painting Diogo did of Moema went to Europe! She became famous and our beach filled up with people wanting to marry

her. But Moema didn't want to be a wife. She just wanted to be a lover. Diogo taught me how to love … and I taught him tenderness.]

127 [[T]hat day, at sunset, we saw land, first a very high and round mountain and other lower ranges to the south and plains with great forests.]

128 [And we were happy now … which is better than forever.]

[Caramuru: Is it ready?
Paraguaçu: Just about.
C: And how does it end?
P: We kiss … and … the end.
C: How original!
P: I just have to write it.
C: Wait! Isn't it our story?
P: Yeah.
C: Then first we have to kiss … and then you write.]

129 [The story of Caramuru and Paraguaçu is based on real facts, and also on other stories, in part real, in part invented. It's true that they got married in France. It's true that they lived in Brazil. And it's true that they became legend.]

Notes

Introduction

1. See Rolena Adorno for similar observations regarding literature treating the colonial period (905, 907–08). Helen Tiffin locates a comparable tendency in other post-colonial contexts, arguing that "the rereading and rewriting of the European historical and fictional record are vital and inescapable tasks" (95).

2. By "colonial films" I mean films set in Latin America's colonial period. I use this term throughout for the sake of efficiency.

3. I am not the first to characterize cinematic production about the colonial period in terms of cannibalism. See, for example, Williams, Alcides Freire Ramos, and Madureira (*Cannibal Modernities*). For example, Madureira characterizes *Como era gostoso*'s relationship to its source text in terms of cannibalization (127). For a concise history of anthropophagy as cultural strategy and the broad-reaching symbolic viability of Andrade's articulation of it, see João César de Castro Rocha's essay "Let Us Devour Oswald de Andrade: A Rereading of the *Manifesto antropófago*," the introductory article of "Anthropophagy Today?", a special issue of *Nuevo Texto Crítico*, published in 1999. For a more recent re-evaluation of Oswaldian anthropophagy, see Luis Madureira's incisive 2005 essay "A Cannibal Recipe to Turn a Dessert Country into the Main Course: Brazilian *Antropofagia* and the Dilemma of Development." For a re-evaluation of Brazilian *modernismo* and the part played by Andrade, among others, see Randal Johnson's insightful articles "Brazilian Modernism: An Idea Out of Place?" (1999) and "Tupy or Not Tupy: Cannibalism and Nationalism in Contemporary Brazilian Literature and Culture" (1987). Regarding the reimergence of cannibalism in 1960s and 1970s Brazil, see, for example, Randal Johnson's essay "Cinema Novo and Cannibalism: *Macunaíma*" (1995); Stam and Xavier's "Transformation of National Allegory: Brazilian Cinema from Dictatorship to Redemocratization" (esp. 306–08); and Shohat and Stam's section "Modernist Anthropophagy," in *Unthinking Eurocentrism* (307–12). A fundamental resource for the topic of cannibalism in Latin America in general is Carlos Jáuregui's groundbreaking book *Canibalia: Canibalismo, Calibanismo, antropofagia cultural y consumo en América Latina* [*Canibalia: Cannibalism, Cabelism, Cultural Anthropophagy, and Consumption in Latin America*] (2008). Now and henceforth, title translations in brackets are my translation.

4. Ella Shohat has called Oswald de Andrade and other Brazilian *modernistas* "postcolonial hybrids *avant la lettre*" (135). The results of intercultural contact has been theorized in an array of assessments of Latin American culture originating in Spanish America, Brazil, and the United States that have attempted to describe with no lasting consensus through other sundry permutations of anthropophagy, as well as through concepts such as transculturation, syncretism, hybridity, misplaced ideas, the in-between, mimicry, heterogeneity, and *mestizaje/mestiçagem*.

5. Here and henceforth, title translations appearing in brackets are mine. Other title translations are of published editions of the work in question.

6. Andrade turns a cannibalistic eye not only on colonialism, but also on what we might call neo-colonialism. For him and his Brazilian *modernista* companions, anthropophagy was a way of coming to terms with their emulation of avant-garde Europe while remaining uniquely Brazilian. Rocha signals both the Romantic anticipation of this battle cry of the *modernistas*—explaining that nineteenth-century novelist José de Alencar "reinstated anthropophagy as an intrinsically positive idea-force" (8)—and the Tropicalist return to anthropophagy in the 1960s and 1970s. With regard to Tropicalism, he writes: "Highly influenced by Modernism, and above all by a national/cosmopolitan dialectic which constituted the core of the *Manifesto antropófago*, Tropicalism revived anthropophagy" (9).

7. As Shohat and Stam, in *Unthinking Eurocentrism,* put it in a section on Columbus, "Cinematic recreations of the past reshape the imagination of the present, legitimating or interrogating hegemonic memories and assumptions" (62).

8. A notable exception is Shohat and Stam's 1994 *Unthinking Eurocentrism: Multiculturalism and the Media,* which identifies and subdivides a corpus of films about the Conquest in various sections of the book (e.g., "Revisionist Film and the Quincentennial" [71–77] and "Slavery and Resistance" [77–81]). See also Cynthia Leigh-Stone's brief but informative 1996 article "The Filming of Colonial Spanish America," which reviews ten films made in and outside Latin America.

9. Useful surveys and filmographies dealing with Latin American films about the colonial period have been produced. In 1994, an important volume was published by the Cineteca Nacional in Mexico: *Los mundos del Nuevo Mundo* [*Worlds of the New World*]. The editors, on the back cover of the book, emphasize that their text is intended to facilitate research on such thematically important, but understudied, films (Calderón et al. n. pag.). Significant, as well, is Rafael de España's 2002 *Las sombras del Encuentro* [*The Shadows of the Encounter*]. And Luís Trelles provides a wide-reaching history of Spain's and Spanish America's cinematic production on the colonial period in *Imágenes cambiantes* [*Changing Images*] (1996).

10. The majority of research on colonial films has been conducted by historians. Examples include partial coverage of the colonial period in collections of essays such as Donald F. Stevens's 1997 volume *Based on a True Story: Latin American History at the Movies* (which covers chiefly films produced by non-Latin American directors), and Mariza de Carvalho Soares and Jorge Ferreira's 2001 collection *A História Vai ao Cinema: Vinte Filmes Brasileiros Comentados por Historiadores* [*History Goes to the Movies: Twenty Brazilian Films Commented on by Historians*]. Additionally, Robert A. Rosenstone devotes a chapter of his 1995 book *Visions of the Past: The Challenge of Film to Our Idea of History* to

Latin American historical cinema, and Natalie Zemon Davis highlights films such as Tomás Gutiérrez Alea's *La última cena* in her study from 2000, *Slaves on Screen: Film and Historical Vision.*

11. Somewhat more similar to the analytical spirit of the reading that I perform here, but more narrow in its scope, is Emperatriz Arreaza's 1996 book *Redescubriendo el descubrimiento* [*Rediscovering the Discovery*], which, through a Marxist analysis, takes into account the contemporary political and cultural implications of how the discovery specifically is replayed in films and other cultural texts from Latin America and the United States. Even more relevant are both Bruce Williams's 1999 article "To Serve Godard: Anthropophagical Processes in Brazilian Cinema," which focuses on two films, and Alcides Freire Ramos's 2002 book *Canibalismo dos fracos* [*Cannibalism of the Weak*], which studies one in detail. They carry out analyses of Brazilian historical film about the colonial period that intersect with my own in recognizing, albeit in ways distinct from this book, the relevance of the critical tradition of cultural cannibalism for understanding how cinema reconfigures the past. Important as well, but nonetheless different from my treatment of colonial films, are Stam's historically and generically expansive, yet geographically focused, 1997 book *Tropical Multiculturalism: A Comparative History of Race in Brazilian Cinema and Culture*; Santiago Juan-Navarro and Theodore Robert Young's edited volume *A Twice-Told Tale: Reinventing the Encounter in Iberian / Iberian American Literature and Film* (2001), a valuable contribution, but one that focuses more on literature than film; essays from the 1993 volume *Mediating Two Worlds: Cinematic Encounters in the Americas,* ed. John King, Ana M. López, and Manuel Alvarado (e.g., Franco, Xavier); and Yari Pérez Marín's study "Lecturas en celuloide: El personaje indígena latinoamericana en el 'cine de época'" ["Celluloid Readings: The Latin American Indigenous Character in Period Films"]. See also Cileine I. Lourenço's "Negotiating Africanness in National Identity: Studies in Brazilian and Cuban Cinema" (1998); Luisela Amelia Alvaray's "Signs of History: Difference in Audiovisual Accounts of 'Discovery and Conquest'" (2004), which looks at European, US, and Spanish American reflections on the past related to the 1992 quincentenary of the Spanish arrival in the Americas; and Claudia Barbosa Nogueira's "Journeys of Redemption: Discoveries, Re-discoveries, and Cinematic Representations of the Americas" (2006). With regard to novels about the colonial period, see, for example, Kimberle S. López's 2002 book *Latin American Novels of the Conquest: Reinventing the New World*, which links such historical novels to the quincentenary and the millennium.

12. Even Nicolás Echevarría's 1991 *Cabeza de Vaca* exemplifies that motives to produce colonial films typically originated outside of the context of the quincentenaries. Despite the year of its release, partial funding by the Comisión del Quinto Centenario [Commission of the Quincentenary], and association of the historical figure Álvar Núñez

Notes to Pages 5–7

Cabeza de Vaca with the quincentenary, the film was initially slated for release in 1986, rather than 1991 (Pérez Turrent 112).

13. For instance, Eduardo Rossoff, the director of *Ave María*, attributes current cinematic interest in the colonial period to a sense of millennial crisis (Ramírez Hernández, "Ave María" 10).

14. For a study of *La monja alférez* that takes these contextual factors into consideration, see Gordon, "The Domestication of the Ensign Nun."

15. The government's support of historical films acted as one means of censorship, by allowing and attempting to contain the cinematic revival of the nation's historical patrimony (Peña 202; Pereira dos Santos, "Le cinema novo" 72).

16. Censorship, especially since 1968, had become particularly fierce in Brazil ("Reasons behind Fade of Brazil's 'Cine Novo'" 68).

17. He has commented that the government did provide funding for historical film, but only films that they found to be consistent with the ideals that they were trying to promote (Mraz, "Pereira dos Santos" 645). Pereira dos Santos recalls that at first the censors were not inclined to accept such a "nudist colony" (Paranaguá, "Nelson Pereira dos Santos" 17), but that ultimately the film—fifteen minutes leaner—was approved in Brazil (Paranaguá, "Nelson Pereira dos Santos" 18). See also Sadlier (58) for an account of Pereira dos Santos's navigation of government censorship.

18. Zuzana Pick has observed that interest in race in Latin American cinema intensified in the 1970s and took on a more critical tone (8), a new concern that directors, especially in Brazil and Cuba, realized in the context of historical films (126).

19. *O Guarani* and *Iracema*, novels by the nineteenth-century Brazilian writer José de Alencar set in the colonial period, have been cinematically adapted a number of times and illustrate the lasting fascination in Brazil with the nation's colonial past. See Stam for a discussion of such "Indianist" films ("Cross-cultural Dialogisms" 178). Gustavo A. García briefly mentions *Tiempos Mayas* [*Mayan Times*] (11), and Andrés de Luna, who authored an informative chapter on Mexican historical cinema, "The Labyrinths of History," included in the volume edited by Paulo Antonio Paranaguá, *Mexican Cinema*, makes a similarly limited mention of the film *Cuauhtémoc* (174). Luís Trelles Plazaola, who gives a slightly more detailed plot summary of this last film (54), opines that *Cuauhtémoc* supported "el espíritu de reafirmación y defensa de lo nacional" ["the spirit of reaffirmation and defense of the national"] (54). Aurelio de los Reyes, in *Cine y sociedad en México, 1896–1930* [*Cinema and Society in Mexico, 1896–1930*], writes that the film exalts the indigenous population (226), and that historical cinema in Mexico began with *Cuauhtémoc* (208). G. García calls *Cuauhtémoc* optimistic and categorizes it with several films that he calls "nationalist reaffirmationists" (12–13).

20. E.g., *La noche de los mayas* (*Night of the Mayas*; Mexico, 1939, dir. Chano Urueta); *Ganga Zumba* (Brazil, 1963, dir. Carlos Diegues); *Xica*

da Silva (Brazil, 1976, dir. Diegues); *Ajuricaba: O Rebelde da Amazônia (Ajuricaba (Brazil)*; Brazil, 1977, dir. Oswaldo Caldeira); *Quilombo* (Brazil, 1984, dir. Diegues); *Túpac Amaru, el último Inca (Túpac Amaru, The Last Inca;* Peru, 1984, dir. Federico García Hurtado); *Chico Rei* (Brazil, 1985, dir. Walter Lima Júnior); *El otro Francisco (The Other Francisco*; Cuba, 1975, dir. Sergio Giral); *Nuevo mundo*; *La última cena*; *La otra conquista*; and *Brava Gente Brasileira.*
21. E.g., *Como era gostoso*; *Cabeza de Vaca*; *La otra conquista*; *Jericó (Jericho*; Venezuela, 1990, dir. Luis Alberto Lamata); *Cautiverio feliz*; *Hans Staden* (Brazil, 1999, dir. Luiz Alberto Pereira); *Brava Gente Brasileira*; *Caramuru: A Invenção do Brasil.*
22. E.g., *La virgen que forjó una patria (The Saint That Forged a Country*; Mexico, 1942, dir. Julio Bracho); *Inconfidência Mineira ([The Mineiran Conspiracy]*; Brazil, 1948, dir. Carmen Santos); *Os Inconfidentes (The Conspirators*; Brazil, 1972, dir. Joaquim Pedro de Andrade); *Independência ou Morte ([Independence or Death!]*; Brazil, 1972, dir. Carlos Coimbra); *Tiradentes, O Mártir da Independência ([Tooth-puller, The Martyr of Independence]*; Brazil, 1976, dir. Geraldo Vietri); *Bolívar, sinfonía tropikal [sic] ([Bolívar, Tropikal Symphony]*; Venezuela, 1979, dir. Diego Risquez); *Tiradentes ([Tooth-puller]*; Brazil, 1999, dir. Oswaldo Caldeira); and *Gertrudis Bocanegra* (Mexico, 1992, dir. Ernesto Medina).
23. E.g., *Anchieta Entre o Amor e a Religião ([Anchieta: Between Love and Religion]*; Brazil, 1932, dir. Arturo Carrari); *El santo oficio (The Holy Office;* Mexico, 1974, dir. Arturo Ripstein); *La última cena*; *Anchieta, José do Brasil ([Anchieta: Joseph of Brazil]*; Brazil, 1977, dir. Paulo César Saraceni); *Nuevo mundo*; *Sermões, A História de Antônio Vieira ([Sermons: The Story of Antônio Vieira]*; Brazil, 1989, dir. Júlio Bressane); *Jericó*; *Fray Bartolomé de las Casas* aka *La leyenda negra ([Fray Bartolomé de las Casas* aka *The Black Legend]*; Mexico, 1993, dir. Sergio Olhovich); *Kino* aka *La leyenda del padre negro ([Kino* aka *The Legend of the Black Father]*; Mexico, 1993, dir. Felipe Cazals); *Ave María*; *Palavra e Utopia ([Word and Utopia]*; Portugal and Brazil, 2000, dir. Manoel de Oliveira).
24. E.g., *Sor Juana Inés de la Cruz* (Mexico, 1935, dir. Ramón Peón); *La monja alférez* (Mexico, 1944, dir. Emilio Gómez Muriel); *Xica da Silva*; *Yo, la peor de todas (I, The Worst of All*; Argentina, 1990, dir. María Luisa Bemberg); *Carlota Joaquina, Princesa do Brazil (Carlota Joaquina, Princess of Brazil*; Brazil, 1995, dir. Carla Camurati); *Ave María*; and *Desmundo* (Brazil, 2002, dir. Alain Fresnot).
25. E.g., *Christophe Colomb* aka *La vida de Cristóbal Colón y su descubrimiento de América Latina (The Life of Christopher Columbus and His Discovery of America*; France and Spain, 1916, dir. Gérard Bourgeois); *Colón* aka *España y sus grandezas: Colón (Columbus* aka *Spain and Its Grandeur*; Spain, 1949, dir. Fernando Fernández Ibero); *Christopher Columbus* (UK, 1949, dir. David MacDonald); *Christopher Columbus:*

The Discovery (UK/USA/Spain, 1992, dir. John Glen); and *1492: Conquest of Paradise* (UK/USA/France/Spain, 1992, dir. Ridley Scott).

26. See Robert Rosenstone's insightful evaluation of diverse national approaches to representing history on film in his chapter "Re-visioning History: Contemporary Filmmakers and the Construction of the Past," in *Visions of the Past: The Challenge of Film to Our Idea of History*.

27. I have in mind films such as Cuban director Sergio Giral's *El otro Francisco*, praised for good reason by historians like Robert Rosenstone (185–86) and John Mraz ("Recasting Cuban Slavery" 104). I would argue that such self-reflective films also adroitly direct their adaptational dialogue and craft devices that determine a spectator's interpretation, even if their urgent goal is to raise consciousness and debunk the deceptions of traditional approaches to history.

28. Such a study might find inspiration in Robert Stam's notion of "intertextual dialogism." As Stam asserts, "[a]daptations, then, can take an activist stance toward their source novels, inserting them into a much broader intertextual dialogism [...] In the broadest sense, intertextual dialogism refers to the infinite and open-ended possibilities generated by all utterances within which the artistic text is situated..." ("Beyond Fidelity" 64).

29. See Joanne Hershfield ("Assimilation and Identification") for an analysis of how the process of Álvar Núñez Cabeza de Vaca's assimilation in the film *Cabeza de Vaca* encourages a re-evaluation of New World identity and otherness.

30. The boom in Mexico's cinema industry in the 1940s, at the center of its Golden Age, was partly due to the support that the United States, through the Office of the Coordinator for Inter-American Affairs, redirected from Argentina to Mexico. Specifically, the OCIAA facilitated raw film stock and investments in film studios, after Mexico sided with Allied forces during World War II (Fein 129).

31. Rockefeller's Office of the Coordinator for Inter-American Affairs also produced a number of documentaries in order to promote cultural understanding among the nations of the Americas, and Mexico and Brazil stand out as the main subject of the OCIAA's films. Many of these can be accessed through "The Internet Moving Images Archive: Movie Collection" (http://www.archive.org/movies/index.html), a section of *The Internet Archive* (http://www.archive.org) that contains hundreds of digitized films from the Prelinger Collection related to North American culture in the twentieth century. Among the OCIAA's films on Latin America, and Brazil and Mexico in particular, are: *Brazil Gets the News* (1942); *The Day Is New* (1942), a film about Mexico City; *Brazil at War* (1943); *Good Neighbor Family* (1943); and *Gracias Amigos* (1944).

32. See Carl Mora's discussion of the favorable reception in Latin America of the two Disney films (73–74).

33. See, for example, Earl Fitz's 2002 article in *Hispania*, in which he indicts the tendency among scholars of "Latin American" literature to exclude or treat superficially Brazilian texts and encourages scholars to take advantage of understudied but abundant connections between Brazilian and Spanish American cultures (440–42).

34. Ana López points out the ubiquity and popularity of Mexican films in Brazil, and throughout Spanish-speaking Latin America (7). And Brazilian filmmaker and critic Alex Viany has spoken of the influence of Mexican films on Brazilian directors (Schvarzman, "Humberto Mauro" n. pag.).

35. With respect to Spanish and Spanish American cinema, Luís Trelles confirms that Mexican cinema has shown the most interest in the colonial period (51).

Chapter One
Re-creating Caminha: The Earnest Adaptation of Brazil's Letter of Discovery in *Descobrimento do Brasil* (1937)

1. The films coincide in considering the colonial period an ideal site to comment on the nation, although they vary widely in their approach, ranging from a somewhat problematic attempt to adapt faithfully a tale of European captivity among the Tupinambá (*Hans Staden*), to an invented tale of an eighteenth-century indigenous rebellion against the Portuguese (*Brava Gente Brasileira*), to a would-be comedic effort to retell the story of a foundational love affair—in this case a threesome composed of a young Portuguese man and two indigenous women (*Caramuru*). Such an intentioned fascination with colonial encounters, although most notably realized by *Cinema Novo* directors such as Nelson Pereira dos Santos and Carlos Diegues in the 1960s and 1970s, was inaugurated in Brazil's silent period, when several adaptations were produced of the nineteenth-century Romantic novels *O Guarani* and *Iracema*, both set in the colonial period. Stam argues that "[l]ike the 'Indianist' novelists, the film-makers saw Brazil as the product of the fusion of the indigenous peoples with the European element into a new entity called 'the Brazilian'" ("Cross-cultural Dialogisms" 178).

2. *Descobrimento do Brasil* was the most ambitious film produced to date about the colonial period—it was preceded in sound cinema only by *O caçador de diamantes* [*The Diamond Hunter*] (1934), an eighteenth-century story of adventure—and had a budget exceeding that of all previous Brazilian films. For an extensive examination of the importance of Mauro for Brazilian cinema, see Sheila Schvarzman's 2003 *Humberto Mauro e as imagens do Brasil* [*Humberto Mauro and the Images of Brazil*].

3. For other readings of Mauro's film and other versions of the story of initial Portuguese presence in Brazil see, for example, Schvarzman (*Humberto Mauro*), Stam (*Tropical Multiculturalism*), Gatti, and Morettin.

4. See Skidmore (*Brazil* 5–7) for a discussion of the much-debated and unresolved claim that the Portuguese intentionally "discovered" Brazil.

5. Citations are from the Cortesão edition of the "Carta." Translations are from *The Voyage of Pedro Álvares Cabral to Brazil and India from Contemporary Documents and Narratives.*

6. In his 1994 edition of the *Carta*, Jaime Cortesão explains that attempts to imagine the Brazilian nation have perennially depended on Caminha's letter as a fundamental source (15). Elsewhere, Cortesão refers to the tradition of calling the letter Brazil's "birth certificate" (*A Carta* [1943] 3). Several critics have discussed how the letter has been used as a vehicle for nationalist rhetoric (see, for example, Cunha and Braga-Pinto).

7. When I speak of *ideology*, I follow the broad definition offered by Stuart Hall: "By ideology I mean the mental frameworks—the languages, the concepts, categories, imagery of thought, and the systems of representation—which different classes and social groups deploy in order to make sense of, define, figure out and render intelligible the way society works" (26).

8. Stam similarly argues that the film "sacralizes European conquest" and portrays an "infantilized" indigenous population that "embrace[s] Christianity and the culture of Europe as irresistibly persuasive" (*Tropical Multiculturalism* 8). Mauro's portrayal of the encounter deviated from the "nativist" reading of the *Carta*, which reached an apogee in Brazil's Romantic period. During the era just following Brazil's relatively smooth but somewhat qualified independence from Portugal, nineteenth-century writers attempted to reject Portuguese parentage and to locate the roots of modern national identity in "native" Brazil by exploiting the frequent instances in which Caminha's text exalts the natives as well as the land. A key example of the exaltation of the Brazilian landscape characteristic of the period is Gonçalves Dias's "Canção do Exílio" ["Song of Exile"], which he wrote while studying in Coimbra. Mauro coincides with the "nativists" in considering Caminha's letter a source of national pride. However, while Mauro celebrated the Portuguese, he presented a condescending portrait of the Amerindians.

9. Oswald de Andrade also carried out his own brief poetic adaptation of Caminha's letter, though the composition maintains a clear ironic distance from the letter (*Pau-Brasil* 69–70).

10. Oswald de Andrade was not the only modernist writer in Brazil to attempt to define the nation's identity by reexamining the colonial period and instrumentalizing the Brazilian native. See Johnson's informative study "Tupy or Not Tupy: Cannibalism and Nationalism in Contemporary Brazilian Literature and Culture," which discusses at length Andrade's *Antropofagia*, and distinguishes its approach to identity from that of another group, *Verde-Amarelo* (later *Anta*), initiated by authors such as Plínio Salgado and Cassiano Ricardo. *Verde-Amarelo* shared with Andrade "a concern with overcoming Brazil's imitativeness and dependence on Europe" (Johnson, "Tupy" 43), but resurrected a neo-Indianism (47) reminiscent of the Brazilian Romantics, and upheld a naïve vision of the encounter and a paternalistic stance with regard to Brazil's indigenous population that anticipated a similar view evident in Mauro's film.

11. *Descobrimento do Brasil* was not entirely out of place at the end of the twentieth century. Mauro's project anticipated the inevitable, if problematic, celebratory (rather than critical) side of the quincentenary.

12. Despite the film's condescending attitude toward the native population of Brazil, Mauro's attention to linguistic and ethnographic detail does reflect a real respect.

13. Since the photocopies provided to me by the Cinemateca in Rio de Janeiro often did not include page numbers, I do not reference the pagination of the following sources: Capovilla, Merten, Pina, Aquino, "Há 50 Anos" ["Fifty Years Ago"], and "O Descobrimento do Brasil" ["The Discovery of Brazil"].

14. More recent criticism concurs with G. Ramos's critique: see Maurice Capovilla (n. pag.) and Stam (*Tropical Multiculturalism* 8).

15. As I will discuss shortly, the majority of the film's intertitles are quotations from Caminha's letter. For an examination of how the First Mass has been periodically instrumentalized, see Cunha.

16. A native wood, pau-brasil, was one of the Portuguese colony's first and most important natural resources, and one that the Portuguese quickly exploited. To wit, Mauro's film dedicates several minutes to a collaborative felling of the first tree to the amazed delight of the natives.

17. Only the letter describes the men as naked, a discrepancy that I will address later.

18. The letter describes how the pair briefly runs away and returns in the nude: "[V]ieram os outros que nós leváramos, os quais vinham já nus e sem carapuças" (Caminha 160); "[C]ame the others whom we had brought. These were now naked and without caps" (14).

19. Caminha also writes: "Mas junto a ele, lançavam os barris que nós tomávamos; e pediam que lhes dessem alguma coisa. Levava Nicolau Coelho cascavéis e manilhas. E a uns dava um cascavel, a outros uma manilha, de maneira que com aquele engodo quase nos queriam dar a mão. Davam-nos daqueles arcos e setas por sombreiros e carapuças de linho ou por qualquer coisa que homem lhes queria dar" (160–61); "They did not actually enter the boat, but from near by, threw them in by hand and we took them, and they asked us to give them something. Nicolao Coelho had brought bells and bracelets and to some he gave a bell and to others a bracelet, so that with that inducement they almost wished to help us. They gave us some of those bows and arrows for hats and linen caps, and for whatever we were willing to give them" (14–15).

20. The passage to which I refer is: "ali por então não houve mais fala nem entendimento com eles, por a berberia deles ser tamanha que se não entendia nem ouvia ninguém" (Caminha 161); "Then for the time there was no more speech or understanding with them, because their barbarity was so great that no one could either be understood or heard" (15). Cortesão provides the following interpretation in a note: "Carolina Michaëlis observa que *berberia* está aqui por *barbaria*, falta de civilização que, naquela conjuntura, se traduzia por vozear excessivo" (205); ["Carolina Michaëlis observes that *berberia* is here for *barbaria* [barbarity], lack of civilization which, in that context, was attributed to them for excessive yelling"].

21. Although Mauro mentions Mestre João in his narrative, he says nothing about such readings on shore with his instrument. The likely source for Mauro's invented intertitle comes from a letter that João himself wrote to the king: "Senhor: O bacharel mestre João, físico e cirurgião de Vossa Alteza, beijo vossas reais mãos. Senhor: porque, de tudo o cá passado, largamente escreveram a Vossa Alteza, assim Aires Correia como todos os outros, somente escreverei sobre dois pontos. Senhor: ontem, segunda-feira, que foram 27 de abril, descemos em terra, eu e o piloto do capitão-mor e o piloto de Sancho de Tovar; tomamos a altrua do sol ao meio-dia e achamos 56 graus, e a sombra era setentrional, pelo que, segundo as regras do astrolábio, julgamos estar afastados da equinocial por 17º, e ter por conseguinte a altura do pólo antártico em 17°, segundo é manifesto na esfera" (qtd. in P. R. Pereira 67–68); "Señor: I, the bachelor Master John, physician and surgeon of Your Highness, kiss your hands. Señor: because Arias Correa as well as all the others have written to Your Highness at length concerning all that happened here, I shall write only regarding two points. Señor: yesterday, Monday, which was the 27th of April, we went on shore, I and the pilot of the chief captain and the pilot of Sancho de Tovar; and we took the height of the sun at midday; and we found 56 degrees, and the shadow was north. By this, according to the rules of the astrolabe, we judged that we were 17 degrees distant from the equinoctial and consequently had the height of the Antarctic pole in 17 degrees, as is manifest in the sphere" (36–37).

22. See Stam (*Tropical Multiculturalism* 8) for a similar interpretation.

23. Similarly, at the beginning of the film, Mauro repeatedly uses the cinematic convention of a map that shows Portugal on the right and Brazil clearly marked and labeled as such on the left, accompanied by an animated ship that travels unswervingly along a direct route to the new Portuguese colony, as if the route were predetermined. The final shot of the film is complementary: the camera shows the Portuguese that have remained behind leaning against the cross, implying that Portugal, supported by and supporting the religion that they have brought to the New World, is there to stay.

24. Roquette-Pinto and Mauro, along with Taunay, also collaborated in the production of *Bandeirantes* (1940), another film treating and glorifying the colonial period (see Capovilla n. pag.).

25. *Descobrimento do Brasil*'s association with renowned intellectuals has led several critics to locate the primary responsibility for the film's message not with Mauro, but with the experts (and government official) mentioned in the credits (Capovilla). Schvarzman talks about how Mauro found himself "sob a influência de Roquette-Pinto" ["under the influence of Roquette-Pinto"] ("Humberto Mauro" n. pag.). Hernani Heffner, as well, makes reference to how Mauro put himself "sob a esfera de influência de Roquette-Pinto" ["under the sphere of influence of Roquette-Pinto"] (18). The influence exerted by Roquette-Pinto and others does illustrate that *Descobrimento do Brasil* formed part of a network of projects at work in Brazil in 1937, but in no way minimizes Mauro's profound involvement in the design of the film. Director (*and* screenplay writer) Mauro possessed acute and first-hand knowledge of the *Carta* and therefore undoubtedly played a substantial role in reading and rewriting the colonial text.

26. Luís de Pina also likens certain sequences to silent film, and lauds the "evidência visual dos factos. E os factos são preparados e construídos de modo a revelar ao público o lado interior, desconhecido, da aventura" (n. pag.); ["visual evidence of the facts. And the facts are prepared and constructed in such a way as to reveal to the audience the interior, unknown side of the adventure"]. I agree with Pina regarding the importance of the visual elements in the film: the verbal silence of Mauro's work encourages the viewer to consider carefully the significance of the image, as in the case of silent film. The lack of dialogue also foregrounds the thematic progression of Villa-Lobos's score. However, the aim of the director to privilege the visual exceeds the simple, revelatory concern to which Pina refers. To my mind, Mauro, a veteran director of silent film, uses silence principally as part of his persuasive apparatus.

27. One relatively recent review of the film argues that life on board Cabral's ship "é descrita com uma preocupação de verdade humana e de rigor na reconstrução histórica" (Pina n. pag.); ["is described with a concern for human truth and rigorous historical reconstruction"]. Perhaps Pina's faith in the veracity of Mauro's imagining of the everyday existence of the crew indicates the effectiveness of the director's persuasive efforts.

28. In fact, early in the letter, Caminha points out that he will leave the communication of navigational details to others: "Da marinhagem e singraduras do caminho não darei aqui conta a Vossa Alteza, porque o não saberei fazer, e os pilotos devem ter esse cuidado" (156); "I shall not give account here to Your Highness of the ship's company and its daily runs, because I shall not know how to do it, and the pilots must have this in their charge" (5).

29. While with the INCE, the director filmed nearly two hundred educational documentaries (Mauro, "O Mundo" 196). His tenure with the government agency lasted for thirty years (Miranda 364), a period that in interviews later in life Mauro avoided discussing (Schvarzman, "Humberto Mauro" n. pag.).

30. Carlos Roberto de Souza points to the influence of Mauro's Christian beliefs on his work in cinema (90).

31. Critics have arrived at a virtual consensus that *Descobrimento do Brasil* conveys the "versão oficial [da história brasileira] da ditadura de Getúlio Vargas" ["official version [of Brazilian history] of the dictatorship of Getúlio Vargas"], as a 1996 review of the film puts it ("*O Descobrimento do Brasil*" n. pag.). To be fair, Mauro did encourage others to add to the retelling of Brazil's story. On October 31, 1937, *O Globo* quotes the director as saying: "Esperamos que não só instituições oficiais, mas particulares sigam esse exemplo e contribuam para a cultura da nossa terra" (qtd. in "Há 50 Anos" n. pag.); ["We hope that not only official institutions, but also private ones, follow this example and contribute to the culture of our land"].

32. In fact, the anthropologist's efforts had led to the establishment of the agency (Miceli 153n24). The Minister of Education and Public Health, Gustavo Capanema—who saw rushes of *Descobrimento do Brasil* and found them impressive (Heffner 19)—led many of the government's efforts to produce an "official culture," but, it should be noted, Capanema tolerated among the writers that he recruited ideologies that differed from that of the Vargas regime; Sérgio Miceli explains that the minister "erigiu uma espécie de território livre infenso às salvaguardas ideológicas do regime, valendo enquanto paradigma de um círculo de intelectuais subsidiados para a produção de uma cultura oficial" (161); ["built a kind of free zone within the ideological safeguards of the regime, which he based on the paradigm of taking advantage of a circle of subsidized intellectuals for the production of an official culture"]. Heitor Villa-Lobos, who wrote the score for Mauro's film, also had ties to Capanema, heading as he did the musical production of the Ministry of Education and Public Health (Heffner 19). Nonetheless, as part of the Estado Novo's educational reforms, Vargas asked Capanema, as Levine writes, "to inculcate the regime's values" and "to instill a common and affirmative sense of national identity" (59). Capanema "commissioned textbooks to stress national unity" and altered school curricula "to encourage national pride, discipline, good work habits, family values, thrift, and morality" (Levine 59).

33. Roquette-Pinto invited Mauro to join the organization in 1936, as the director was completing the filming of *Descobrimento do Brasil* (Mauro, "O Mundo" 196).

34. Decree 21.240, a set of policies signed into law in 1932 that affected the film industry, hoped to capture the influential potential of cinema and deploy it to emblematize the ideal nation for the masses (Johnson, *The Film Industry* 47). For a detailed treatment of the historical relationship between the Brazilian government and the cinema industry, see Johnson, *The Film Industry*.

35. The pamphlet *O Brasil é Bom* [*Brazil Is Good*] begins by implicating the children who read it in its own indoctrination: "Menino: Lê êste livrinho com ateção. Aprende êstes ensinamentos. Si teu pai e teus irmãosinhos sabem lêr, faze como que êles o leiam comtigo. Si êles não sabem lêr, prestarás um serviço ao teu Brasil, lendo-o em voz alta para que êles o ouçam e aprendam o que nêle se ensina" (Departamento Nacional de Propaganda n. pag.); ["Child: Read this book with attention. Learn these lessons. If your father and your little siblings know how to read, make sure they read it with you. If they don't know how to read, do a service to your Brazil by reading it aloud so that they hear it and learn what is taught in it"].

36. The Portuguese historian Jaime Cortesão refers to Vargas's "elevada compreensão das origens portuguesas do Brasil" ["elevated comprehension of Brazil's Portuguese origins"] and commends his dedication to the study of Brazilian history (*Cabral* 10).

37. No date appears on this pamphlet, which is D.I.P. publication #145. However, *Brasil dos Nossos dias*, #138, is dated 1940, which puts the date of publication of *Quem foi que disse?* at 1940 or slightly later.

38. The questions and answers that structure this pamphlet are directed "ao homem do povo, ao trabalhador, ao menino pobre, que não póde comprar livros, ao soldado e ao marinheiro que, por defenderem a Pátria, nos momentos de perigo ...." (Departamento de Imprensa e Propaganda, *Quem* 5); ["to the common man, to the worker, to the poor child, who cannot buy books, to the soldier and to the sailor who, because they are defending the Fatherland in moments of danger ..."].

39. Vargas coincides with Romantic nativism in attempting to inspire national pride by means of instrumentalizing the *Carta*'s praise of the Brazilian terrain (e.g., the first stanza of Gonçalves Dias's "Canção do Exílio").

40. For further study of Vargas's manipulation of history and culture through propaganda see, for example: Lúcia Lippi Oliveira, Mônica Pimenta Velloso, and Ângela Maria Castro Gomes, *Estado Novo: Ideologia e Poder* [*Estado Novo: Ideology and Power*]; Maria Helena Rolim Capelato, *Multidões em Cena: Propaganda Política no Varguismo e no Peronismo* [*Masses on Stage: Political Propaganda in Varguism and Peronism*]; and Angela de Castro Gomes, *História e Historiadores: A Política Cultural do Estado Novo* [*History and Historians: The Cultural Politics of the Estado Novo*].

41. Boris Fausto explains that the Church arranged popular support for the government, and in return, Vargas favored Catholicism through his policies (333). See also Miceli (51).

42. Roquette-Pinto, Gilberto Freyre, and others saw racism in such a heterogeneous country as a threat to "national unity" and the "Brazilian family." See Skidmore (*Black into White* 206 and "Racial Ideas" 20, 26).

43. Skidmore observes generally of the period that "[t]he 1920s and 1930s in Brazil saw a consolidation of the whitening idea and its implicit acceptance by the idea makers and social critics" ("Racial Ideas" 19).

44. Freyre's interpretation of the Portuguese colony in the Americas is not uncommon. Historian Leonardo Arroyo, for example, calls the "primeiros contactos" ["first contacts"] "idílicos" ["idyllic"] and writes that the Portuguese captivated the natives "com bondade, cordialidade, bom trato" (26) ["with kindness, cordiality, [and] good treatment"].

Chapter Two
Exoticizing the Nation in *Cabeza de Vaca* (1991) and *Como era gostoso o meu francês* (1971)

1. My citations from *Naufragios* come from the Roberto Ferrando edition, which is based on the version printed in 1555 in Valladolid. Translations are from *Castaways: The Narrative of Alvar núñez Cabeza de Vaca*.

2. In order to avoid confusion, I will refer to the writer and protagonist of *Naufragios* as Álvar Núñez, and the protagonist of the film as Cabeza de Vaca.

3. *Como era gostoso* does incorporate references to several other colonial intertexts, in contrast to Luiz Alberto Pereira's 1999 film *Hans Staden*, an adaptation specifically of Staden's text. See Darlene Sadlier's discussion of the other intertexts of *Como era gostoso* (e.g., Durand de Villegaignon, Jean de Léry, and André Thevet) (59–62) in her insightful reading of the film. Sadlier also sees Staden as the chief basis for the film. Despite some basic changes to the plot—for example, Staden, a German, is replaced by a Frenchman who, unlike the figure on which he is based, is eaten at the end of the film—it is clear that the film primarily derives from Staden's account. See also de Sousa's article, which compares Staden's text extensively with the film. There are many specific parallels between Staden's text and Pereira dos Santos's film, some of which are discussed in the body of the text. Here are a few examples: both characters (Staden and Jean from the film) are captured by the same tribe, the Tupinambá (allied with the French), while in the company of Portuguese (allied with another tribe, the Tupinikin) as artillerymen, but under very different circumstances; the national origin of both is questioned, but with different results; a visiting Frenchman refuses, at first, to help both of the protagonists; both use "magic" in the attempt to ameliorate their predicament; and the same particular chief, Cunhambebe, appears, though in somewhat different conditions. See also Williams for distinct reflections on sources for *Como era gostoso*.

4. The director echoes the Brazilian modernists' valuation of the Tupinambá's anthropophagy, as famously articulated in Oswald de Andrade's "Manifesto antropófago" (1928).

5. Some critics have questioned the verisimilitude of *Como era gostoso*'s portrayal of the Tupinambá. For example, although Greenspun recognizes "an attempt at verisimilitude" and says that "[i]n portraying its Indians, it exercises great care ... ," he concludes that "[t]he verisimilitude, of course, is something of a joke. The Indians are middle-class white Brazilians (ordinary men and exceptionally beautiful, young women) stripped down and reddened up for the occasion" (34.1); and another critic makes the following concurring comment: "The Indians seems to have body makeup and an old galleon is obviously a model" (Rev. of *Como era gostoso* 14 July 1971 n. pag.). Allen agrees with the previous assessment, stating that "[t]he anthropological ambiance is doubtful, seemingly

more fairy tale than fact ..." (66). Many others dissent, however, and find *Como era gostoso* to be an accurate and impartial portrait of the Tupinambá. Such was Pereira dos Santos's aim with the film, which he has called "cinéma anthropologique," an evaluation confirmed by criticism on the film (Paranaguá, "Nelson Pereira dos Santos" 18; Martin 64–65). De Sousa, for example, insists that, "[b]ased on anthropological research, and even with dialogue in Tupi, the movie offers an ethnography of Tupinambá culture" (90). With regard to *Como era gostoso* presenting the Tupinambá's cultural practices, specifically cannibalism, as contextually justified, I quote de Sousa's summary of the tribe's obligatory process of assimilation: "The prisoner's assimilation into Tupinambá culture lasts approximately eight months and takes place in steps: (1) the women at first see Jean as a worthless slave, the embodiment of everything they hate: they tease and insult him; (2) the women accept the prisoner's company; (3) the prisoner is given a wife, Seboipep; (4) the Tupinambá men accept Jean as one of their own; (5) finally, the tribe consumes the prisoner in a cannibal feast. The prisoner's status improves as his execution nears: worthless slave, a womanish man who cannot enjoy the company of other males, a brave warrior, *the food that sustains the tribe and the blood that quenches the tribe's revenge against the enemy*" (92; emphasis added).

6. My understanding of self-exoticizing in *Cabeza de Vaca* and *Como era gostoso* is partly informed by Stephanie Merrim's definition of the term in her article "Spectacular Cityscapes of Baroque Spanish America." Roberto González Echevarría points to one instance in colonial Spanish America of what I am calling self-exoticizing. He discusses the example of Espinosa Medrano, *Lunarejo*, who like other writers at the time, "resentfully" appropriated the pejorative denomination *Indiano* (153) and used typically exotic American elements in order to paint a self-portrait. González Echevarría explains: "*Lunarejo* calls himself a quill from the Indian Orb, straining the commonplace synecdoche feather-quill-poet to identify himself with the singularity of the plumage of those American birds whose extravagant colors were so admired by Europeans. The exorbitance—I use the word here in its most literal sense—of the place from which he writes contributes to *Lunarejo*'s strangeness, to his exoticism. Drawing frontiers becomes increasingly emphatic, and crossing them, therefore, a greater and greater feat, even if only a verbal one. It is clear that Espinosa Medrano's self-definition issues from his resentment, born of feelings of alienation and estrangement provoked by the disdain of Europeans. His self-definition, even his naming of himself and his group, is always based on how the Europeans name Americans. *Lunarejo*'s is a reflexive sense of being strange" (153–54).

7. While I am reading this and other colonial films generally as anthropophagous in terms of its adaptational strategy, Sadlier (71–72) articulates a different and no less valid reading of *Como era gostoso* in light of anthropophagy. She argues that "[t]he ritual of cannibalism becomes a metaphor for a paradoxical kind of modern consumerism that regards whatever is 'devoured' as an alien substance and is careful to resist being utterly transformed by it. The consumption of any foreign element, the film seems to argue, ought to become a discriminating, proactive, even aggressive strategy; it should be highly selective about what it takes in, and it should ingest the foreign only to strengthen the local community" (72). Stam has also written that the film "performs an 'anthropophagic' critique of European colonialism" ("Cabral" 216).

8. Hershfield holds that the tone in the final scenes of *Cabeza de Vaca* is the culmination of a gradual reversal of the exotic representation of indigenous peoples, corresponding to Cabeza de Vaca's degree of assimilation within indigenous culture ("Assimilation and Identification" 20).

9. Santiago Juan-Navarro has recently made a similar observation, yet attributes the misreading to the film itself. He points out, "[t]he film purports to be historically and anthropologically rigorous, and benefits from a display of backing that is unusual in Hispanic cinema. However, such an apparent faithfulness to the historical record collapses as soon as one takes a closer look at Cabeza de Vaca's text" (76).

10. Griffith, for example, calls *Como era gostoso* an attack on "oppressive imperialism" (12).

11. For a more detailed critical assessment of *Cabeza de Vaca* see, for example, Rabasa (e.g., 62).

12. Recall that for *Como era gostoso* Pereira dos Santos consulted Humberto Mauro regarding dialogue in Tupi.

13. Griffith, among others, confirms this perspective on the Tupinambá in the film: "Nevertheless, the natives are not put on the level of the colonists, because they remain completely guileless—nakedly guileless, if you will" (12); he later adds: "The cannibals' words and actions, however blunt or violent, are always straightforward rather than duplicitous, and justified by law and custom rather than motivated by greed" (12).

14. Richard Peña, for example, argues that the film counters the likely reflex to view Jean as the "hero" and the indigenous as the villains: "Pereira dos Santos plays on the audience's expectations; knowing full well that the Brazilian audience would identify with the Frenchman as a 'hero,' he continually undercuts the ease of this identification" (203).

15. My citations from Staden's text come from the 1937 Brazilian edition, titled *Viagem ao Brasil: Versão do texto de Marburgo, de 1557*.

16. Note 47 (61) in Staden's text explains the meaning of the word.

17. Xavier highlights this correlation, as well (201).

18. Consistent with the film's point of view, it has also been said that all of the Europeans in the film look alike, whereas the Tupinambá are individualized. Griffith writes: "This is only one of many sly reversals: not only do white Europeans all look alike, but whereas colonists force clothes on the natives before exploiting their natural resources, the prisoner soon strips and shaves and then sells his knowledge of artillery for war with a rival tribe—all to placate his captors" (12).

19. Staden manages to convince the Tupinambá that he has sway over his God's supernatural powers. When illness befalls the tribe, he explains that the illness is the result of the tribe's wanting to eat him (86). He reflects in his narrative that "Agora Deus está commigo" (85) ["God is with me today"]. On a broader level, Staden later assures his captors that nothing bad will happen to them if they refrain from eating human flesh: "Eu disse-lhe que não havia perigo si não comesse mais carne de gente" (87); "I also told him that he was not in danger, but that he should not eat human flesh anymore" (71).

20. The VHS cover distributed by Sagres foregrounds an antique woodcut showing the full body of a woman who is eating the arm of a person.

21. Perhaps an allusion to the moment before Jean, in Pereira dos Santos's 1971 *Como era gostoso,* is killed and eaten.

22. Ferrando, in a footnote to his edition of *Naufragios*, argues: "Resulta curioso que Álvar Núñez, que ha contado numerosos casos de antropofagia entre españoles, no cite ninguno entre los indígenas" (89); ["It is curious that Álvar Núñez, who has recounted numerous cases of anthropophagy among Spaniards, does not cite any among the indigenous people"]. In another edition of the text, it is suggested that cannibalism was not practiced by the indigenous peoples with whom the explorer came into contact (Favata and Fernández 130), which would certainly explain the explorer's silence on the subject.

23. Rabasa (59–62) also reads critically the film's character Mala Cosa.

24. See Adorno (*Polemics* 256–62) for a different reading of the character of Mala Cosa in the narrative.

25. Like *Cabeza de Vaca*'s protagonist, Staden repeatedly insists on his superiority over the Tupinambá "savages." Moreover, he also attempts to sway the natives with song—reinforcing Staden's commonality with *Cabeza de Vaca*'s protagonist—but his efforts are quite futile. In reaction to a discussion of which parts of him each person would eat, Staden writes: "Depois obrigaram-me a cantar e cantei versos religiosos. Queriam elles que eu os traduzisse. Disse então que tinha cantado do meu Deus. Elles respondiam que meu Deus era excremento, isto é, na lingua delles, —*Teuire*" (79); "After this I had to sing to them, and I sang spiritual songs [psalms]. Then I had to explain them in their language. Then I said I have sung about my God. They said that my God was a piece of dirt, in their language this is called Teuire [teõuira]" (64). From the standpoint of Staden's narrative and within his sixteenth-century European context, his story would surely serve to reinforce the author's suggestion of Tupinambá savagery. In a more contemporary context, the same scenario might imply entirely the opposite: the rejection of the universal appeal and validity of European culture.

26. The directors' manipulations of visual perspectives can be viewed in terms of a long-standing filmic paradigm, studied by Laura Mulvey in her seminal essay "Visual Pleasure and Narrative Cinema," in which the gaze of a film's male characters controls the presentation of the female body, thereby affecting how the audience sees the women. Mulvey provides

a valuable basis for the consideration of the visual orientation active in *Cabeza de Vaca* and *Como era gostoso*.

27. As Sadlier says: "It is important to note that the people in the film seem naked rather than nude. As John Berger and others have pointed out, 'nudity' is a form of dress—a fetishized, artfully composed imagery of the human body that has a long history in European art. By contrast, dos Santos shows us people without clothes" (73).

28. "[C]uando llegué cerca de los ranchos que ellos tenían, yo vi el enfermo que íbamos a curar que estaba muerto, porque estaba mucha gente al derredor de él llorando y su casa deshecha, que es señal que el dueño estaba muerto; y ansí, cuando yo llegué hallé el indio los ojos vueltos y sin ningún pulso, y con todas señales de muerto, según a mí me paresció, y lo mismo dijo Dorantes. Yo le quité una estera que tenía encima, con que estaba cubierto, y lo mejor que pude supliqué a nuestro Señor fuese servido de dar salud a aquél y a todos los otros que de ella tenían necesidad; y después de santiguado y soplado muchas veces, me trajeron su arco y me lo dieron ... y lleváronme a curar otros muchos que estaban malos de modorra ... y a la noche se volvieron a sus casas, y dijeron que aquel que está muerto y yo había curado en presencia de ellos, se había levantado bueno y se había paseado, y comido, y hablado con ellos" (Cabeza de Vaca 98).

"[W]hen I came near to their settlements I saw the sick man whom we were going to heal, who was dead, for many people were around him weeping and his house had been pulled down, which is a sign that its owner has died. And so when I got there I found the Indian with his eyes rolled up and without any pulse and with all the signs of being dead, as it seemed to me, and Dorantes said the same. I took off a reed mat with which he was covered, and as best I could implored Our Lord to be pleased to give health to that man and all others who had need of it.

"And after I had made the sign of the cross and blown on him many times, they brought me his bow and gave it to me, [...] and took me to heal many others who were lying in a stupor [...] And that night they returned to their homes and said that the man who was dead and whom I had healed had stood up in their presence entirely well and had walked and eaten and spoken with them" (72).

Chapter Three
Reimagining Guadalupe in *Nuevo mundo* (1976) and *La otra conquista* (1998)

1. As Miguel León-Portilla writes: "Tonantzin, que significa 'Nuestra madre' [...] era el nombre con que los nahuas llamaban a la Madre de los dioses. Ella, Tonantzin, había sido adorada precisamente en el Tepeyac, adonde desde mediados del siglo XVI muchos seguían yendo en busca de la que comenzó a llamarse Nuestra Señora de Guadalupe" (13);

["Tonantzin, which means 'Our mother' [...] was the name with which the Nahuas called the Mother of their gods. She, Tonantzin, had been worshipped precisely at Tepeyac, where since the mid-sixteenth century many continued to go in search of the one that began to be called Our Lady of Guadalupe"].

2. Despite having received government funding (from CONACINE), "'[l]a película fue censurada de manera indirecta porque las autoridades mexicanas de la época [...] y en especial el Instituto de Radio, Televisión y Cinematografía, dirigido por Margarita López Portillo, no apreciaron la manera como eran presentados los españoles, la Iglesia y la Inquisición, dijo [...] Gonzalo Lora, productor del filme" (A.F.P. 3); ["[t]he film was censured in an indirect way because the Mexican authorities of the era [...] and especially the Radio, Television and Cinematography Institute, directed by Margarita López Portillo, did not appreciate the way that Spaniards, the Church, and the Inquisition were presented, said Gonzalo Lora, producer of the film"]. See also IPS (n. pag.), which explains that López Portillo, in an effort to suggest that censorship did not exist in Mexico, showed the film with no fanfare in a few out-of-the-way theaters; still, authorities did not allow the film to participate in festivals like Cannes, which had selected it, and the government, as co-producer, was able to lock the film away. David Maciel explains that during the Echeverría sexenio (1970–76), the government invested heavily in the cinema industry and even encouraged directors, in a departure from the policies of previous administrations, to deal with politics and social issues (203). Yet "[i]t had been evident that three particular issues in commercial cinema would not be tolerated by government officials. First, there was the religious question, especially if a national religious symbol was involved, such as the Virgin of Guadalupe" (203). Given that climate, Maciel argues that Retes practiced self-censorship, drastically altering an award-winning screenplay, which provoked the writer to have his name removed from the credits (205). Even with these changes, the film was prohibited by the government.

3. Elsewhere he insists on the continuing relevance of the Encounter and on the importance of recognizing Mexico as a hybrid culture (Ramírez Hernández, "*La otra*" 1).

4. David Brading cites the quick and broad significance of Guadalupe for Mexico in the seventeenth century. He explains that the cult of Our Lady of Guadalupe at Tepeyac "attracted the devotion of both creoles and Indians, nobles and commoners, and soon extended across all the dioceses of New Spain. The significance of this cult was that it affirmed that the Mother of god had chosen the Mexican people, no matter what their race, for her especial protection" (Brading, *The First America* 3–4). Stafford Poole underscores the ever widening appeal of Guadalupe: "After the city of Mexico chose Guadalupe as its principal patron in 1737, this patronage was extended to all New Spain and Guatemala (1746) and later (1757) to all Spanish dominations throughout the world" (3). One review of *La otra conquista* ties Guadalupe to other mestiza Virgins around Latin America (A.F.P. 3).

5. Poole points out that the account of the apparition "was not published until 1648 by the Oratorian priest Miguel Sánchez. In the following year another account, commonly known today by the Nahuatl name *Nican mopohua*, was published by the vicar of Guadalupe, Luis Laso de la Vega, with the Indians as its intended audience" (1). Brading agrees that the author of the *Nican mopohua* was Laso de la Vega—who based this Nahua version of the tale on Miguel Sánchez's 1648 book—and not Antonio Valeriano, a native disciple of Sahagún, as Edmundo O'Gorman has famously argued in his book *Destierro de sombras* (Brading, *Mexican Phoenix* 360). Brading therefore argues that Miguel Sánchez and Laso de la Vega are the "true founders of the Guadalupe tradition" (*Mexican Phoenix* 360). He does take issue, however, with the exclusive emphasis that Poole places on the Baroque period when considering the dissemination of the Guadalupe myth, arguing that there was indeed early indigenous devotion following 1531 (*Mexican Phoenix* 351–55).

6. As Poole puts it elsewhere: "The criollos were the new chosen people; no other people had a picture of the Virgin that she had personally painted; God had not done the like for any other nation" (2).

7. To recognize the long-standing and varied history of colonial cinema in Latin America, one need only take into consideration the much earlier *Nuevo mundo*, or, going back farther, recall films such as Emilio Gómez Muriel's 1944 reconsideration of the iconic Catalina de Erauso, in *La monja alférez*, starring the no-less iconic María Félix. See Gordon, "The Domestication of the Ensign Nun," for further discussion of this film. In Brazil, the many different adaptations of *Iracema*, from the silent period through the second half of the twentieth century, illustrate the same point.

8. One review of *Nuevo mundo* underscores Retes's "larga investigación, recurriendo a documentos históricos de los conquistadores. Por eso no se trata de una película novelada ni maniqueísta; aunque describe implacablemente los excesos de la Colonia" (A.F.P. 3); ["substantial research, consulting historical documents of the Conquistadors. Therefore it is not a question of a fictional or a Manichean film; although it implacably describes the excesses of colonialism"]. Gustavo Moheno writes of *La otra conquista* that "[f]ar from adapting a history lesson for the screen, though, Carrasco proposes a very stylized paraphrase (What is fiction? What is reality?) of the mixture of races, basing scenes on proven facts and using historical figures like Hernán Cortés and Tecuichpo (the oldest daughter of Moctezuma) as key characters in a remarkable fictitious drama, rich in ideas and interpretations" (n. pag.).

9. Carrasco sees *La otra conquista* as an invitation "a la reflexión sobre una etapa formativa y crucial de nuestra historia: la década que siguió a la conquista española de México, entre el 13 de agosto de 1521 (la caída oficial de México-Tenochitlán) y los sucesos guadalupanos de

1531" ("Entrevista" n. pag.); ["to reflect on a formative and crucial era of our history: the decade that followed the Spanish conquest of Mexico, between August 13, 1521 (the official fall of Mexico-Tenochtitlán) and the Guadalupan events of 1531"].

10. Poole underscores the variable and ultimately ambiguous nature of Guadalupe within Mexican society: "If Guadalupe is a powerful national symbol, it is also an ambiguous one. Like Tonantzin, she symbolizes destruction and the fulfillment of apocalyptic liberation and submission" (6).

11. Carrasco has said of the film: "Lo importante con *La otra conquista* es mostrar una visión conciliatoria en la que los mexicanos aceptemos que somos parte de ese sincretismo, por lo que no podemos rechazar nuestro lado indígena o español" (qtd. in Hernández 59); ["The important thing with *La otra conquista* is showing a conciliatory perspective within which Mexicans accept that we are part of that syncretism, and because of which we cannot reject our Indigenous or Spanish side"].

12. The image of Guadalupe has been attributed to a native painter, Marcos de Aquino (Brading, *Mexican Phoenix* 10).

13. Readers will recall the monumental closing extreme long shot of *Cabeza de Vaca*, in which dozens of indigenous slaves are depicted carrying a massive silver cross through an empty desert.

14. A quality shared by Juan Mora Catlett's *Retorno a Aztlán* (1990).

15. Shohat and Stam discuss such complexities of perspective in *Unthinking Eurocentrism* (e.g., in the sections "Perspective, Address, Focalization" and "Negotiating Spectatorship").

16. Two possible intertexts for this scene within colonial Mexican cinema are Arturo Ripstein's 1974 *El santo oficio* and Eduardo Rossoff's much later *Ave María*, which feature the Spanish colonial machine burning at the stake subaltern figures.

17. This exchange anticipates a similar one at the end of Rossoff's *Ave María*, which similarly considers the creation of a religious icon in Mexico based on either a European or indigenous (or mestiza) woman, and weighs the implications of the choice.

18. The name Topiltzin, a Nahuatl honorific, used to name Quetzalcoatl, emphasizes the figure's symbolic importance in the film.

19. Carrasco offers this more detailed explanation of the title: "El título tiene que ver principalmente con tres temas: primero, la conquista religiosa o espiritual que se dio aparte de la conquista militar. Segundo, la Conquista de México enfocada en un protagonista indígena (el escribano azteca Topiltzin, hijo natural del emperador Moctezuma), es decir la historia no oficial, la otra cara de la moneda. Tercero, la conquista que llevó a cabo la cultura indígena al hacer suya la religión europea; por ejemplo, la forma en que la Virgen de Guadalupe integra el culto de la Diosa Madre azteca con la Virgen María" ("Interview" 66); ["The title mainly has to do with three topics: First, the religious or spiritual conquest that went on apart from the military conquest. Second, the Conquest of Mexico focalized through an indigenous character (the Aztec scribe Topiltzin, natural child of the emperor Moctezuma); in other words the non-official history, the other side of the coin. Third, the conquest that indigenous culture carried out upon making European religion theirs; for example, the way in which the Virgin of Guadalupe integrates the cult of the Aztec Mother Goddess with the Virgin Mary"]. The first theme to which he refers likely alludes to Robert Ricard's *The Spiritual Conquest of Mexico: An Essay on the Apostolate and the Evangelizing Methods of the Mendicant Orders in New Spain, 1523–1572,* first published in 1933.

20. He writes: "A menudo se ha representado a las culturas indígenas de tiempos de la Conquista como sociedades pasivas, como si nada más se hubiesen adaptado a las imposiciones españolas sin ofrecer demasiada resistencia cultural. *La otra conquista* presenta una cultura indígena creativa, con capacidad crítica, que a pesar de un sinfín de pérdidas asume un papel activo en su propio destino" ("Interview" 66); ["Indigenous cultures from the time of the Conquest have often been represented as passive societies, as if they had simply accepted Spanish impositions without offering too much cultural resistance. *La otra conquista* presents a creative indigenous culture, one with critical capacity, and which despite innumerable losses assumes an active role in its own destiny"].

21. Poole, a Catholic priest, contests this view: "The very existence of a shrine or temple at Tepeyac dedicated to Tonantzin is open to question, as is the nature and identity of the mother goddess herself. If indeed Guadalupe became the binding force of the new nation, she did so not in 1531 but two hundred years later. My research shows clearly that for the first century of its existence, beginning in 1648, the devotion to Guadalupe based on the apparition story was a criollo phenomenon in which any Indian role was tangential. There was no spontaneous surge of Indians toward Guadalupe/Tonantzin in the sixteenth century, no mass conversions, no consoling acceptance of a new mother goddess. Rather, there seems to have been a more or less planned effort to propagate the devotion among the Indians only in the eighteenth century" (10). Brading (*Mexican Phoenix*) disagrees with Poole's view of sixteenth-century indigenous interaction with the figure of Guadalupe.

22. See Chipman, *Moctezuma's Children,* for detail on this historically grounded figure.

23. For negative reviews that call attention to this or other aspects of the film, see Carro and García Tsao. For favorable evaluations of the film, see Moheno, Subirats, and Salvador Velasco.

Chapter Four
Sor Juana Inés de la Cruz and the
Retooling of a National Icon in *Ave María* (1999)

1. Partido Revolucionario Institucional [Institutional Revolutionary Party].

2. Partido Acción Nacional [National Action Party] and Partido Verde Ecologista de México [Ecologist Green Party of Mexico].

3. As has been the case with many recent Latin American films such as *Cabeza de Vaca*, *Ave María* was a co-production. It received 20 percent of its funding from Spain; several of the actors are also Spanish (see Peguero, "*Ave María*, historia" 40). A document produced by the Spanish Ministerio de Educación y Cultura gives some of the details of the arrangement (Armas Serra n. pag.).

4. Camille Thomasson wrote the screenplay and later collaborated with Rossoff in its revision (Ciuk, "Los Fantasmas" 37).

5. *Ave María* principally intersects with the life of Sor Juana, rather than with her literature; however, to engage with the poet's biography is to engage with her texts, for the one is arguably a function of the other.

6. The spelling of the last name finds confirmation in a number of the English subtitles.

7. The exception would be Gregorio Gransden, who compares María to Sor Juana, yet correctly and consistently calls her María.

8. Dávalos, in an article that she wrote *before* seeing the film, also calls the protagonist "María Inés," but notably refers to María's father as "el duque don Juan Inés" ("Se filma" 15); ["Duke Don Juan Inés"], the possible result of hearing the full name pronounced in an interview. Silvia Garcilaso, who writes in 1998, and Joel Hernández Espinosa, who writes in 2000, just days before the premiere, do not mention Sor Juana and call Tere López-Tarín's character María Inés, as well. However, as in Dávalos's case, they arguably treat Inés as a last name, since the protagonist appears elsewhere in the articles as simply María.

9. A similar device is used in Gabriel Retes's *Nuevo mundo* and Salvador Carrasco's *La otra conquista*.

10. "Recent criticism, on the basis of persuasive, though not conclusive, new evidence, has tended to push her birth date back three years, from 1651 to 1648" (Trueblood 2). Sabat-Rivers, however, argues for 1651 as the birth date of Sor Juana (275).

11. Previous cinematic treatments of the writer include: *Sor Juana Inés de la Cruz* (1935); *El secreto de la monja* ([*The Secret of the Nun*]; 1939); *Constelaciones* (1978); and Nicolás Echevarría's 1987 docu-drama *Las trampas de la fe* [*The Traps of Faith*], based explicitly on Paz's *Sor Juana Inés de la Cruz o las trampas de la fe*.

12. Alan Trueblood confirms that "Sor Juana's ruling passion was intellectual. It is evident that what most engaged her was the impassioned pursuit of 'beauties with which to stock the mind,' to paraphrase [Sonnet #146]. One need not read between the lines of the *Reply to Sor Philothea* to see that her choice of conventual life over marriage was one of mind over heart and body—over motherhood and domesticity" (12).

13. María's technical leanings may represent a partial symbolic fusion of Sor Juana with Carlos de Sigüenza y Góngora, a friend of the nun-writer and noted intellectual.

14. The lens comes to signify the envy that separates María from her peers. When one of the nuns shatters the protagonist's possession, a conflict between the two contributes to the religious community condemning María for excessive pride.

15. Extratextual reading guides are often a tactic employed in the persuasive apparatus of colonial films, as we can observe, for example, in *Descobrimento do Brasil* and *Caramuru: A Invenção do Brasil* (dir. Guel Arraes, 2001). See chapters 1 and 5, respectively, for a discussion of this aspect of the films.

16. Joel Hernández Espinosa writes that "una vez más la recreación del pasado colonial de México demuestra ser un tema por demás espinoso pero interesante que seguramente a los amantes de nuestra historia les fascinará" (27); ["once again the re-creation of Mexico's colonial past proves to be a thorny but interesting topic that will certainly fascinate those who love our history"].

17. Trueblood characterizes the nun: "For of all the memorable Hispanic voices of the latter half of the seventeenth century—and they were not lacking in those dominions on which the sun never set—Sor Juana's most clearly pierces constraints to proclaim the will and the right of the individual—and particularly of the individual woman—to realize herself intellectually, artistically, and emotionally" (1).

18. Pardo (4) agrees, and Lorena Ríos Alfaro echoes the allegorical interpretation of the film and writes that *Ave María* "resulta en una metáfora del mundo actual" (24); ["results in a metaphor of the real world"].

19. Gransden, on the other hand, evaluates *Ave María*'s allegorical critique of present-day injustices in less convinced terms (12).

20. For a synthesis of the *Neptuno* and its background, see Sabat-Rivers 289. Merrim points out that throughout the *Neptuno*, "Sor Juana ingeniously manipulates her sources to create an image of Neptune that profiles the ideal leader she hopes the new viceroy will be and to exalt learned women through the figure of Isis, goddess of wisdom. These manipulations reflect Sor Juana's intellectual and personal agendas" (*Early Modern* 232).

21. Merrim explains: "For with the *Neptuno* Sor Juana indelibly establishes herself as an intellectual with an extraordinary depth of knowledge on a specific subject. Propelled by the personal and political motivations discussed at the end of my first chapter, she also establishes her value as an icon of Culture to be supported by the Marquis de la Laguna. Isis becomes her mask and the *Neptuno* another act of self-fashioning in a public context as Sor Juana almost imperceptibly writes herself into the text: 'Este, Señor, triunfal arco, / que artificioso compuso más el estudio de amor / que no *el amor del estudio*' [4.403; italics mine] [...]. In the *Neptuno* as well as in the *P[rimero] S[ueño]*, Sor Juana subdues her 'I' but blazons her will to signature" (*Early Modern* 232).

22. Rossoff says: "No trato de corregir nada de la historia con esta película, por eso no hablamos de aspectos históricos sino de cierta gente y de algo que pudo suceder ya que se permitía el abuso hacia la mujer" (qtd. in de la Cruz Polanco 7); ["I do not attempt to correct any aspect of history with this film, and for that reason we do not speak of historical aspects, but rather of certain people and of something that could have happened since abuses toward women were permitted"].

23. Ayala Blanco confirms the critically religious tone of the film, calling it "iconoclasta" (100) ["iconoclast"].

24. On echoes of Sor Juana in recent Mexican fiction by women, see Hind.

25. As Margo Echenberg explains: "[I]n every instance in which the issue of renown appears in Sor Juana's writing, it is accompanied by an invective against the manipulation of her public image *and* a self-image of her own design" (177; emphasis in original).

26. All quotations of Sor Juana are taken from Alfonso Méndez Plancarte's edition of her *Obras completas*. The page number in the parenthetical citations follows the volume number. Translations followed by a page number are from *A Sor Juana Anthology*; otherwise, they are mine, unless explicitly noted.

27. Merrim characterizes Sor Juana's endeavor as "a desperate final effort to combat praise and fame" (*Early Modern* 176).

28. Trueblood points out the following: "the last two years of her life are marked by complete silence, preceded by what appears to be her last poem [...] unfinished and probably dating from late 1692, when the second volume of her works would have reached her from Spain. Perhaps all is not rhetorical convention in the self-deprecation with which she meets the eulogies of the 'pens of Europe'" (10). As Sabat-Rivers points out, "[l]a fama de sor Juana crecía en la Nueva España y en la Península a la par que sus problemas" (278); ["Sor Juana's fame grew in New Spain and in the Peninsula on par with her problems"]. For thorough and insightful examinations of Sor Juana's fame, see Merrim (*Early Modern* 29–37 and 138–90) and Echenberg (173–222).

29. Sor Juana had also enjoyed the protection of the previous Viceroy and Vicereine, the Marquis and Marquise de Mancera, whose term ended in 1673. As Trueblood writes: "Their protection and that of their successors would serve to hold at bay critical voices motivated by religious zeal and voices of the invidious carping against her worldliness" (6). The Marquis and Marquise de Mancera, Trueblood continues, "were succeeded by the Archbishop of the city of Mexico, Friar Payo Enríquez de Ribera, with whom Sor Juana was on good terms. But the period of her closest relations with the viceregal court and of her plenitude as writer and scholar began in 1680 when Friar Payo was succeeded by Tomás Antonio de la Cerda, Marquis de la Laguna, and his wife, María Luisa, who was Countess de Paredes in her own right" (6).

30. "There are two principal hypotheses with regard to the Bishop's motivation. Clearly there was rivalry between him and Aguiar y Seijas, whom documents prove to have been made Archbishop of Mexico in preference to Santa Cruz. In publishing a confutation of an eminent Jesuit Archbishop, Santa Cruz was indirectly attacking the Jesuit Archbishop, covering his traces, perhaps with intentional transparency, in the prefatory letter [...]. On this view, Sor Juana, to her detriment, is a missile in an undeclared war, and Santa Cruz appears willing to violate her confidence (for she obviously had no expectation of publication) for his own purposes. A second hypothesis holds that the Bishop saw a storm brewing between the unbending misogynist cleric and the proud cloistered nun who dared to point her words and her interests toward the world beyond the convent walls. On this reading, the Bishop's covering letter is a lightning rod intended to deflect the thunderbolt he saw coming from the Archbishopric of the capital city now that Sor Juana no longer could count on strong viceregal protection" (Trueblood 7–8).

31. "With the departure of the Marquis and Marquise de la Laguna in 1688, storm clouds began to gather for Sor Juana. Her relations with the new viceregal couple, the Count and Countess de Galve, while cordial, were more ceremonial, less close, to judge by the formal nature of the few compositions in which the two figure" (Trueblood 7). "The publication of her poetry [in Madrid by the Marquise de la Laguna] in 1689, while it consolidated her fame outside of New Spain, seems to have increased resentment of her preeminence and her womanhood in the literary and clerical establishment at home in Mexico. The episode of the *Missive Worthy of Athena* in the end distanced her from Santa Cruz, who seems to have withdrawn his support when, instead of heeding his advice and turning to heavenly muses, she firmly defended her cultivation of earthly ones. The hostility of Aguiar y Seijas was evidently exacerbated by her unwitting role as pawn in the feud between him and Santa Cruz. Rather than an organized cabal against her there was simply a recrudescence of the ecclesiastic pressures that had been there from the start. Sor Juana must have felt increasingly vulnerable" (Trueblood 10). Years earlier, Sor Juana's "Autodefensa espiritual" ["Spiritual Self-defense"] anticipates the crisis that culminates with the *Respuesta*; in the "Autodefensa" Sor Juana responds to attacks by her confessor, Antonio Núñez de Miranda, which "seem to have been ignited to a considerable degree by the nun's fame" (Merrim, *Early Modern* 153). "In the 'Autodefensa' we see Sor Juana having reached that dreaded juncture in which *fama*, dangerous enough in itself for a woman, has with Núñez's slander become outright *mala fama*" (154).

32. María's questions clearly recall points that Sor Juana makes in the *Respuesta*. In reference to the first question, I would cite Sor Juana's similar, if more subtle, argument: "¿[Q]ué inconveniente tiene que una mujer anciana, docta en letras y de santa conversación y costumbres, tuviese a su cargo la educación de las doncellas?" (4.465); "[W]hat drawback could there be to having an old woman, well-versed in letters and pious in conversation and way of life, in charge of the education of maidens?" (233). With regard to María's second question, Sor Juana writes: "Pues por la—en mí dos veces infeliz—habilidad de hacer versos, aunque fuesen

sagrados, ¿qué pesadumbres no me han dado o cuáles no me han dejado de dar? Cierto, señora mía, que algunas veces me pongo a considerar que el que se señala—o le señala Dios, que es quien sólo lo puede hacer—es recibido como enemigo común, porque parece a algunos que usurpa los aplausos que ellos merecen o que hace estanque de las admiraciones a que aspiraban, y así le persiguen" (4.452–53); "Why, for the ability (doubly infelicitous in my case) to compose verse, even when it was sacred verse, what nastiness have I not been subjected to, what unpleasantness has not come my way! I must say, Madam, that sometimes I stop and reflect that anyone who stands out—or whom God singles out, for He alone can do so—is viewed as everyone's enemy, because it seems to some that he is usurping the applause due them or deflecting the admiration which they have coveted, for which reason they pursue him" (219).

33. Trueblood writes that the fact that Sor Juana's "brilliance aroused envy from the beginning is clear from her verse" (4).

34. Document 410 begins, "Juana Inés de la Cruz, la más indigna e ingrata criatura de cuantas crió vuestra Omnipotencia, y la más desconocida de cuantas crió vuestro amor, parezco ante vuestra divina y sacra Majestad, [...] prostrada con toda reverencia de mi alma [...]" (4.520); ["Juana Inés de la Cruz, the most unworthy and ungrateful creature of all that Your Omnipotence created, and the most unknown of all that Your love created, appears before Your divine and sacred Majesty [...] prostrated with all of the reverence of my soul"].

35. Additionally—as was conversely the case with Emilio Gómez Muriel's 1944 film *La monja alférez*, which associates Catalina de Erauso with the iconic actress María Felix (see Gordon, "The Domestication")—by tying María to an existing Mexican icon, the film's protagonist is better positioned as a national icon and therefore a suitable vehicle for a political message. Interestingly, *La monja alférez* transformes the historical (but Spanish) figure into a Mexican icon.

36. The telescope in *Ave María* recalls the visual role played by the *astrolábio* in *Descobrimento do Brasil*, during the moments of early contact on shore between technologically advanced, benign Portuguese and primitive, playful indigenous people.

37. Perhaps Rossoff combines alluring shots of María with her deification in order to slip her into the familiar, and thus readable, virgin/slut dichotomy. I would add that, unlike *Yo, la peor de todas*, the director in no way implies that María is a lesbian. Despite the film's anti-Catholic attitude, it appears that María's sexualization must remain heterosexual in order to preserve her potential as a Mexican icon.

38. Octavio Paz, in his 1988 book on Sor Juana, calls the writer's father an "enigma" (65). Rossoff takes full advantage of the paternal *tabula rasa* of the film's intertext and amplifies in this scene María's ideological turnaround by codifying María's father as the archetypical oppressor of the indigenous population in Mexico ("Nadie fue tan eficaz como Inez a la hora de someter a los Indios"; ["No one was more effective than Inez when it came to subjugating the Indians"], a figure with whom María initially identifies.

39. María's tactics in the confession scene remind me of Merrim's description of Sor Juana's two-pronged counter to the slander leveled at her. In reference to *Los empeños de una casa* [*The House of Trials*], Merrim writes that the "speech of the idealized heroine Leonor can thus be seen as a personal statement by Sor Juana in a political context, one that counters public slander with a public self-defense. In it Sor Juana not only replays her crisis, but also recasts her story and, conceivably in response to the crisis, refashions her own image" (*Early Modern* 156). María declares the nature of her new image by appropriating a Church space, and finally transcends her condemnation that took place in another Church space.

40. María has now entirely assumed through indigenous mysticism a syncretic identity, a move for which Sor Juana provides a degree of precedent. While the poet claims no indigenous parentage, it is worth noting that she also participated, with others, in the beginnings of a sense of independent Creole identity through poetic displays of American pride. One oft-cited example is her Romance #37, in which she writes, "[…] nací / en la América abundante, / […] / que en ninguna parte más / se ostenta la tierra Madre" (1.103); ["I was born in abundant America […] In no other place does Mother Earth flaunt herself more"]. Notable, as well, and in even more intimate dialogue with *Ave María* is her Romance #51, in which the poet associates herself with what she casts as exotic American imagery: "¿Qué mágicas infusiones / de los Indios herbolarios / de mi Patria, entre mis letras / el hechizo derramaron?" (1.160); ["What magical infusions from Indian herbalists of my Fatherland did spill a spell among my letters?"]. Sor Juana attributes the success of her poetry and literary fame to the mystical indigenous element in her country. Trueblood writes of this poem: "Sor Juana occasionally brings unprecedented touches of indigenous exoticism into the literary canon: the (Indian) 'herb-doctors of my country' figure instead of Medea as casters of spells" (16).

41. Rossoff's choice to have María raped before her execution merits examination. María, a mestiza, is already tacitly one of the *hijas de la chingada*, one of the children of La Malinche. However, her violation in this scene, foreshadowed by her earlier rescuing of an indigenous victim of rape, fuses María with the figure of Malinche. Up to this point, the film has taken María's racial constitution as a starting point and attributed the peaceful unification of the Mexican people to religious syncretism. Perhaps the film is unable to dodge, as in the case of Sor Juana, the irresistible invitation to associate María with Malinche, or perhaps the film is postulating a vicious circle of abuse and oppression within which any attempt to define Mexican identity spins.

42. Sor Juana's death, according to Echenberg, produced an analogous outcome: "following her death, Sor Juana's image as Mexico's Tenth Muse and as a religious model becomes crystallized: the image of the person has all but evanesced. Her person has given way to her persona; her myth has eclipsed her life" (221).

43. Jorge Ayala Blanco also draws the parallel with Christ, referring to María's "largas pausas en negro al término de cada estación de su Via Crucis" (100); ["long pauses in black on finishing each station of her Via Crucis"]. Echenberg shows how in the *Respuesta* Sor Juana "describes a martyrdom triggered by applause and akin to Christ's while adopting a self-image that, surprisingly enough, warranted fame" (193).

44. Sor María's "exaltation of the Virgin as equal to Christ and as a queen of wisdom, can be seen to bear on Sor Juana's [text]" (Merrim, *Early Modern* xii).

45. Pardo describes María as "tan altiva y hermosa como las imágenes españolas de la Virgen, una María que después se convertirá en una mártir de los indígenas cuando recupere sus raíces y se desprenda de los bienes materiales" (4); ["just as haughty and beautiful as the Spanish images of the Virgin, a María who later becomes a martyr of the indigenous when she recuperates her roots and relinquishes her material possessions"].

46. Ironically, María's becoming "diferente de ti y de mí" ["different from you and me"] coincides with her becoming an icon of the Mexican population.

Chapter Five
Inverted Captivities and Imagined Adaptations in *Brava Gente Brasileira* (2000) and *Caramuru: A Invenção do Brasil* (2001)

1. A possible inspiration for this invention is *Viagem ao Brasil de Alexandre Rodrigues Ferreira: a expedicão philosophica pelas Capitanias do Pará, Rio Negro, Mato Grosso e Cuyabá* [*Alexandre Rodrigues Ferreira's Voyage to Brazil: The Philosophical Expedition through the Captaincies of Pará, Rio Negro, Mato Grosso and Cuiabá*].

2. The boy's aborted path of resistance recalls one of *La otra conquista*'s proposals of resistance. Although at the end of *La otra conquista*, protagonist Topiltzin and his dedication to Aztec culture and religion are annihilated by the syncretic inertia of the Catholic Church, from the beginning of the film he is shown to resist heroically Spanish domination. Topiltzin eludes the first attempt to capture him and is only taken into custody after his brother betrays him. Moreover, when Cortés erases his name (calling him Tomás) and sentences him to indoctrination, he immediately begins plotting, with his half-sister, the legitimate heir of Moctezuma, to forge Cortés's name on a self-damning letter to the king.

3. The "Notas de produção" ["Production Notes"] declare: "A proposta não é criar um épico, mas opor duas lógicas. A da civilização indígena e a portuguesa. Ambas se desagregando no choque cultural. O 'selvagem,' visto pelo português como incapaz de articular um pensamento, é capaz de elaborar uma estratégia militar utilizando-se da fraqueza manifesta do inimigo. De outro lado, a dualidade do colono branco que, ao final da vida, pede à Coroa proteção para sua família indígena. Se não esiste pecado do lado debaixo do Equador, não existe também retorno"; ["The goal is not to create an epic, but to oppose two ways of thinking. That of the indigenous civilization, and that of the Portuguese. Both break down as cultures clash. The 'savage,' seen by the Portuguese as incapable of articulating a thought, is capable of devising a military strategy that exploits the manifest weakness of the enemy. On the other side, the duality of the white colonist who, at the end of his life, asks the Crown for protection for his indigenous family. If sin doesn't exist below the Equator, nor does there exist a way back"]. In the "Making of ..." documentary, the actress that plays Ánote, Luciana Rigueira, says that the character "é a ligação entre o mundo indígena e o mundo dos brancos na época" (Murat, *Brava Gente* [DVD] n. pag.); ["is the link between the world of the indigenous people and the world of the whites in that era"].

4. Diogo and the other non-indigenous characters complicate easy categorizations of heroes and villains in colonial Brazil. Many Brazilian colonial films, such as those treating the Inconfidência Mineira—e.g., *Os Inconfidentes*, 1972, dir. Joaquim Pedro de Andrade—favor people of Portuguese descent born in Brazil—who represent a spirit of resistance—over newly arrived Portuguese—who represent oppression. In *Brava Gente*, Diogo, through his adverse relationship with the brutal Brazilian-born *mestiço* soldier Capitão Pedro, helps to embody another side of the complex and sometimes tense relationship in the period between newly arrived Portuguese and people born in Brazil.

5. The actor who plays Pedro, Floriano Peixoto, comments on the interesting genesis and importance of this character: "Quando a Lúcia encontrou com um menino índio que tinha aspecto de branco, ficou fascinada e resolveu incorporá-lo ao roteiro. Isso enriqueceu muito o meu personagem, já que se estabelece uma relação intensa entre o personagem do menino e o Pedro, que tenta levá-lo para a cultura dos brancos, a qualquer preço" ("Notas de produção," Murat, *Brava Gente* [DVD] n. pag.); ["When Lúcia found an Indian boy who looked white, she became fascinated and decided to incorporate him into the screenplay. This greatly enriched my character since an intense relationship develops between the character of the boy and Pedro, who tries to pull him into the culture of the whites at whatever cost"].

6. See Kornis (e.g., 97) on TV Globo's long-standing predilection for producing historical television programs and the commentary on Brazilian national identity that such programs have realized.

7. Amado writes that the historical "Caramuru was able to command the respect of the indigenous peoples after discharging a firearm into the air. Such weapons were unknown to the Indians, who terrified, prostrated themselves at his feet" (783). This event, which appears in most narratives about Caramuru (784), occurs in Arraes's film as well. Amado explains that the Tupi word *Caramuru* is "variously translated as 'son of fire,' 'son of thunder,' 'man of fire,' 'sea dragon,' 'Brazilian river fish similar to the moray eel,' 'great river,' 'he who can speak the Indians' language'" (783–84).

8. As Stam writes: "The attempt at a contrapuntal, polyperspectival approach sketched out in the overture sequence is compromised, unfortunately, by a number of features of the miniseries" ("Cabral" 208).

9. In an interview, director Guel Arraes confirms that he sees the film as characteristic of his generation, "marcada pela retomada nos anos setenta das teses dos modernistas sobre a cultura brasileira" ("Entrevista" n. pag.); ["marked by the recuperation in the 1970s of the [Brazilian] modernists' theses about Brazilian culture"], within which loomed large the topic of anthropophagy. Stam describes that era in Brazilian film as "the third 'oral-cannibalistic-tropicalist-allegorical' phase of *Cinema Novo* (1968–1971), during which filmmakers turned for inspiration to the modernist writers of the 1920s and especially to Oswald de Andrade's notion of 'anthropophagy'" ("Cabral" 215). Instead of seeing *Caramuru* as either a generational residue or cultural anachronism—a possible interpretation of Arraes's comment—I see the film's return to anthropophagy as a de facto argument for the continuing viability of cannibalism as a cultural trope in Brazil.

10. In the earlier Caramuru narratives, a Portuguese imperial perspective tended to dominate; the plot elements were devised by Portuguese authors, and circulated by and to the Portuguese population (Amado 786). Lisa Voigt, in her study of Santa Rita Durão's 1781 *Caramuru*, acknowledges the presence of the Portuguese colonizing enterprise in the text—"the 'home' invented in *Caramuru* is unquestionably part of the Portuguese empire, not the forerunner of an independent nation-state" (312)—but takes issue with criticism that focuses exclusively on such elements (e.g., 266–67). She signals as well a significant American patriotic bent in the epic poem: "In the *Reflexões prévias* to the poem, [...] [Durão] writes, [...] 'The events of Brazil are no less deserving of a Poem than those of India. Love for my homeland incited me to write this one'" (265; translation by Voigt). She continues: "Álvares is presented as the heroic founder of the Portuguese colony, but only after he has experienced captivity among and integration with the Tupinambá Indians, taking both an Amerindian wife (Paraguaçu) and name (Caramuru). [Durão's] *Caramuru* also relates the couple's voyage to France, where they are married and Paraguaçu is baptized before the French court. By tracing their displacement to Europe and back to Brazil, Durão redefines the colony as 'home' and inscribes the origins of Brazilian culture in the transculturated characters of a Portuguese ex-captive and a converted Amerindian noblewoman. [...] [H]is affirmations of patriotism in the poem's preface and his favorable depiction of Brazil and its native inhabitants in *Caramuru* have secured him a place as one of the founding fathers in the national literary canon and a precursor to the Indianist tendency of Brazilian Romanticism" (265–66).

11. Amado (787–89) catalogues the references in Brazil, Portugal, France, and England to this historical figure from the sixteenth century to the present, emphasizing the diversity of genres through which Caramuru has been portrayed (e.g., chronicles, historiography, poetry, plays, novels).

12. Amado cites the seventeenth-century Jesuit Simão de Vasconcellos, who claims Diogo Álvares was of noble birth (790–91). Voigt points out that some contemporaries of Durão considered Álvares to be "a 'fugitive' or treasonous 'coward'" (275). The historical figure likely reached what is now the state of Bahia, Brazil, sometime between the early years of the sixteenth century and the 1530s (not before Cabral) (Amado 783).

13. Amado points out that Santa Rita Durão's epic poem, which coincides with the basic plot line established by Vasconcellos (Amado 797), "showed himself to be an ardent defender of monogamy. From the beginning, Caramuru possessed only one wife, Paraguaçu. The other women were only in love with him, among them 'the poor Moema,' drowned when she threw herself into the sea with the others after Diogo departed for France with Paraguaçu" (798). Moema, an invented character, began to emerge as part of the story before Durão (Amado 798; or Voigt 286–91). Earlier texts (e.g., Vasconcellos and Rocha Pita), however, acknowledged a lack of monogamy on Diogo/Caramuru's part, even if they claimed that Paraguaçu held a privileged place among other women (Amado 811).

14. Carlos Alberto Mattos sees *Caramuru*'s humorous approach to historical cinema as an emerging genre, "revitalizada" ["revitalized"] by Carla Camurati's 1995 film *Carlota Joaquina, Princesa do Brazil* (7), a film that has been singled out in criticism as one of the watersheds in recent Brazilian cinema, marking the beginning of what has been dubbed the *Retomada*, or Recuperation, a period of cinematic revival that began in the mid-90s and continues today.

15. As Amado observes with regard to retellings of the tale in general: "a number of changes were made by reordering the events in the story, emphasizing different passages and characters, targeting differing audiences, and altering the themes and uses of the story" (792). Notwithstanding the importance of Vasconcellos as a hub of narrative recycling regarding Diogo/Caramuru, he was not unique. Other early sources include a report by Francisco de Avila on the ship *São Gabriel* (1526); a report by Captain Diogo de Garcia (1526); a letter from Pero Lopes to Martim Afonso de Souza (1531); a deposition by Herrera (1535); a letter from Pero de Campo Tourinho to King Dom João III (1546); and a letter from Manuel da Nóbrega (1555) (Amado 806). One later commentary, which appears in the 1817 publication in which Pero Vaz de Caminha's letter of discovery was first published, argues that liberties taken in Vasconcellos's retelling of Caramuru's story begot liberties in subsequent versions of the tale: "segundo o que eu pude ver, [Vasconcellos] foi o primeiro, que divulgou (mais de cento e cincoenta anos depois) as aventuras de Diogo Alves Corrêa o *Caramurú* quazi em fórma de Novella; e os posteriores consideraram-se authorizados para enfeitalla; o que faz encontrar nesta historia incoherencias, e paradóxos" (Ayres de Casal 88); ["according to what I have managed to see, [Vasconcellos] was the first to divulge (more than 150 years later) the adventures of Diogo Alves Corrêa, the *Caramurú*, almost in the form of a novella; and those who came after him considered themselves authorized to embellish it, which has led to incoherence and paradox in this story"].

16. Stam lists some of the intertexts of the miniseries in addition to that of José de Santa Rita Durão's *Caramuru: Poema Épico do Descobrimento da Bahia*: "Gabriel Soares de Sousa, Gregório de Mattos, Sebastião da Rocha Pita, Francisco Adolfo de Varnihagen, Arthur Lobo d'Ávila, João de Barros, Claude d'Abbeville, Robert Southey" ("Cabral" 207).

17. Globo has achieved, in fact, a dynamic whereby television's alimentation of cinema is facilitated. Carlos Diegues has observed that this is not typically the case in Brazilian media, and argues that the survival of the cinema industry depends on Brazil's interweaving more effectively the two industries, as is officially done in other countries (30). He proposes that Brazil "integrate the film and television industries, through new resources, in order to stimulate the growth of both and their international expansion" (34).

18. Mattos has described the TV-cinema anthropophagy analogy from the opposite perspective: "De alguma maneira também, é a televisão devorando o cinema e lambendo os beiços. Primeira minissérie inteiramente rodada em HDTV (TV de alta definição) entre nós, simultaneamente à experiência similar de George Lucas com o novo episódio de *Guerra nas estrelas*, *A invenção do Brasil* foi exibida em abril do ano passado, como parte das comemorações pelos 500 anos do Descobrimento" (7); ["In some way as well it's television devouring cinema and licking its lips. The first miniseries filmed in HDTV (high definition TV) among us, simultaneously with the experience of George Lucas with the new episode of *Star Wars*, *A invenção do Brasil* was shown in April of last year, as part of the commemoration of the 500th anniversarty of the Discovery"].

19. Mattos takes a critical view of the centrality of the three-way sexual dynamic in the film: "Desse triângulo inaugural, teria nascido nossa suposta licenciosidade amorosa. A sacanagem seria o nosso grande mito de origem. Assim como essa mania de se apaixonar perdidamente por tudu o que vem de fora" (7); ["From that inaugural triangle, our alleged amorous licentiousness is supposed to have been born. Promiscuity would be our great myth of origin. Just like that obsession with becoming madly passionate about everything that arrives from outside Brazil"].

20. Mattos evaluates the nature of the film's humor and its role: "A língua, exercitada à exaustão (como linguagem, não como sexo), é a base de um humor até fácil, mas inegavelmente contagiante" (7); ["Tongues exercised to exhaustion (as in language, not sex), is the basis of a rather simple humor, but undeniably contagious"]. He continues: "Isso não quer dizer que *Caramuru* seja uma anti-aula de tolices. Pelo contrário, é inteligente até onde o modelo permite. O público cai nas graças de seu anacronismo brincalhão, especialmente no que diz respeito às duas índias-de-Ipanema e seu pai Itaparica. Tudo se justifica pelo código lúdico aplicado homogeneamente no filme inteiro" (7); ["That is not to say that *Caramuru* is an unedifying lesson in foolishness. On the contrary, it's intelligent up to the point that the model allows. The audience responds to the humor of its playful anachronism, especially in regards to the two Indian-Girls-from-Ipanema and their father Itaparica. Everything is justified by the ludic code applied homogeneously to the entire film"].

21. See also Mônica Brincalepe Campo, who analyzes the miniseries (both the documentary and narrative portions) as well as the screenplay of the miniseries, and proposes to elucidate how this audiovisual text interacts with and exhibits history.

22. In reference to the combination of documentary and narrative in the miniseries, Stam comments: "*Invenção do Brasil* brilliantly interweaves maps, paintings, archival footage, digital simulacra, staged scenes, all backed up by the highly syncretic music which evokes the 'multi-nation' cultures at the roots (routes) of Brazil" ("Cabral" 207).

23. Though Diogo only becomes Caramuru part-way through the film, I will refer to him with that name from here on in order to avoid confusion.

24. By "filmmakers," I mean to refer not only to director Arraes, but also to others who contributed to the creation of the film. Often I have in mind the inclusion of Jorge Furtado, co-writer of the film and director of the documentary portion of the miniseries and the DVD.

25. For a cogent analysis of the miniseries that highlights both the successes and shortcomings of Arraes's polygeneric experiment, see Stam, "Cabral" 206–08.

26. Nevertheless, Arraes points out the following: "surpreendentemente, o filme está mais leve e mais popular do que a minissérie, enquanto devia ser o contrário" ("Entrevista" n. pag.); ["surprisingly, the film is lighter and more popular than the miniseries, though the contrary should be the case"].

27. "—Eu gosto do formato docudrama. Mas no cinema, achei que poderia criar rejeição. É sempre arriscado interromper uma história, cortar o envolvimento do espectador" (qtd. in Biaggio 8); ["I like the docudrama format. But a cinematic context, I thought that it might be rejected. It's always a risk to interrupt the story, to break the involvement of the spectator"].

28. In an interview, Arraes defines *Caramuru* as a "comédia romântica histórica narrada em tom de fábula. Embora o encontro de Caramuru e Paraguaçu se baseie em fatos reais, trabalhamos as referências da História com muita liberdade" ("Entrevista" n. pag.); ["romantic historical comedy narrated in the tone of a fable. Though the encounter of Caramuru and Paraguaçu is based on real facts, we worked very freely with historical references"]. Later he adds that they wished to "narrar em tom de comédia uma história que tem como pano de fundo aquela época" (n. pag.);

["narrate in a comedic tone a story that has that era as a backdrop"]. He summarizes by saying that "*A Invenção do Brasil*, na falta de um termo melhor, é uma obra pop, com as vantagens, desvantagens e imperfeições do gênero" (n. pag.); ["*A Invenção do Brasil*, for lack of a better term, is a pop text, with the advantages, disadvantages, and imperfections of the genre"].

29. In an interview, soundtrack composer Lenine highlights the contribution that the soundtrack makes to connecting past to present in the film: "[C]hegamos à conclusão de que tínhamos pouco tempo para compor e produzir uma trilha original. Sendo assim, decidimos 'descobrir' o universo musical de Caramuru e Paraguaçu, garimpando fonogramas existente, tentando fazer um paralelo da música do Velho Mundo com a do Novo Mundo e buscando, principalmente, similaridades e consonâncias [...] O objetivo sempre foi a contemporaneidade" (n. pag.); ["[W]e arrived at the conclusion that we had little time to compose and produce an original soundtrack. That being the case, we decided to 'discover' a musical universe of Caramuru and Paraguaçu, mining existing recordings, attempting to create a parallel between the music of the Old World and the New World and seeking out, principally, similarities and consonances [...] The objective was always contemporaneity"]. In another comment that evokes the spirit of the anthropophagy of Brazilian *modernismo*, with regard to intercultural exchange between Europe and Brazil, he says: "Na parte da Europa foi intencional a procura por algum Brasil na música de outros países. Foi assim que chegamos a Maria João e Mario [*sic*] Laginha ou aos Fabolous [*sic*] Trobadors, por exemplo. Qualquer semelhança não é mera coincidência" (n. pag.); ["In the part that takes place in Europe the search for some Brazil in the music of other countries was intentional. That's how we decided on Maria João and Mário Laginha or the Fabulous Trobadors, for example. Any similarity is not mere coincidence"].

30. *Macunaimês* serves as an adjective through which Arraes means to convey an intertextual/anthropophagic relationship with Mário de Andrade's *Macunaíma: O herói sem nenhum caráter*, published in the same year (1928) as Oswald de Andrade's "Manifesto antropófago," and "widely recognized as a vital practical enactment of what Oswald de Andrade put forth in theoretical terms in his manifesto" (K. López, "*Modernismo*" 28). K. López's analysis of Andrade's *Macunaíma* helps to elucidate the analogy we find here between Arraes's project and *anthropofagia*: "*Macunaíma* embodies the central contradiction of the Modernist movement: it strives to define a Brazilian identity by incorporating popular speech and indigenous myths, but also seeks to create a cosmopolitan literature for international export" ("*Modernismo*" 25).

31. Despite the film's liberal attitude with regard to historical fidelity, the liner notes of the DVD still call the film a "primorosa recriação de época" ["pristine period re-creation"] and thus celebrate a quality often appreciated by viewers of historical films. Moreover, a web-based advertisement for the screenplay of the initial Rede Globo miniseries version of the story authorizes as faithful the film's interaction with history:

"A narrativa inventada por Guel Arraes e Jorge Furtado reconstitui a época áurea dos descobrimentos portugueses, percorrendo a Lisboa quinhentista e o litoral dionisíaco do Brasil recém-descoberto. Hábitos, costumes, práticas sexuais: as diferenças entre os europeus e os índios são exploradas a partir de um ponto de vista original e divertido, com a irreverência que costuma marcar as produções da dupla nos últimos 10 anos" (Arraes, *Caramuru* [DVD] n. pag.); ["The narrative invented by Guel Arraes and Jorge Furtado reconstructs the golden age of Portuguese discoveries, spanning Lisbon of the 1500s and the Dionysiac coast of the recently discovered Brazil. Habits, customs, sexual practices: the differences between Europeans and Indians are explored from an original and entertaining point of view, with the irreverence that tends to mark the productions of the pair over the last 10 years"].

32. Kornis provides background for this articulation of quality, specifically with regard to TV Globo's products, explaining that during the 1970s politics within the company pushed for technically polished programs: "o chamado 'padrão Globo de qualidade'" ["the so-called Globo pattern of quality"],which has been continued over the course of decades (102). The review later qualifies somewhat its glowing evaluation of the film: "Embora pensado como filme desde a sua concepção, 'Caramuru' tropeça em características intrínsecas do veículo que o originou" (Almeida 7); ["Though it was thought of as a film since its conception, 'Caramuru' trips over intrinsic characteristics of the vehicle that gave it origin"]. Almeida specifies this critique of the film's adaptational strategy in this way: "'Caramuru' rearranja o pop" (7); ["'Caramuru' rearranges pop"].

33. With regard to recent Rede Globo productions, Kornis indicates that from the 1990s to today, Globo's discourse emphasizes the idea that the company's fictional production "retrata o 'caráter brasileiro'" (113); ["portrays the 'Brazilian character'"].

34. Not all reviews of the film, of course, were as favorable. Carlos Alberto Mattos adopts a more independent and critical stance toward the film in a review for another newspaper, *Jornal do Brasil*. Referring to the lack of knowledge of the historical basis for the legend of Caramuru and Paraguaçu, he writes that the film "deita e rola nessa areia fofa. Toma todas as licenças—poéticas ou não—para oferecer, digamos assim, a primeira comédia romântica vivida em solo pátrio" (7); ["lies down and rolls around in that soft sand. It takes licenses—poetic and not—to offer, we might say, the first romantic comedy experienced on national soil"].

35. See Kornis on Globo's historical television programs.

36. Mulvey, in a 2003 essay about Brazilian film, makes a similar observation about the implications of new technologies and cinema: "Now anyone, with the simple touch of a digital button can stop and think about the complexities of moving images with the same space for reflection on time that has long been offered by the still photograph" ("Then and Now" 268).

37. Nonetheless, Diegues argues in a 2003 article that the ancillary markets of Brazilian cinema, such as DVD, are still drastically underdeveloped (25–26).

38. Stam points out elements in the documentary portion of the original miniseries that help to make the connection between past and present: "Throughout Arraes/Furtado deploy anachronism as a device, linking Cabral to Neil Armstrong, Renaissance maps to satellite TV, and the Voyages of Discovery to a theme park ride" ("Cabral"207).

39. Stam also calls attention to the shift in point of view ("Cabral" 207), but feels that a "Eurocentric perspective" predominates in the film (208).

40. For a concise evaluation of anthropophagy in *Macunaíma*, see Stam ("Cabral" 215) and K. López. And for a more detailed study of the 1969 film, see Johnson ("Cinema Novo").

41. The film here underscores the director's claimed inspiration in the character Macunaíma: the words "No fundo da mata virgem" reference the beginning of Mário de Andrade's novel.

42. Her characterization of the Brazilian landscape recalls one of the intertitles from Mauro's 1937 *Descobrimento do Brasil*: "Os descobridores rasgam a matta virgem, a procura do lenho para a Cruz"; ["The discoverers scour the virgin forest in search of wood for the cross"].

43. Walter Lima Júnior's 1985 film *Chico Rei*, which re-creates the historical/legendary tale of an eighteenth-century African king who was taken captive, sold into slavery in Brazil, and eventually bought his liberty, concludes with a similar comment. The Afro-Brazilian narrator of the film, who speaks from an undefined period in the past, declares as the film closes: "Todo que a gente sabe é que ele tornou a ser rei, rei de uma festa que conta a sua glória, rei da congada, que os negros do Brasil ainda hoje cantam e dançam"; ["All we know is that he became king, king of a festival that recounts his glory, king of the *congada*, which Brazilian blacks still sing and dance today"]. For an analysis of this film see Gordon, "The Slave."

44. Arraes insists that the film "nasce de um sentimento de amor pelo Brasil, de querer gostar de ser brasileiro, o que permite também uma irreverência à História, com respeito mas com criatividade" ("Entrevista" n. pag.); ["was born from love for Brazil, from wanting to like being Brazilian, which enables also an irreverence toward History, with respect but with creativity"]. Arraes has said that he and screenplay co-writer Jorge Furtado wanted to "contar um pouco desta fábula meio à modernista, neo-tropicalista, aplicada ás cores, música, elementos de chanchada, que são as principais influências da nossa geração. E esta mistura nos possibilitaria também falar do Brasil de hoje" ("Entrevista" n. pag.); ["narrate a bit of this fable in a sort of [Brazilian] modernist, neo-Tropicalist way, with regard to colors, music, elements of the [comedic and often musical cinematic genre popular in Brazil in the 1930s, 1940s, and 1950s, the] chanchada, which are the principal influences of our generation. And this mixture would also make it possible for us to talk about the Brazil of today"].

Works Cited

Adorno, Rolena. "La estatua de Gonzalo Guerrero en Akumal: Íconos culturales y la reactualización del pasado colonial." *Revista Iberoamericana* 42.176–77 (July–Dec. 1996): 905–09.

———. *The Polemics of Possession in Spanish American Narrative*. New Haven and London: Yale UP, 2007.

A.F.P. [l'Agence France-Presse]. "Tuvo Buena Acogida en el Festival de Arcachón, el Filme Mexicano Nuevo Mundo." Rev. of *Nuevo mundo*, dir. Gabriel Retes. *Excelsior* 2 Sept. 1992: 3, 7.

Allen, T. "What's Cooking, Comrade?" Rev. of *Como era gostoso o meu francês*, dir. Nelson Pereira. *Village Voice* 28 Aug. 1978: 66.

Almeida, Eros Ramos de. "Invenção é 'O auto.'" *O Globo* 9 Nov. 2001: Rio Show 7.

Althusser, Louis. "Ideology and Ideological State Apparatuses (Notes towards an Investigation)." *Lenin and Philosophy and Other Essays*. Trans. B. Brewster. New York: Monthly Review P, 1971.

Alvaray, Luisela Amelia. "Signs of History: Difference in Audiovisual Accounts of 'Discovery and Conquest.'" Diss. UCLA, 2004.

Amado, Janaína. "Mythic Origins: Caramuru and the Founding of Brazil." *Hispanic American Historical Review* 80.4 (2000): 783–811.

Anderson, Benedict. *Imagined Communities*. London: Verso, 1991.

Andrade, Joaquim Pedro de, dir. *Macunaíma*. Difilm; Filmes do Sêrro; Grupo Filmes; Condor Filmes. VideoFilmes, 1969.

Andrade, Mário de. *Macunaíma: O herói sem nenhum caráter*. Ed. Telê Porto Ancona Lopez. [Paris]: ALLCA XX, 1988.

Andrade, Oswald de. "Manifesto antropófago." In "Anthropophagy Today?" Special issue of *Nuevo Texto Crítico* 12.23/24 (Jan.–Dec. 1999 [1928]): 25–31.

———. *Pau-Brasil*. 5th ed. São Paulo: Globo, 1991.

———. *A Utopia Antropofágica*. São Paulo: Globo / Secretaria de Estado da Cultura, 1990.

Aquino, Tacilda. "Em defesa da memória do cinema." *Folha de Goiáz* 23 Nov. 1983: n. pag.

Armas Serra, Beatriz de. "Memo to the Secretaria de Gobernación, Dpto. de Cinematografía." 13 Dec. 1999. Spanish Ministerio de Educación y Cultura. Mexican Cinetec, Mexico City.

Arraes, Guel, dir. *Caramuru: A Invenção do Brasil*. Globo Filmes. Columbia Tristar Home Entertainment. Film, 2001. DVD, 2002.

Works Cited

Arraes, Guel. "Entrevista: Guel Arraes." *Webcine*. Internet. Available: http://www.webcine.com.br/notaspro/npcaramu.htm. Accessed 20 July 2007. N.d. N. pag.

Arraes, Guel, and Jorge Furtado, dirs. *A Invenção do Brasil* [miniseries]. Rede Globo 2000.

Arreaza Camero, Emperatriz E. *Redescubriendo el descubrimiento*. Maracaibo: Astro Data, 1996.

Arroyo, Leonardo. *A Carta de Pero Vaz de Caminha: Ensaio de Informação à Procura de Constantes Válidas de Método*. 2nd ed. São Paulo: Melhoramentos / Instituto Nacional do Livro / Ministério da Educação e Cultura, 1976.

Autran, Arthur. "Roquette Pinto, Edgard." *Enciclopédia do Cinema Brasileiro*. Ed. Fernão Ramos and Luiz Felipe Miranda. São Paulo: SENAC São Paulo, 2000.

"Ave María (1999)." *The Internet Movie Database*. Internet. Available: http://us.imdb.com/Title?0185897. Accessed 7 Apr. 2002.

"Ave Maria [*sic*]." *The Latin American Video Archive*. N.d. Internet. Available: http://www.lavavideo.org. Accessed 7 Apr. 2002.

Aviña, Rafael. "Cabeza de Vaca." Rev. of *Cabeza de Vaca*, dir. Nicolás Echevarría. *Dicine* 38 (Mar. 1991): 12.

Ayala Blanco, Jorge. "Rossoff y la inteligencia cegada." Rev. of *Ave María*, dir. Eduardo Rossoff. *El financiero* 8 May 2000: Cultura 100.

Ayres de Casal, Manuel. *Corografia brazilica, ou, Relação historico-geografica do reino do Brazil, composta e dedicada a Sua Magestade fidelissima por hum prebitero secular do gram priorado do Crato* [...] Rio de Janeiro: Impressão regia, 1817.

Barriga Chávez, Ezequiel. "Desde la Butaca: *Ave María*." Rev. of *Ave María*, dir. Eduardo Rossoff. *Excelsior* 12 May 2000: Espectáculos 10.

Bemberg, María Luisa, dir. *Yo, la peor de todas*. GEA Cinematográfica, First Run Features, 1990.

Bhabha, Homi K. *The Location of Culture*. London and New York: Routledge, 1994.

Biaggio, Jaime. "Nova reinvenção de Guel Arraes: Diretor de 'O auto da compadecida' leva a série 'A invenção do Brasil' ao cinema." *O Globo* 7 Nov. 2001: Segundo Caderno 8.

Brading, David A. *The First America: The Spanish Monarchy, Creole Patriots, and the Liberal State, 1492–1867*. Cambridge and New York: Cambridge UP, 1991.

———. *Mexican Phoenix: Our Lady of Guadalupe: Image and Tradition across Five Centuries*. Cambridge: Cambridge UP, 2001.

Braga-Pinto, César. "Portugal Revisited, Brazil Rediscovered." *Global Impact of the Portuguese Language*. Ed. Asela Rodríguez de Laguna. New Brunswick and London: Transaction Publishers, 2001.

Caillois, Roger, Pedro Henríquez Ureña, and Germán Arciniegas. "Do the Americas Have a Common History?" *Journal of Latin American Cultural Studies* 9.3 (2000): 357–65.

Calderón, Eligio, et al. *Los mundos del Nuevo Mundo: El Descubrimiento, la Conquista, la Colonización y la Independencia de los Países Americanos, desde Alaska a la Patagonia, a través de la Mirada Cinematográfica. Catálogos y Paráfrasis*. México: Cineteca Nacional, 1994.

Caminha, Pêro Vaz de. *Carta*. Ed. Jaime Cortesão. Lisbon: Imprensa Nacional–Casa da Moeda, 1994.

———. "Letter of Pedro Vaz de Caminha to King Manuel, 1 May 1500." *The Voyage of Pedro Álvares Cabral to Brazil and India from Contemporary Documents and Narratives*. Trans., introd., ed. William Brooks Greenlee. London: The Hakluyt Society, 1938. 3–33.

Campo, Mônica Brincalepe. "*A Invenção do Brasil*: Proposta de narrativa da História no meio Audiovisual." Intercom—Sociedade Brasileira de Estudos Interdisciplinares da Comunicação. XXVIII Congresso Brasileiro de Ciências da Comunicação—Uerj—5 a 9 de setembro de 2005. Available: http://www.intercom.org.br/papers/nacionais/2005/resumos/R1603-1.pdf. Accessed 19 Feb. 2009.

Camurati, Carla, dir. *Carlota Joaquina, Princesa do Brasil*. Elimar Produções Artísticas, Europa Filmes, 2001.

Canby, Vincent. "On the Road with Cabeza de Vaca." Rev. of *Cabeza de Vaca*, dir. Nicolás Echevarría. *New York Times* 23 Mar. 1991: 12A.

Capelato, Maria Helena Rolim. *Multidões em Cena: Propaganda Política no Varguismo e no Peronismo*. Campinas, São Paulo: Papirus, 1998.

Capovilla, Maurice. "O Descobrimento do Brasil e Bandeirantes de Humberto Mauro." Rio de Janeiro: Cinemateca, 1962. N. pag.

"Caramuru—Brazil Reinvented, a Film by Guel Arraes." 2005. Internet. Available: http://www.brasilemb.org/cultural/washington_events.shtml. Accessed 20 July 2007. N. pag.

Works Cited

Carr, Jay. "Finally, an Honest Portrayal of the New World." Rev. of *Cabeza de Vaca*, dir. Nicolás Echevarría. *Boston Globe* 30 Oct. 1992: 32.

Carrasco, Salvador. "Entrevista con Salvador Carrasco." Internet. Available: http://www.jornada.unam.mx/1999/abr99/990418/sem-salvador.html. N. pag.

———. Interview. Press book for *La otra conquista*. [Rpt. in Cineteca Mexican internal document A03688: 66–67.]

———, dir. *La otra conquista*. Carrasco & Domingo Films S.A. de C.V.; ADO Entertainment (associate producer); CONACULTA; FONCA; Foprode; Fundacion Miguel Aleman; IMCINE; Salvastian Pictures; Secretaria de Desarrollo Social; Tabasco Films; Trata Films. Union Station Media; Starz Home Entertainment, 1998.

Carro, Nelson. "La otra conquista." Rev. of *La otra conquista*, dir. Salvador Carrasco. *Tiempo Libre* 10 Apr. 1999: 987 2.

Cervo, Amado Luiz, and José Calvet de Magalhães. *Depois das Caravelas: As relações entre Portugal e Brasil 1808–2000*. Brasília: Editora Universidade de Brasília, 2000.

Chanan, Michael. "New Cinemas in Latin America." *The Oxford History of World Cinema*. Ed. Geoffrey Nowell-Smith. New York: Oxford UP, 1997.

Chipman, Donald E. *Moctezuma's Childrem: Aztec Royalty under Spanish Rule, 1520–1700*. Austin: U of Texas P, 2005.

Ciuk, Perla. "'Ave María, no es una película que te haga pensar, sino sentir': Eduardo Rossoff." Rev. of *Ave María*, dir. Eduardo Rossoff. *Unomásuno* 6 May 2000: 30.

———. "Los Fantasmas del Roxy: Ave María." Rev. of *Ave María*, dir. Eduardo Rossoff. *Unomásuno* 3 May 2000: 37.

Clifford, James. *The Predicament of Culture: Twentieth-Century Ethnography, Literature, and Art*. Cambridge, MA: Harvard UP, 1988.

Columbus, Christopher. *Textos y documentos completos*. Ed. Consuelo Varela and Juan Gil. Madrid: Alianza, 1995.

Como era gostoso o meu francês, Rev. of. Dir. Nelson Pereira dos Santos. *Variety* 14 July 1971.

Cortesão, Jaime. *Cabral e as origens do Brasil*. Rio de Janeiro: Edição do Ministro das Relações Exteriores, 1944.

———, introd. and ed. *Carta*. By Pêro Vaz de Caminha. Lisbon: Imprensa Nacional–Casa da Moeda, 1994.

Works Cited

———. *A carta de Pero Vaz de Caminha*. Lisboa: Imprensa Nacional–Casa da Moeda, 1994.

———. Preface. *A Carta de Pero Vaz de Caminha*. Rio de Janeiro: Livros de Portugal, 1943.

Couto, José Geraldo. "'Descobrimento' de Mauro é mais lírico do que épico." Rev. of *Descobrimento do Brasil*, dir. Humberto Mauro. *Folha de São Paulo* 1 Oct. 1998: n. pag.

Cruz Polanco, Fabián de la. "'Ave María,' nueva visión del cine mexicano sobre el papel de la mujer en la época colonial." Rev. of *Ave María*, dir. Eduardo Rossoff. *Excelsior* 23 Apr. 2000: 7.

Cunha, Eneida Leal. "A estampa originária da dependência." *Brasil/Brazil* 13 (1995): 61–69.

Dávalos, Patricia E. "*Ave María*, historia colonial sobre intolerancia, amor, fe [...] y bostezos." Rev. of *Ave María*, dir. Eduardo Rossoff. *La crónica* 5 May 2000: 17.

———. "Se filma en la ex hacienda del Conde de Regla la película *Ave María*, coproducción México-España." *La crónica* 17 Aug. 1998: 15.

Davis, Natalie Zemon. *Slaves on Screen: Film and Historical Vision*. Cambridge, MA: Harvard UP, 2000.

Denby, D. "Same Old Stuff." Rev. of *Cabeza de Vaca*, dir. Nicolás Echevarría. *New York* 25 (8 June 1992): 58–59.

Departamento de Imprensa e Propaganda [D.I.P.]. *Brasil dos Nossos días* (D.I.P. #138). Rio de Janeiro: Jornal do Commercio Rodrigues & Cia., 1940.

———. *Quem foi que disse? Quem foi que fez?* (D.I.P. #145). Rio de Janeiro: Graph. Metrôpole, 1940.

Departamento Nacional de Propaganda [D.N.P.]. *O Brasil é Bom*. Rio de Janeiro: Officina Graphica Mauá, 1938. N. pag.

"O Descobrimento do Brasil." Rev. of *Descobrimento do Brasil*, dir. Humberto Mauro. *A Tarde* 1996: n. pag.

Dias, Gonçalves. *Poesia e Prosa Completas*. Rio de Janeiro: Nova Aguilar, 1998.

Diegues, Carlos. "The Cinema That Brazil Deserves." *New Brazilian Cinema*. Ed. Lúcia Nagib. London and New York: I. B. Tauris in association with The Centre for Brazilian Studies, U of Oxford, 2003. 23–35.

Durão, José de Santa Rita. *Caramuru: Poema épico do descobrimento da Bahia*. Lisbon: Na Regia officina typografica. 1781.

Works Cited

Echenberg, Margo. "On 'Wings of Fragile Paper': Sor Juana Inés de la Cruz and the *Fama y obras póstumas* (1700)." Diss. Brown U, 2000.

Echevarría, Nicolás, dir. *Cabeza de Vaca*. Producciones Iguana; IMCINE; American Playhouse; Channel Four Films; Cooperativa José Revueltas; Fondo de Fomento a la Calidad Cinematográfica; Gobierno del Estado de Coahuila; Gobierno del Estado de Nayarit; Grupo Alica; Sociedad Estatal Quinto Centenario; Sociedad Estatal para la Ejecucion de Programas del V Centenario; Televisión Española (TVE); Universidad de Guadalajara; New Horizons, 1991.

———. Interview. "La conquista según Nicolás Echevarría." By Leonardo García Tsao. *Dicine* 38 (Mar. 1991): 8–11.

Erauso, Catalina de. *Vida i sucesos de la monja alférez: Autobiografía atribuida a Doña Catalina de Erauso*. Ed. Rima de Vallbona. Tempe: Arizona State U, 1992.

España, Rafael de. *Las sombras del Encuentro: España y América: cuatro siglos de Historia a través del Cine*. Badajoz: Departamento de Publicaciones de la Diputación Provincial de Badajoz, 2002.

Fausto, Boris. *História do Brasil*. São Paulo, SP, Brasil: Edusp: Fundação para o Desenvolvimento da Educação, 1994.

Favata, Martin A., and José B. Fernández, trans. and eds. *The Account: Álvar Núñez Cabeza de Vaca's "Relación."* Houston: Arte Público P, 1993.

Fein, Seth. "From Collaboration to Containment: Hollywood and the International Political Economy of Mexican Cinema after the Second World War." *Mexico's Cinema: A Century of Film and Filmmakers*. Wilmington, DE: Scholarly Resources, 1999. 123–64.

Ferguson, Norman, dir. *The Three Caballeros*. Walt Disney Pictures. Buena Vista Home Entertainment, 1945.

Fernández, Enrique. "Cabeza de Vaca." *Village Voice* 37 (26 May 1992): 72.

Fernández de Oviedo, Gonzalo. *Sumario de la natural historia de las Indias*. Ed. Manuel Ballesteros. Madrid: Historia 16, 1986.

Ferrando, Roberto, ed. *Naufragios y Comentarios*. By Álvar Núñez Cabeza de Vaca. Madrid: Historia 16, 1985.

Ferreira, Alexandre Rodrigues, José Paulo Monteiro Soares, Cristina Ferrão, and António José Landi. *Viagem ao Brasil de Alexandre Rodrigues Ferreira: a expedição philosophica pelas Capitanias do Pará, Rio Negro, Mato Grosso e Cuyabá*. Petrópolis, Brazil: Kapa, 2008.

Works Cited

Fitz, Earl. "Internationalizing the Literature of the Portuguese-Speaking World." *Hispania* 85.3 (Sept. 2002): 439–48.

Franco, Jean. "High-tech Primitivism: The Represetation of Tribal Societies in Feature Films." *Mediating Two Worlds: Cinematic Encounters in the Americas*. Ed. John King, Ana M. López, and Manuel Alvarado. London: BFI Publishing, 1993. 81–94.

Freyre, Francisco de Britto. *Nova Lusitânia: História da guerra brasílica*. Lisbon: Oficina de Joam Galram, 1675.

Freyre, Gilberto. *Casa-grande & senzala: formação da família brasileira sob o regime da economia patriarcal*. 18th ed. Rio de Janeiro: J. Olympio, 1977.

———. *Conferencias na Europa*. Rio de Janeiro: Ministerio da Educação e Saude / Serviço Gráfico, 1938.

Fuentes, Fernando de, dir. *La devoradora*. Producciones Grovas 1946.

Gallegos, José Luis. "Actuación Estelar de Ana Torrent y Damián Alcázar; Dirección de Eduardo Rossoff." *Excelsior* 23 July 1998: 4.

García, Gustavo A. "In Quest of a National Cinema: The Silent Era." *Mexico's Cinema: A Century of Film and Filmmakers*. Ed. Joanne Hershfield and David R. Maciel. Wilmington, DE: Scholarly Resources, 1999. 5–16.

García Riera, Emilio. *Breve historia del cine mexicano: Primer siglo: 1897–1997*. México: Ediciones Mapa SA de CV, 1998.

———. *Historia documental del cine mexicano*. 1st ed. México, DF: Era, 1969.

García Tsao, Leonardo. "La verdadera conquista de *La otra conquista*." Rev. of *La otra conquista*, dir. Salvador Carrasco. *La Jornada* 23 May 1999: Jornada Semanal 12.

Garcilaso, Silvia. "Una historia en torno a la fe y la libertad." *El Nacional* 16 Aug. 1998: 41.

Gatti, André, and Inimá Simões. "Censura." *Enciclopédia do Cinema Brasileiro*. Ed. Fernão Ramos and Luiz Felipe Miranda. São Paulo: SENAC São Paulo, 2000.

Gatti, José. "(Re)discoveries of Brazil." *Ilha do desterro* 32 (1997): 163–76.

Gomes, Angela de Castro. *História e Historiadores: A Política Cultural do Estado Novo*. Rio de Janeiro: Fundação Getúlio Vargas, 1996.

Gómez Muriel, Emilio, dir. *La monja alférez*. Clasa Films Mundiales. Noda Audio Visual, 1944.

Works Cited

González Echevarría, Roberto. *Celestina's Brood: Continuities of the Baroque in Spanish and Latin American Literature.* Durham: Duke UP, 1993.

González Echevarría, Roberto, and Enrique Pupo-Walker, eds. *The Cambridge History of Latin American Literature.* Vol. 1: *Discovery to Modernism.* Cambridge: Cambridge UP, 1996.

Gordon, Richard A. "The Domestication of the Ensign Nun: *La monja alférez* (1944) and Mexican Identity." *Hispania* 87.4 (Dec. 2004): 675–81.

———. "Recreating Caminha: The Earnest Adaptation of Brazil's Letter of Discovery in Humberto Mauro's *Descobrimento do Brasil* (1937)." *MLN* 120.2 (2005): 408–36.

———. "The Slave as National Symbol in Cuban and Brazilian Cinema: Representing Resistance and Promoting National Unity in *La última cena* and *Chico Rei*." *Journal of Latin American Cultural Studies* 15.3 (Dec. 2006): 301–20.

Gransden, Gregorio. "Ave María." Rev. of *Ave María*, dir. Eduardo Rossoff. *Excelsior* 7 May 2000: 12.

Greenlee, William Brooks, trans., introd., and ed. *The Voyage of Pedro Álvares Cabral to Brazil and India from Contemporary Documents and Narratives.* London: The Hakluyt Society, 1937.

Greenspun, Roger. Rev. of *Como era gostoso o meu francês*, dir. Nelson Pereira. *New York Times* 17 Apr. 1973: 34:1.

Griffith, James. "Overlooked and Underrated: How Tasty Was My Little Frenchman." Rev. of *Como era gostoso o meu francês*, dir. Nelson Pereira. *Take One* 4 (1979): 12.

"Há 50 Anos." *O Globo* 31 Oct. 1987: n. pag.

Habib, Sérgio. "Graciliano Ramos fala de Humberto Mauro." *Jornal de Brasília* 10 Feb. 1979: n. pag.

Hall, Stuart. "The Problem of Ideology: Marxism without Guarantees." *Stuart Hall: Critical Dialogues in Cultural Studies.* Ed. D. Morley and K. Chen. New York: Routledge, 1996. 25–46.

Hartl, John. "How Do You Solve a Problem Like 'Ave María'?" Rev. of *Ave María*, dir. Eduardo Rossoff. *The Seattle Times* 4 June 2000: M2.

Heffner, Hernani. "Notas sobre *O descobrimento do Brasil* de Humberto Mauro." *Restauração de O descobrimento do Brasil.* Ed. André Andries. Rio de Janeiro: Funarte, 1997. 16–19.

Hernández, Jesús. "Memorias de un mestizaje." Rev. of *La otra conquista*, dir. Salvador Carrasco. *El Financiero* 23 Mar. 1999: Cultura 59.

Hernández Espinosa, Joel. "*Ave María*, el castigo a la mujer por su inteligencia y sabiduría." Rev. of *Ave María*, dir. Eduardo Rossoff. *El día* 30 Apr. 2000: 27.

Hershfield, Joanne. "Assimilation and Identification in Nicolás Echevarría's *Cabeza de Vaca*." *Wide Angle* 16.3 (1995): 6–24.

———. "Race and Ethnicity in the Classical Cinema." *Mexico's Cinema: A Century of Film and Filmmakers*. Ed. Joanne Hershfield and David Maciel. Wilmington, DE: Scholarly Resources, 1999. 81–100.

Hind, Emily. "The Sor Juana Archetype in Recent Works by Mexican Women Writers." *Hispanófila* 141 (May): 89–103.

Holanda, Sérgio Buarque de. *Raízes do Brasil*. Rio de Janeiro: Livraria José Olympio, 1976.

"Icon." *Webster's Third New International Dictionary of the English Language*. Unabridged. 1986.

IPS. "*Nuevo mundo*, dirigida por Retes y prohibida aquí, se exhibirá en Alemania." Rev. of *Nuevo mundo*, dir. Gabriel Retes. *Uno más uno* 9 Sept. 1992: n. pag.

Jáuregui, Carlos A. *Canibalia: Canibalismo, calibanismo, antropofagia cultural y consumo en América Latina*. Madrid and Frankfurt: Iberoamericana/Vervuert, 2008.

Johnson, Randal. "Brazilian Modernism: An Idea Out of Place?" *Modernism and Its Margins: Reinscribing Cultural Modernity from Spain and Latin America*. Ed. Anthony L. Geist and José B. Monleón. New York and London: Garland, 1999. 186–214.

———. "Cinema Novo and Cannibalism: *Macunaíma*." *Brazilian Cinema*. Ed. Randal Johnson and Robert Stam. New York: Columbia UP, 1991. 178–90.

———. *The Film Industry in Brazil: Culture and the State*. Pittsburgh: U of Pittsburgh P, 1987.

———. "Tupy or Not Tupy: Cannibalism and Nationalism in Contemporary Brazilian Literature and Culture." *On Modern Latin American Fiction*. Ed. John King. London and Boston: Faber and Faber, 1987. 41–59.

Juana Inés de la Cruz. *Obras completas*. Ed. Alfonso Méndez Plancarte and Alberto G. Salceda. 4 vols. México: Fondo de Cultura Económica, 1951–57.

Works Cited

Juana Inés de la Cruz. *A Sor Juana Anthology*. Ed. and trans. Alan S. Trueblood. Cambridge, MA: Harvard UP, 1988.

Juan-Navarro, Santiago. "Constructing Cultural Myths: Cabeza de Vaca in Contemporary Hispanic Criticism, Theater, and Film." *A Twice-Told Tale: Reinventing the Encounter in Iberian / Iberian American Literature and Film*. Ed. Santiago Juan-Navarro and Theodore Robert Young. Newark: U of Delaware P, 2001. 67–79.

Juan-Navarro, Santiago, and Theodore Robert Young. *A Twice-Told Tale: Reinventing the Encounter in Iberian / Iberian American Literature and Film*. Newark: U of Delaware P, 2001.

Kornis, Mônica Almeida. "Ficção televisiva e identidade nacional: o caso da Rede Globo." *História e cinema*. Ed. Maria Helena Capelato et al. São Paulo: Alameda, 2007. 97–114.

Lazcano, Hugo. "Intolerancia de dos culturas." *Reforma* 11 Sept. 1998: 2.

Leigh-Stone, Cynthia. "The Filming of Colonial Spanish America." *Colonial Latin American Review* 5.2 (1996): 315–20.

Lenine. Interview. N.d. Internet. Available: http://www.webcine.com.br/notaspro/npcaramu.htm. Accessed 20 July 2007. N. pag.

León-Portilla, Miguel. *Tonantzin Guadalupe. Pensamiento náhuatl y mensaje cristiano en el 'Nican Mopohua.'* Mexico City: El Colegio Nacional/Fondo de Cultura Económica, 2000.

Levine, Robert M. *Father of the Poor? Vargas and His Era*. Cambridge, Engl.: Cambridge UP, 1998.

Lima Júnior, Walter, dir. *Chico Rei*. Art-4; POProduções. Globo Vídeo,1985.

López, Ana M. "A Cinema for the Continent." *The Mexican Cinema Project*. Ed. Chon A. Noriega and Steven Ricci. Los Angeles: UCLA Film and Television Archive, 1994. 7–12.

López, Kimberle S. *Latin American Novels of the Conquest : Reinventing the New World*. Columbia: U of Missouri P, 2002.

———. "*Modernismo* and the Ambivalence of the Postcolonial Experience: Cannibalism, Primitivism, and Exoticism in Mário de Andrade's *Macunaíma*." *Luso-Brazilian Review* 35.1 (1998): 26–38.

Lourenço, Cileine I. "Negotiating Africanness in National Identity: Studies in Brazilian and Cuban Cinema." Diss. The Ohio State U, 1998.

Luna, Andrés de. "The Labyrinths of History." *Mexican Cinema*. Ed. Paulo Antonio Paranaguá. Trans. Ana M. López. London: British Film Institute, 1995. 171–79.

Maciel, David. "Cinema and the State in Contemporary Mexico, 1970–1999." *Mexico's Cinema: A Century of Filmmakers.* Ed. Joanne Hershfield and David R. Maciel. Wilmington, DE: Scholarly Resources, 1999. 197–232.

Madureira, Luis. *Cannibal Modernities: Postcoloniality and the Avant-Garde in Caribbean and Brazilian Literature.* Charlottesville: U of Virginia P, 2005.

———. "A Cannibal Recipe to Turn a Dessert Country into the Main Course: Brazilian *Antropofagia* and the Dilemma of Development." *Luso-Brazilian Review* 41.2 (2005): 96–125.

Martin, Marcel. "Qu'il etait bon mon petit français." *Ecran* 25 (May 1974): 64–65.

Matamoros, Mauricio. "En *Ave María* la intolerante Nueva España se asemeja a nuestra modernidad." Rev. of *Ave María*, dir. Eduardo Rossoff. *Unomásuno* 25 Apr. 2000: 34.

Mattos, Carlos Alberto. "Licenças poéticas de Caramuru: Nas telas, sob a direção de Guel Arraes, a comédia da vida privado do primeiro português a pisar no Brasil." *Jornal do Brasil* 14 Nov. 2001: Caderno B 7.

Mauro, Humberto, dir. *Descobrimento do Brasil.* Instituto de Cacau da Bahia; Ministério da Educação e Saúde; Instituto Nacional de Cinema Educativo; Ministério da Educação e Cultura. Funarte, 1937.

———. "O Mundo e as Idéias de Humberto Mauro." *Humberto Mauro: Sua vida / sua arte / sua trajetória no cinema.* Rio de Janeiro: Artenova / EMBRAFILME, 1978. 101–234.

Mendoza González, Jessica. "Entre religiosa y pagana." Rev. of *Ave María*, dir. Eduardo Rossoff. *El Universal* 28 Apr. 2000: 1.

Merrim, Stephanie. *Early Modern Women's Writing and Sor Juana Inés de la Cruz.* Nashville: Vanderbilt UP, 1999.

———. "Spectacular Cityscapes of Baroque Spanish America." *Literary Cultures of Latin America: A Comparative History.* Vol. 3. Ed. and introd. Mario J. Valdés and Djelal Kadir. Oxford, Engl.: Oxford UP, 2004. 31–57.

Merten, Luiz Carlos. "Humberto Mauro redescobre o Pais." *O Estado de São Paulo* 19 July 1996: n. pag.

Mestre João. "Letter of Master John to to King Manuel, 1 May 1500." *The Voyage of Pedro Álvares Cabral to Brazil and India from Contemporary Documents and Narratives.* Trans., introd., ed. William Brooks Greenlee. London: The Hakluyt Society, 1938. 36–40.

Works Cited

Miceli, Sérgio. *Intelectuais e Classe Dirigente no Brasil (1920–1945)*. São Paulo and Rio de Janeiro: Difel/Difusão, 1979.

Miranda, Luiz Felipe. "Mauro, Humberto." *Enciclopédia do Cinema Brasileiro*. Ed. Fernão Ramos and Luiz Felipe Miranda. São Paulo: SENAC São Paulo, 2000.

Moheno, Gustavo. "The Other Conquest." *Cine Premiere* (Apr. 1999). Internet. Available: http://www.theotherconquest.com/site/reviews/content_cine.html. Accessed 10 Apr. 2002.

Monroy, Manuel H. "Impactó el Filme 'Ave María.'" Rev. of *Ave María*, dir. Eduardo Rossoff. *Excelsior* 28 Apr. 2000: 1.

Monteiro, Elis. "'Caramuru' e a reinvenção do cinema: Captado em alta definição, novo filme de Guel Arraes rende-se à era do cinema digital." *O Globo* 12 Nov. 2001: Informática. N. pag.

Mora, Carl J. *Mexican Cinema: Reflections of a Society: 1896–1980*. Berkeley: U of California P, 1982.

Morettin, Eduardo Victorio. "Produção e formas de circulação do tema do Descobrimento do Brasil: uma análise de seu percurso e do filme *Descobrimento do Brasil* (1937), de Humberto Mauro." *Revista Brasileira de História* 20.39 (2000): 135–65.

Mraz, John. "Pereira dos Santos, Nelson." *International Dictionary of Film and Filmmakers* Vol. 2: *Directors*. Ed. Nicholas Thomas. 2nd ed. Chicago: St. James P, 1991.

———. "Recasting Cuban Slavery: *The Other Francisco* and *The Last Supper*." *Based on a True Story: Latin American History at the Movies*. Ed. Donald F. Stevens. Wilmington, DE: Scholarly Resources, 1997. 103–22.

Mulvey, Laura. "Then and Now: Cinema as History in the Light of New Media and New Technologies." *The New Brazilian Cinema*. London and New York: I.B. Tauris in association with The Centre for Brazilian Studies, U of Oxford, 2003. 261–69.

———. "Visual Pleasure and Narrative Cinema." *Screen* 16.4 (1975): 6–18.

Murat, Lúcia, dir. *Brava Gente Brasileira*. BigDeni Filmes; Costa do Castelo Filmes; Quanta Centro de Produções Cinematográficas; Skylight Cinema Foto Art; Taiga Films. Europa Filmes. Film, 2000. DVD, 2001.

Nájera-Ramírez, Olga. "Engendering Nationalism: Identity, Discourse and the Mexican Charro." *Anthropology Quarterly* 67.1 (1994): 1–14.

Nemer, Ana Rita, Sérgio Arena, and Joaquim Eufrasino. "Letreiros." *Restauração de O descobrimento do Brasil*. Ed. André Andries. Rio de Janeiro: Funarte, 1997. 13.

Nogueira, Claudia Barbosa. "Journeys of Redemption: Discoveries, Rediscoveries, and Cinematic Representations of the Americas." Diss. U of Maryland, College Park, 2006.

Núñez Cabeza de Vaca, Álvar. *Castaways: The Narrative of Álvar Núñez Cabeza de Vaca*. Ed. Enrique Pupo-Walker. Trans. Frances M. López-Morillas. Berkeley: U of California P, 1993.

Núñez Cabeza de Vaca, Álvar. *Naufragios y Comentarios*. Ed. Roberto Ferrando. Madrid: Historia 16, 1985.

Oliveira, Francisco de. "Fronteiras Invisíveis." Text distributed to announce his presentation in the pamphet produced for the conference *Oito Visões da América Latina: Perto de um Mundo Distante*. CCBB. Rio de Janeiro. 15–29 June 2004.

Oliveira, Lúcia Lippi, Mônica Pimenta Velloso, and Ângela Maria Castro Gomes. *Estado Novo: Ideologia e Poder*. Rio de Janeiro: Zahar, 1982.

Paranaguá, Paulo Antonio. "Nelson Pereira dos Santos: Trajectoire d'un dépouillement." *Positif* 298 (Dec. 1985): 13–19.

———. "Pasado y presente en el cine latinoamericano: Jalones para una reflexión." *La historia y el cine*. Ed. Esteve Riambau and Joaquim Romaguera. Barcelona: Fontamara, 1983.

Pardo, Laura. "Un heroico rosario." Rev. of *Ave María*, dir. Eduardo Rossoff. *Reforma* 5 May 2000: 4.

Pavão, Jadyr. "Cenas do passado: Sobre qual 'Descobrimento do Brasil,' emfim, falava Humberto Mauro?" 2000. Internet. Available: http://www.valor.com.br/valoreconomico/matteria. asp?id=563805. Accessed 21 July 2001.

Paz, Octavio. *Sor Juana*. Trans. Margaret Sayers Peden. Cambridge, MA: Harvard UP, 1988.

———. *Sor Juana Inés de la Cruz o las trampas de la fe*. Barcelona: Seix Barral, 1982.

Peguero, Raquel. "*Ave María*, historia 'sensual de represión,' será filmada en Hidalgo." *La Jornada* 23 July 1998: 40.

———. "*Ave María* no será una película religiosa sino histórica: Rosoff [sic]." *La Jornada* 17 Aug. 1998: 29.

Peixoto, Floriano. Interview. Press book for *Brava Gente Brasileira*.

Peña, Richard. "Como era gostoso o meu francês." *International Dictionary of Film and Filmmakers*—Vol. 1: *Films*. Ed. Nicholas Thomas. 2nd ed. Chicago: St. James, 1991.

Pereira, Paulo Roberto, ed. *Os três únicos testemunhos do descobrimento do Brasil*. 2nd ed. Rio de Janeiro: Lacerda, 1999.

Works Cited

Pereira dos Santos, Nelson, dir. *Como era gostoso o meu francês.* Condor Filmes; Luiz Carlos Barreto Produções Cinematográficas. Sagres [Brazil], New Yorker Video [US], 1971.

———. Interview. "Le cinema novo: Une histoire vieille de dix ans." By J. Frenais. *Cinéma* Oct. 1976: 70–74.

———. Interview. "Nelson Pereira dos Santos." By Julianne Burton. *Cinema and Social Change in Latin America: Conversations with Filmmakers.* Austin: U of Texas P, 1986.

Pérez Marín, Yarí. "Lecturas en celuloide: El personaje indígena latinoamericano en el 'cine de época.'" Unpublished ms.

Pérez Turrent, Tomás. "Crises and Renovations (1965–1991)." *Mexican Cinema.* Ed. Paulo Antonio Paranaguá. Trans. Ana M. López. London: British Film Institute, 1995. 94–116.

Pick, Zuzana M. *The New Latin American Cinema: A Continental Project.* Austin: U of Texas P, 1993.

Pina, Luís de. "O Descobrimento do Brasil (1937): Un filme de Humberto Mauro." *489° Aniversário da Descoberta do Brasil.* Lisbon: Cinemateca Portuguesa, 1989. N. pag.

Poole, Stafford. *Our Lady of Guadalupe: The Origins and Sources of a Mexican National Symbol, 1531–1797.* Tucson: U of Arizona P, 1995.

Rabasa, José. *Writing Violence on the Northern Frontier: The Historiography of Sixteenth-Century New Mexico and Florida and the Legacy of Conquest.* Durham and London: Duke UP, 2000.

Ramírez Hernández, Rocío. "'Ave María' levanta el vuelo." *Novedades* 22 July 1998: 10.

———. "*La otra conquista* muestra la visión de los vencidos." Rev. of *La otra conquista*, dir. Salvador Carrasco. *Novedades* 1 Apr. 1999: Espectáculos 1.

Ramos, Alcides Freire. *Canibalismo dos fracos.* Bauru, São Paulo: EDUSC, 2002.

Ramos, Graciliano. "Uma Tradução de Pero Vaz." *Humberto Mauro: Sua vida / sua arte / sua trajetória no cinema.* Rio de Janeiro: Editora Artenova / EMBRAFILME, 1978. 66–68.

"Reasons behind Fade of Brazil's 'Cine Novo.'" *Variety* 31 Mar. 1976: 68.

Rego, A. da Silva. *Relações Luso-Brasileiras (1822–1953).* Lisbon: Panorama, 1966.

Retes, Gabriel, dir. *Nuevo mundo.* Corporación Nacional Cinematográfica (CONACINE); S.T.P.C. de la R. M. Vanguard Cinema, 1976.

Works Cited

Reyes, Aurelio de los. *Cine y sociedad en México: 1896–1930*. Vol. 1: *1896–1920*. México: Universidad Nacional Autónoma de México and Instituto de Investigaciones Estéticas, 1996.

Ricard, Robert. *The Spiritual Conquest of Mexico: An Essay on the Apostolate and the Evangelizing Methods of the Mendicant Orders in New Spain, 1523–1572*. Trans. Lesley Byrd Simpson. Berkeley: U of California P, 1966 [1933].

Ríos Alfaro, Lorena. "El principal reto en el cine es la dirección." *Unomásuno* 16 Aug. 1998: 24.

Rivers, Kenneth. "Alfred Hitchcock's WWII French Films and the Limits of Propaganda." N.d. Internet. Available: http://www.imagesjournal.com/issue09/features/wwiifrench/. Accessed 29 Oct. 2001.

Rocha, João César de Castro. "Let Us Devour Oswald de Andrade: A Rereading of the *Manifesto antropófago*." "Anthropophagy Today?" Special issue of *Nuevo Texto Crítico* 12.23/24 (Jan.–Dec. 1999): 5–19.

Rocha Pita, Sebastião da. *Historia da America portugueza, desde o anno de mil e quinhentos do seu descobrimento, até o de mil e setecentos e vinte e quatro*. Lisboa occidental: Na officina de Joseph Antonio da Sylva, 1730.

Rosenstone, Robert A. *Visions of the Past: The Challenge of Film to Our Idea of History*. Cambridge, MA and London: Harvard UP, 1995.

Rossoff, Eduardo, dir. *Ave María*. Manga Films; Foprocine; IMCINE; Lestes Films. DistriMax, 1999.

Sabat-Rivers, Georgina. "Sor Juana Inés de la Cruz." *Historia de la Literatura Hispanoamericana*. Vol. 1: *Época colonial*. Ed. Luis Íñigo Madrigal. 2nd ed. Madrid: Cátedra, 1992. 275–94.

Sadlier, Darlene J. *Nelson Pereira dos Santos*. Urbana and Chicago: U of Illinois P, 2003.

Said, Edward W. *Orientalism*. New York: Pantheon, 1978.

Salazar Hernández, Alejandro. "*Ave María*, cinta sobre la tolerancia y la justicia." *El Nacional* 23 July 1998: 43.

Saragoza, Alex M., with Graciela Berkovich. "Intimate Connections: Cinematic Allegories of Gender, the State and National Identity." *The Mexican Cinema Project*. Ed. Chon A. Noriega and Steven Ricci. Los Angeles: UCLA Film and Television Archive, 1994. 25–32.

Schvarzman, Sheila. *Humberto Mauro e as imagens do Brasil*. São Paulo: UNESP, 2003.

Works Cited

Schvarzman, Sheila. "Humberto Mauro e a constituição da memória do cinema brasileiro." 2001. Internet. Available: http://www.mnemocine.com.br/cinema/historiatextos/hmauro.htm. Accessed 21 July 2001.

Shohat, Ella. "Notes on the "Post-Colonial." *The Pre-Occupation of Postcolonial Studies*. Ed. Fawzia Afzal-Khan and Kalpana Seshadri-Crooks. Durham and London: Duke UP, 2000. 126–39.

Shohat, Ella, and Robert Stam. *Unthinking Eurocentrism: Multiculturalism and the Media*. London and New York: Routledge, 1994.

Skidmore, Thomas E. *Black into White: Race and Nationality in Brazilian Thought: With a Preface to the 1993 Edition and Bibliography*. Durham: Duke UP, 1993.

———. *Brazil: Five Centuries of Change*. New York: Oxford UP, 1999.

———. "Racial Ideas and Social Policy in Brazil, 1870–1940." *The Idea of Race in Latin America, 1870–1940*. Ed. and introd. Richard Graham. Austin: U of Texas P, 1990.

Soares, Mariza de Carvalho, and Jorge Ferreira. *A História Vai ao Cinema: Vinte Filmes Brasileiros Comentados por Historiadores*. Rio de Janeiro: Record, 2001.

Sommer, Doris. *Foundational Fictions: The National Romances of Latin America*. Berkeley: U of California P, 1991.

Sousa, G. U. de. "Theatrics and Politics of Culture in Sixteenth-Century Brazil." *Journal of Dramatic Theory and Criticism* 8.2 (Spring 1994): 89–102.

Souza, Carlos Roberto de. "À Espera de Discípulos." *Humberto Mauro: Sua vida / sua arte / sua trajetória no cinema*. Rio de Janeiro: Artenova / EMBRAFILME, 1978. 88–91.

Souza, Márcio. "Um novo descobrimento." *Restauração de O descobrimento do Brasil*. Ed. André Andries. Rio de Janeiro: Funarte, 1997. 5.

Staden, Hans. *Hans Staden's True History: An Account of Cannibal Captivity in Brazil*. Ed. and trans. Neil L. Whitehead and Michael Harbsmeier. Durham and London: Duke UP, 2008.

———. *Viagem ao Brasil; Versão do texto de Marburgo, de 1557*. Ed. Theodoro Sampaio. Rio de Janeiro: Officina Industrial Graphica, 1930.

Stallybrass, Peter, and Allon White. *The Poetics and Politics of Transgression*. Ithaca: Cornell UP, 1986.

Stam, Robert. "Beyond Fidelity: The Dialogics of Adaptation." *Film Adaptation*. Ed. James Naremore. New Brunswick, NJ: Rutgers UP, 2000. 54–78.

Works Cited

———. "Cabral and the Indians: Filmic Representations of Brazil's 500 Years." *The New Brazilian Cinema.* Ed. Lúcia Nagib. London and New York: Tauris in association with The Centre for Brazilian Studies, U of Oxford, 2003. 205–28.

———. "Cross-cultural Dialogisms: Race and Multiculturalism in Brazilian Cinema." *Mediating Two Worlds: Cinematic Encounters in the Americas.* Ed. John King, Ana M. López, and Manuel Alvarado. London: BFI Publishing, 1993. 175–91.

———. *Tropical Multiculturalism: A Comparative History of Race in Brazilian Cinema and Culture.* Durham, NC: Duke UP, 1997.

Stam, Robert, and Ismail Xavier. "Transformation of National Allegory: Brazilian Cinema from Dictatorship to Redemocratization." *New Latin American Cinema.* Vol. 2: *Studies of National Cinemas.* Ed. Michael T. Martin. Detroit: Wayne State UP, 1997. 295–322.

Stevens, Donald F., ed. *Based on a True Story: Latin American History at the Movies.* Wilmington, DE: Scholarly Resources, 1997.

"Strat." Rev. of *Cabeza de Vaca*, dir. Nicolás Echevarría. *Variety* 4 Mar. 1991: 54.

Subirats, Eduardo. "La otra conquista." Rev. of *La otra conquista*, dir. Salvador Carrasco. *Reforma* 28 Oct. 1998: Angel Cultural 3.

Thomas, Kevin. "Mysticism and Wonder Prevail in 'Cabeza.'" Rev. of *Cabeza de Vaca*, dir. Nicolás Echevarría. *Los Angeles Times* 3 July 1992: 17F.

Tiffin, Helen. "Post-colonial Literatures and Counter-discourse." *The Post-colonial Studies Reader.* Ed. Bill Ashcroft, Gareth Griffiths, and Helen Tiffin. London: Routledge, 1995. 95–98.

Trelles Plazaola, Luís. *Imágenes cambiantes: Descubirimiento, conquista y colonización de la América Hispana vista por el cine de ficción y largometraje.* San Juan: Editorial de la Universidad de Puerto Rico, 1996.

Trueblood, Alan S., ed. and trans. *A Sor Juana Anthology.* Cambridge, MA: Harvard UP, 1988.

"Uma leitura original e divertido da História de Caramuru e Paraguaçu." N.d. Internet. Available: http://www.editoras.com/objetiva/303-1.htm. Accessed 20 July 2007.

Varnhagen, Francisco Adolfo de. "O Caramuru perante a História." *Revista Trimestral de História e Geographia ou Jornal do Instituto Histórico e Geográfico Brasileiro* 10.2 (1848): 129–52.

Works Cited

Vasconcellos, Simão de. *Chronica da Companhia de Jesu do Estado do Brasil*. Lisbon: Na officina de Henrique Valente de Oliveira. 1663.

Velasco, Salvador. "La guerra de imágenes en *La otra conquista* de Salvador Carrasco." *Cuadernos Americanos* 87 (2001): 128–32.

Velasco, Sherry M. *The Lieutenant Nun: Transgenderism, Lesbian Desire and Catalina de Erauso*. Austin: U of Texas P, 2000.

Voigt, Lisa. *Writing Captivity in the Early Modern Atlantic: Circulations of Knowledge and Authority in the Iberian and English Imperial Worlds*. Chapel Hill, NC: Omohundro Institute of Early American History and Culture/U of North Carolina P, 2009.

Williams, Bruce. "To Serve Godard: Anthropophagical Processes in Brazilian Cinema." *Literature Film Quarterly* 27.3 (1999): 202–09.

Xavier, Ismail. "Eldorado as Hell: Cinema Novo and Post Cinema Novo—Appropriations of the Imaginary of the Discovery." *Mediating Two Worlds: Cinematic Encounters in the Americas*. Ed. John King, Ana M. López, and Manuel Alvarado. London: BFI Publishing, 1993. 192–203.

Index

1492: Conquest of Paradise (dir. Ridley Scott), 202n25
Acordo Cultural Luso-Brasileiro, 45
adaptation. *See* anthropophagous adaptation
Adorno, Rolena, 197n1, 213n24
A.F.P. (l'Agence France-Presse), 215n2, 216n4, 216n8
Aguiar y Seijas, Francisco, Archbishop, 122, 221n30, 222n31
Ajuricaba: O Rebelde da Amazônia (dir. Oswaldo Caldeira), 201n20
Albuquerque, Cao, 161
Aleijadinho: Paixão, Glória e Suplício (dir. Geraldo Santos Pereira), 4
Alencar, José de, 198n6, 200n19
Alianza por el Cambio (PAN-PVEM), 109, 218n2
alienation. *See* anthropophagous adaptation: and exoticizing
allegory, 15
Allen, T., 72, 210n5
Almeida, Eros Ramos de, 162, 232n32
Alvarado, Manuel, 199n11
Alvaray, Luisela Amelia, 199n11
Amado, Janaína, 153–55, 226n7, 227n10, 228nn11–13 and 15
Anchieta, José do Brasil (dir. Paulo César Saraceni), 24, 201n23
Anchieta Entre o Amor e a Religião (dir. Arturo Carrari), 201n23
Andrade, Joaquim Pedro de, 157, 169
Andrade, Mário de, 164, 169, 231n30, 233n41

Andrade, Oswald de, 2–3, 22, 39, 46, 152, 156, 197n3, 204nn9–10, 210n4, 227n9, 231n30
anthropophagous adaptation, 1–3, 4, 8, 10, 15, 96, 109, 150–76, 177–79
 and authorizing of adaptation, 16, 19, 20–40, 46, 51, 141, 142, 157, 161, 176
 and context of the adaptation, 4, 19, 40–46, 109
 and exoticizing (*also* self-exoticizing, alienation, othering, exoticism, Eurocentrism), 13–14, 28, 47–77, 127, 176, 177, 202n29, 211n6
 and identity, 3, 4
 and nationalism or patriotism, 3
 and persuasion, 19–21, 38, 40, 41, 42, 46, 98, 178
 and resistance, 3
 and source text (real or imaginary), 2, 53
 relationship between film and source text, 16, 111–12
 collusive relationship, 19–46
 consciousness raising, 202n27
 disconnected, 27, 63
 dominant relationship, 1–3, 16–17
 egalitarian relationship, 16–17
 intertextual dialogism, 16–17, 178, 202n28
 invented source, 15, 16, 98, 132–40, 141–76, 177–79
 loose, open, 109–10
 unwieldy, 177–79
anthropophagy. *See* cannibalism

253

Index

Aquino, Tacilda, 24, 39, 205n13
Arciniegas, Germán, 10
Armstrong, Neil, 168, 233n38
Arraes, Guel, 5, 15, 19, 83, 98, 141–76, 220n15, 226n7, 227n9, 230nn24–26 and 28, 231n30, 232n31, 233n44
Arreaza Camero, Emperatriz E., 199n11
Arroyo, Leonardo, 209n44
Autran, Arthur, 41
Ave María (dir. Eduardo Rossoff), 4, 5, 14, 15, 16, 79, 83, 104, 109–40, 143, 144, 150, 177–79, 200n13, 201nn23–24, 217nn16–17, 219nn3 and 5, 220n18, 223n36
Ávila Camacho, Manuel, 5
Aviña, Rafael, 73
Ayala Blanco, Jorge, 112, 115, 116, 221n23, 225n43
Aztecs. *See* Nahua

Bandeirantes (dir. Humberto Mauro), 206n24
Barriga Chávez, Ezequiel, 110, 112
Biaggio, Jaime, 160, 162, 230n27
bien esquivo, El (dir. Augusto Tomayo San Román), 4
Bolívar, sinfonía tropikal (dir. Diego Rísquez), 201n22
Brading, David A., 215n4, 216n5, 217n12, 218n21
Braga-Pinto, César, 204n6
Brava Gente Brasileira (dir. Lúcia Murat), 5, 14, 15, 16, 19, 98, 141–76, 201nn20–21, 203n1, 226nn3–5
Brazil and Mexico, in comparison. *See* comparative Luso-Hispanic studies
Brazil at War, 202n31
Brazil Gets the News, 202n31

Cabeza de Vaca (dir. Nicolás Echevarría), 5, 8, 9, 13, 47–77, 79, 82, 87, 103, 110, 116, 127, 130, 133, 143, 144, 152, 177, 199n12, 202n29, 211n6, 212nn8 and 11, 213n25, 214n26, 217n13, 219n3
Cabeza de Vaca, Álvar Núñez. *See* Núñez Cabeza de Vaca, Álvar
Cabral, Pedro Álvares, 7, 13, 19–21, 23, 25, 43, 45, 87, 127, 151, 168, 204n5, 207n27, 228n12, 233n38
caçador de diamantes, O (dir. Vittorio Capellaro), 203n2
Cafundó (Paulo Betti and Clovis Bueno), 4
Caillois, Roger, 10
Calderón, Eligio, 198n9
Caminha, Pêro Vaz de, 12–13, 16, 19–46, 114, 173, 204nn6 and 8–9, 205nn15 and 18, 207n28, 228n15
Campo, Mônica Brincalepe, 230n21
Canby, Vincent, 67, 68
cannibalism, 47–77, 151–76, 197n4, 198n6, 204n10, 210n4, 211nn5 and 7, 227n9. *See also* anthropophagous adaptation
Capanema, Gustavo, 41, 208n32
Capelato, Maria Helena Rolim, 209n40
Capovilla, Maurice, 205nn13–14, 206n24, 207n25
captivity. *See* colonial films: captivity
Caramuru: A Invenção do Brasil (dir. Guel Arraes), 5, 14, 15, 16, 19, 83, 98, 141–76, 179, 201n21,

254

Index

203n1, 220n15, 226n7, 227n9
Caramuru: Poema Épico do Descobrimento da Bahia (Durão), 15, 153, 229n16
Cárdenas, Lázaro, 5
Carlota Joaquina, Princesa do Brazil (dir. Carla Camurati), 154, 201n24, 228n14
Carr, Jay, 52
Carrasco, Salvador, 4, 14, 79–108, 110, 143, 216nn8–9, 217nn11 and 19, 219n9
Carro, Nelson, 218n23
Casal, Manuel Ayres de, 30
Cautiverio feliz (dir. Cristián Sánchez), 4, 201n21
Cervo, Amado Luiz, 45
Chanan, Michael, 5, 6
Chico Rei (dir. Walter Lima Júnior), 201n20, 233n43
Chipman, Donald E., 218n22
Christophe Colomb (dir. Gérard Bourgeois), 201n25
Christopher Columbus (dir. David MacDonald), 201n25
Christopher Columbus: The Discovery (dir. John Glen), 202n25
Cinema Novo, 5, 6, 56, 157, 203n1, 227n9
Ciuk, Perla, 112, 116, 219n4
Clifford, James, 68–69
Coatlicue, 115, 139
Colón (dir. Fernando Fernández Ibero), 201n25
colonial films. *See also* historical cinema
  allegory, 15
  arrival of Europeans to the New World as theme, 7
  assimilation, 9, 211n5
  captivity, 7, 9, 10, 15, 47–77, 141–76
  as category, 4
  Catholic Church as theme, 7
  and censorship, 41, 200n16
  Church and State, 31, 35, 43, 87, 117, 130, 177
  and civilization and barbarism, 29, 103
  Columbus as theme, 7
  and connecting past and present, 1, 2, 3, 5, 6, 7, 10, 16, 17, 19, 22, 42, 46, 96, 109, 111, 129, 141, 142, 144, 155, 231n29
  conquest and conquistadors as theme, 7
  contact between indigenous and European groups, 1–2, 7, 9, 10, 14, 40, 43, 47–77, 135, 141–76, 203n1
  Creole struggles for independence as theme, 7
  the "discovery" as theme, 7
  evangelization of indigenous people, 20–23, 26–27, 29, 40
  foundational myths, couples, 14–15, 40, 41, 43, 46, 135–36, 141–76, 203n1
  government involvement in, 14, 31, 40–46
  historians writing on, 4
  and Hollywood, 14, 127, 163, 229n18
  iconic, symbolic, mythic, malleable, or legendary figures or texts, 8, 10, 14, 15, 16, 19, 83, 84, 93, 105, 79–40, 151–76, 177–79
  identity, 1, 3, 5, 6, 9, 10, 14, 19, 46, 64, 65, 69, 71, 76–77, 79, 80, 81, 83, 84, 88, 105, 107–08, 111, 118, 120, 126, 129, 132, 148–50, 154–56,

255

colonial films: identity *(continued)* 158, 163–65, 170, 177–79, 202n29, 224n41
    indigenous peoples as theme, 6–7, 9
    inverted power dynamics, 9, 10, 13
    Iracema and *O Guarani* as theme, 7, 200n19, 203n1, 216n7
    Justification for comparing Mexico and Brazil, 10–12
    legacy of the conquest, 9
    mestizaje/mestiçagem, 14, 43–46, 79, 84, 95, 107–08, 109–10, 118, 125–27, 134–37, 142, 149–50, 156, 170, 177, 197n4, 215n3, 224n41, 225n2, 226n4
    military dictatorship, 13
    motives for producing, 4–5
    and nationalism or patriotism, 40–46
    and nudity, 29–30, 125–27, 200n17
    ongoing interest among Latin American filmmakers, 4
    and quincentenaries, 1, 14, 15, 19, 22, 80, 198n8, 199nn11–12
    resistance and rebellion, 7, 13, 15, 149–50, 198n8, 203n1, 225n2
    revisionism, 6, 82
    and science and technology, 29
    and silent era, 34, 216n7
    and television, 15
    transculturation, 9, 15, 106–07
    women in colonial Iberoamerica as theme, 7
colonial past and present. *See* colonial films: and connecting past and present
Columbus, Christopher, 7, 53, 54, 198n7

Comissão Federal de Censura, 41
Como era gostoso o meu francês (dir. Nelson Pereira dos Santos), 5, 6, 8, 9, 13, 14, 24, 47–77, 82, 110, 143, 144, 151, 152, 157, 159, 160, 201n21, 210n3, 210–11n5, 211n7, 212n10, 213n21, 214n26
comparative Luso-Hispanic studies, 10–12
    and Hollywood, 11
Constelaciones, 219n11
contact, intercultural. *See* colonial films: contact between indigenous and European groups
Cortés, Hernán, 97, 102, 216n8, 225n2
Cortesão, Jaime, 204nn5–6, 206n20, 209n36
Cruz Polanco, Fabián de la, 220n22
Cuauhtémoc (dir. Manuel de la Bandera), 7, 200n19
Cunha, Eneida Leal, 204n6

Dávalos, Patricia E., 112, 115, 219n8
Davis, Natalie Zemon, 199n10
Day Is New, The, 202n31
Decree 21.240, 41, 42, 208n34
Denby, D., 67
Departamento de Imprensa e Propaganda, 22, 41, 42, 45, 209nn37–38
Departamento Nacional de Propaganda, 22, 41, 209n35
Descobrimento do Brasil (dir. Humberto Mauro), 5, 7, 11, 12–13, 16, 19–46, 56, 87, 110, 127, 141, 143, 173, 203n2, 205n11, 206n25, 208nn31–33, 220n15, 223n36, 233n42

Desmundo (dir. Alain Fresnot), 4, 201n24
Diário de um novo mundo (dir. Paulo Nascimento), 4
Dias, Gonçalves, 204n8, 209n39
dictatorship. *See* colonial films: military dictatorship; historical cinema: and military dictatorship
Diego, Juan, 14, 81, 82
Diegues, Carlos, 203n1, 229n17, 232n37
Disney, Walt, 11
reception of his films, 202n32
Dom Manuel, 19–21, 40
Durão, José de Santa Rita, 153, 154, 227n10, 228n12, 229n16

Echenberg, Margo, 221n25, 224n42, 225n43
Echevarría, Nicolás, 5, 9, 13, 47–77, 79, 82, 87, 103, 110, 127, 143, 177, 199n12
eighteenth century, 141–76
Encounter. *See* colonial films: contact between indigenous and European groups
Erauso, Catalina de, 216n7
Eréndira ikikunari (dir. Juan Mora Catlett), 4
España y sus grandezas: Colón (dir. Fernando Fernández Ibero), 201n25
Eurocentrism. *See* anthropophagous adaptation: and exoticizing
European and indigenous contact. *See* colonial films: contact between indigenous and European groups
evangelization. *See* colonial films: evangelization of indigenous people

exoticism (or exoticizing). *See* anthropophagous adaptation: and exoticizing

Fausto, Boris, 42, 209n41
Favata, Martin A., 213n22
Ferdinand and Isabel, King and Queen of Spain, 21
Fernández, Enrique, 51
Fernández, José B., 213n22
Fernández de Oviedo, Gonzalo, 53
Fernández de Santa Cruz, Manuel, Bishop of Puebla, 122, 221–22n30
Ferrando, Roberto, 68, 210n1, 213n22
Ferreira, Alexandre Rodrigues, 225n1
Ferreira, Jorge, 198n10
Fitz, Earl, 203n33
Fox, Vicente, 109
Fray Bartolomé de las Casas (dir. Sergio Olhovich), 201n23
Freyre, Gilberto, 43–46, 209nn42 and 44
Furtado, Jorge, 151, 164, 176, 230n24, 232n31, 233n44

Gama, Vasco da, 168
Ganga Zumba (dir. Carlos Diegues), 200n20
García, Gustavo A., 200n19
García Tsao, Leonardo, 218n23
Garcilaso, Silvia, 219n8
Gatti, André, 41
Gatti, José, 203n3
Gertrudis Bocanegra (dir. Ernesto Medina), 201n22
Globo (media conglomerate), 151–76, 208n31, 226n6, 229n17, 231n31, 232nn32–33 and 35
Gomes, Ângela Maria Castro, 209n40
González Echevarría, Roberto, 211n6

257

Index

Good Neighbor Family, 202n31
Gordon, Richard A., 200n14, 216n7, 233n43
Gracias Amigos, 202n31
Gransden, Gregorio, 110, 125, 126, 219n7, 220n19
Greenspun, Roger, 210n5
Gregório de Mattos (dir. Ana Carolina), 4
Griffith, James, 61, 212nn10 and 13 and 18
Guadalupe, the Virgin of, 14, 79–108, 111, 115, 139, 178, 214n1, 215nn2 and 4, 216n5, 217n10, 217–18n19, 218n21
Guaicuru, 141–51
Guaicuru language, 145, 147, 148
  translation of or not, as strategy, 141–51
Guarani, O (dir. Paulo Benedetti, 1912), 7
Guarani, O (dir. Vittorio Capellaro, 1916), 7

Hall, Stuart, 204n7
Hans Staden (dir. Luiz Alberto Pereira), 19, 201n21, 203n1, 210n3
Hartl, John, 112
Heffner, Hernani, 22, 38, 207n25, 208n32
Henríquez Ureña, Pedro, 10–11
Hernández, Jesús, 217n11
Hernández Espinosa, Joel, 219n8, 220n16
Hershfield, Joanne, 52, 202n29, 212n8
historical cinema. *See also* colonial films
  costume drama, 8
  government involvement in, 5–6
  and Hollywood, 8
  and identity, 5, 8
  and indigenous peoples of Latin America, 6–7
  and military dictatorship, 6
  and national unity, 5
  and race, 6
  and silent era, 7
  and social critique, 6
Holanda, Sérgio Buarque de, 44
Hollywood. *See* colonial films: and Hollywood; historical cinema: and Hollywood; comparative Luso-Hispanic studies: and Hollywood
hybridity. *See* colonial films: *mestizaje/mestiçagem*

icons. *See* colonial films: iconic, symbolic, mythic, legendary figures or texts
identity. *See* colonial films: identity
INCE (Instituto Nacional de Cinema Educativo), 39, 40–44, 207n29
Inconfidência Mineira (dir. Carmen Santos), 201n22
Inconfidentes, Os (dir. Joaquim Pedro de Andrade), 201n22, 226n4
Independência ou Morte (dir. Carlos Coimbra), 201n22
indigenous languages. *See* Guaicuru language; Kadiwéu language; Náhuatl; Tupi language
indigenous peoples. *See* colonial films: indigenous peoples, as theme; Guaicuru; Kadiwéu; Nahua; Tupinambá
indigenous and European contact. *See* colonial films: contact between indigenous and European groups
intercultural contact. *See* colonial films: contact between indigenous and European groups

intertext. *See* anthropophagous adaptation: and source text *and* relationship between film and source text
intertextual dialogism. *See* anthropophagous adaptation: relationship between film and source text: intertextual dialogism
IPS, 215n2
Iracema (dir. Vittorio Capellaro), 7
Italian Neo-Realism, 5

jardín de tía Isabel, El (dir. Felipe Cazals), 6
Jáuregui, Carlos, 197n3
Jericó (dir. Luis Alberto Lamata), 201nn21 and 23
Johnson, Randal, 5, 42, 197n3, 204–05n10, 208n34, 233n40
Juan-Navarro, Santiago, 199n11, 212n9
Juana Inés de la Cruz, Sor, 14, 80, 109–40, 150, 179

Kadiwéu, 141, 142, 148
Kadiwéu language, translation of or not, as strategy, 141–51
King, John, 199n11
Kino (dir. Felipe Cazals), 201n23
Kornis, Mônica Almeida, 226n6, 232n32

Lazcano, Hugo, 115, 116, 118
Leigh-Stone, Cynthia, 198n8
Lenine, 160, 231n29
León-Portilla, Miguel, 214n1
Levine, Robert M., 208n32
leyenda del padre negro, La (dir. Felipe Cazals), 201n23
leyenda negra, La (dir. Sergio Olhovich), 201n23

López, Ana M., 199n11, 203n34
López, Kimberle S., 199n11, 231n30, 233n40
López Portillo, Margarita, 215n2
López-Tarín, Tere, 139, 219n8
Lora, Gonzalo, 215n2
Lourenço, Cileine I., 199n11
Luna, Andrés de, 200n19
Lusofonia, 45–46
Luso-Hispanic studies. *See* comparative Luso-Hispanic studies

Maciel, David, 215n2
Madureira, Luis, 197n3
Magalhães, José Calvet de, 45
Mala Cosa, 67–69, 213n23
Martin, Marcel, 211n5
Matamoros, Mauricio, 112, 116
Mattos, Carlos Alberto, 160, 169, 228n14, 229nn18–20, 232n34
Mauro, Humberto, 5, 11, 12–13, 19–46, 52, 56, 87, 110, 114, 127, 141, 143, 173, 203nn2–3, 204n8, 205nn11–12 and 16, 206nn21 and 23–24, 207nn25–27 and 28–29, 208nn31–33, 212n12, 233n42
Meirelles, Victor, 25, 87
Méndez Plancarte, Alfonso, 120, 221n26
Mendoza González, Jessica, 115
Merrim, Stephanie, 211n6, 220nn20–21, 221nn27–28, 222n31, 224n39, 225n44
Merten, Luiz Carlos, 24, 39, 205n13
mestizaje/mestiçagem. *See* colonial films: *mestizaje/mestiçagem*
Mexico and Brazil, in comparison. *See* comparative Luso-Hispanic studies

Index

Miceli, Sérgio, 208n32, 209n41
military dictatorship. *See* colonial films: military dictatorship; historical cinema: and military dictatorship
Ministério da Educação, 40
Miranda, Luiz Felipe, 24, 207n29
Moctezuma, 97, 216n8, 217–18n19, 218n22
Modernism (Brazilian), 50, 152, 169, 197nn3–4, 198n6, 204n10, 210n4, 227n9, 231n29, 233n44
Moheno, Gustavo, 216n8, 218n23
monja alférez, La (dir. Emilio Gómez Muriel), 5, 200n14, 201n24, 216n7, 223n35
Monroy, Manuel H., 117
Monteiro, Elis, 163
Monti, Félix, 162
Mora, Carl J., 202n32
Morettin, Eduardo Victorio, 203n3
Mraz, John, 200n17, 202n27
Mulvey, Laura, 213n26, 232n36
Murat, Lúcia, 5, 15, 19, 98, 141–76, 226nn3 and 5

Nahua, 79–108
Náhuatl
  identity through language acquisition, 129–30
  translation of or not, as strategy, 85, 88–90, 93–94
Nájera-Ramírez, Olga, 5
national icons. *See* colonial films: iconic, symbolic, mythic, legendary figures or texts
national identity. *See* colonial films: identity; historical cinema: and identity
nationalism. *See* colonial films: and nationalism or patriotism
Naufragios (Álvar Núñez Cabeza de Vaca), 13, 47–77, 130

New Latin American Cinema, 5, 6
Nican mopohua, 14, 79–108, 110–11, 216n5
noche de los mayas, La (dir. Chano Urueta), 200n20
Nogueira, Claudia Barbosa, 199n11
Nuevo mundo (dir. Gabriel Retes), 5, 14, 15, 79–108, 110, 137, 146, 178, 201nn20 and 23, 216nn7–8, 219n9
Núñez Cabeza de Vaca, Álvar, 9, 47–77, 85, 130, 199–200n12, 201n21, 202n29, 213n22, 214n28

Office of the Coordinator for Inter-American Affairs, 11, 202nn30–31
O'Gorman, Edmundo, 97, 216n5
Oliveira, Lúcia Lippi, 209n40
othering. *See* anthropophagous adaptation: and exoticizing
otra conquista, La (dir. Salvador Carrasco), 4, 5, 14, 15, 79–108, 111, 116, 143, 144, 145, 150, 178, 201nn20–21, 216nn8–9, 219n9, 225n2
otro Francisco, El (dir. Sergio Giral), 201n20, 202n27

Palavra e Utopia (dir. Manoel de Oliveira), 201n23
PAN-PVEM (Partido Acción Nacional-Partido Verde Ecologista de México). *See* Alianza por el Cambio
Paranaguá, Paulo Antonio, 200nn17 and 19, 211n5
Pardo, Laura, 220n18, 225n45
patriotism. *See* colonial films: and nationalism or patriotism

Index

past and present. *See* colonial films: and connecting past and present
Paz, Octavio, 113, 219n11, 223n38
Peguero, Raquel, 139, 219n3
Peixoto, Floriano, 226n5
Peña, Richard, 200n15, 212n14
Pereira dos Santos, Nelson, 9, 13, 24, 47–77, 82, 110, 143, 151, 157, 200nn15 and 17, 203n1, 210n3, 211n5, 212n12, 213n21
Pérez Marín, Yarí, 199n11
Pérez Turrent, Tomás, 200n12
Pick, Zuzana M., 200n18
Pina, Luís de, 24, 38, 205n13, 207nn26–27
Pindorama (dir. Arnaldo Jabor), 6
polyperspectivality, 89, 99
Poole, Stafford, 79, 82, 215n4, 216nn5–6, 217n10, 218n21
Portuguese, Brazilian vs. Continental, 170
PRI (Partido Revolucionario Institucional), 109, 218n1

Quetzalcoatl, 130, 217n18
Quilombo (dir. Carlos Diegues), 201n20
quincentenaries. *See* colonial films: quincentenaries

Rabasa, José, 212n11, 213n23
Ramírez Hernández, Rocío, 116, 200n13, 215n3
Ramos, Alcides Freire, 197n3, 199n11
Ramos, Graciliano, 22, 25, 39, 45, 46, 205n13
Renha, Lia, 161
Retes, Gabriel, 5, 14, 79–108, 110, 146, 216n8, 219n9
Retorno a Aztlán (dir. Juan Mora Catlett), 79, 116, 217n14

revisionism. *See* colonial films: revisionism
Reyes, Aurelio de los, 200n19
Ricard, Robert, 218n19
Rigueira, Luciana, 226n3
Ríos Alfaro, Lorena, 116, 220n18
Roble de olor (dir. Rigoberto López), 4
Rocha, Gláuber, 6
Rocha, João César de Castro, 197n3, 198n6
Rocha Pita, Sebastião da, 228n13
Rockefeller, Nelson D., 11, 202n31
Romanticism (Brazilian), 50, 198n6, 205n10, 209n39, 227n10
Roquette-Pinto, Edgard, 34, 40–46, 206n24, 207n25, 208n33, 209n42
Rosenstone, Robert A., 198n10, 202nn26–27
Rossoff, Eduardo, 4, 14, 79, 82–83, 104, 109–40, 143, 177, 200n13, 217nn16–17, 220n22, 223n37, 224n41

Sabat-Rivers, Georgina, 219n10, 220n20, 221n28
Sadlier, Darlene J., 200n17, 210n3, 211n7, 214n27
Salazar, Antônio, 45
Saludos Amigos (Disney Studio), 11
Sánchez, Miguel, 216n5
santo oficio, El (dir. Arturo Ripstein), 6, 201n23, 217n16
Saraceni, Paulo César, 24
Schvarzman, Sheila, 22, 203nn34 and 2–3, 207nn25 and 29
secreto de la monja, El, 219n11
self-exoticizing. *See* anthropophagous adaptation: and exoticizing

261

Sermões, A História de Antônio Vieira (dir. Júlio Bressane), 201n23
seventeenth century, 109–40
Shohat, Ella, 197nn3–4, 198nn7–8, 217n15
silent films. *See* colonial films: and silent era; historical cinema: and silent era
Simões, Inimá, 41
sixteenth century, 19–108, 141–76
Skidmore, Thomas E., 43, 44, 204n4, 209nn42–43
Soares, Mariza de Carvalho, 198n10
Sommer, Doris, 15
Sor Juana Inés de la Cruz (dir. Ramón Peón), 201n24, 219n11
soundtrack, 25–26, 35, 127, 160, 161, 231n29
source text. *See* anthropophagous adaptation: and source text *and* relationship between film and source text
Sousa, G. U. de, 58, 59, 60, 210n3, 211n5
Souza, Bernardino José de, 34
Souza, Carlos Roberto de, 207n30
Staden, Hans, 9, 47–77, 212nn15–16, 212–13n19, 214n25
Stallybrass, Peter, 68
Stam, Robert, 6, 16, 25, 197n3, 198nn7–8, 199n11, 200n19, 202n28, 203nn1 and 3, 204n8, 205n14, 206n22, 212n7, 217n15, 227nn8–9, 229n16, 230nn22 and 25, 233nn38–39
Stevens, Donald F., 198n10
"Strat," 51
Subirats, Eduardo, 218n23
subtitles, use or lack of, 85, 88–90, 93–94, 99, 145

syncretism. *See* colonial films: *mestizaje/mestiçagem*
Taunay, Affonso de E., 34, 206n24
Tecuichpo, 97–108, 216n8
as Isabel, 104
television. *See* colonial films: and television
Thomas, Kevin, 51, 67
Thomasson, Camille, 109, 139, 219n4
Three Caballeros, The (Disney Studio), 11
Tiempos Mayas, 7
Tiffin, Helen, 197n1
Tiradentes (dir. Oswaldo Caldeira), 201n22
Tiradentes, O Mártir da Independência (dir. Geraldo Vietri), 201n22
Tonantzin, 79–108, 131, 214n1, 217n10, 218n21
Topiltzin, 97–108, 217n18, 217–18n19
trampas de la fe, Las (dir. Nicolás Echevarría), 219n11
translation of indigenous speech, as strategy. *See* Guaicuru language, translation of or not; Kadiwéu, translation of or not; Náhuatl: translation of or not; Tupi language
Trelles Plazaola, Luís, 198n9, 200n19, 203n35
Tropicalism, 198n6, 233n44
Trueblood, Alan S., 219n10 and 12, 220n17, 221nn28–29, 222nn30–31, 223n33
Túpac Amaru, el último Inca (dir. Federico García Hurtado), 201n20
Tupi language, 24, 39, 170, 212n12

Tupinambá, 2, 47–77, 151–76, 203n1

última cena, La (dir. Tomás Gutiérrez Alea), 6, 199n10, 201nn20 and 23

Vargas, Getúlio, 5, 13, 40–46, 208nn31–32, 209nn36 and 40–41
Varnhagen, Francisco Adolfo de, 229n16
Vasconcellos, Simão de, 153, 228nn12–13
Vega, Luis Laso de la, 81, 216n5
Velasco, Salvador, 218n23
Velloso, Mônica Pimenta, 209n40
Vernet, Horace, 25
Viany, Alex, 203n34
vida de Cristóbal Colón y su descubrimiento de América Latina, La (dir. Gérard Bourgeois), 201n25
Villa-Lobos, Heitor, 25, 26, 207n26, 208n32
Virgin of Guadalupe, the. *See* Guadalupe, the Virgin of

Virgin Mary, 79–108, 131, 132, 143, 217–18n19
virgen que forjó una patria, La (dir. Julio Bracho), 201n22
Voigt, Lisa, 227n10, 228n12

Warhaftige Historia (Hans Staden), 13, 47–77
White, Allon, 68
whitening, 44–46, 209n43
Williams, Bruce, 197n3, 199n11, 210n3

Xavier, Ismail, 6, 197n3, 212n17
Xica da Silva (dir. Carlos Diegues), 200–01n20, 201n24

Yo, la peor de todas (dir. María Luisa Bemberg), 113–14, 123–24, 201n24, 223n37
Young, Theodore Robert, 199n11

Zumárraga, Juan de, Don Fray, Archbishop, 81

263

About the Author

Richard A. Gordon, The Ohio State University, works in the areas of Hispanic and Portuguese-language literatures and cultures and film studies and comparative studies. His research intersects with colonial and post-colonial studies, centering on Brazilian and Spanish-American historical cinema. He is currently writing a book that evaluates the role that films about slavery have played in shaping national identities in Cuba and Brazil. His articles have appeared in *Hispania, MLN, Luso-Brazilian Review, Letras peninsulares, Colonial Latin American Review,* and *Journal of Latin American Cultural Studies.*

www.ingramcontent.com/pod-product-compliance
Lightning Source LLC
Chambersburg PA
CBHW062122300426
44115CB00012BA/1782